Final Confession

FINAL
CONFESSION

The

Unsolved

Crimes

of Phil

Cresta

Brian P. Wallace & Bill Crowley

University Press of New England
HANOVER AND LONDON

University Press of New England
www.upne.com
© 2000 Brian P. Wallace and William Crowley
All rights reserved
First University Press of New England paperback edition 2013
Manufactured in the United States of America
Designed by Ann Twombly
Typeset in Fairfield by Wellington Graphics
ISBN for the paperback edition: 978-1-61168-378-3
ISBN for the ebook edition: 978-1-61168-379-0

For permission to reproduce any of the material in this book, contact
Permissions, University Press of New England, One Court Street,
Suite 250, Lebanon NH 03766; or visit www.upne.com

Originally published in 2000 by Northeastern University Press

The Library of Congress has cataloged the hardcover edition as follows:

Wallace, Brian P., 1949–
    Final confession : the unsolved crimes of Phil Cresta /
Brian P. Wallace & Bill Crowley.
        p. cm.
    ISBN 1-55553-449-X (cloth : alk. paper)
    1. Cresta, Phil.   2. Thieves—Massachusetts—Boston—
Biography.   3. Burglary—Massachusetts—Boston.
4. Organized crime—Massachusetts—Boston.   I. Crowley,
Bill.   II. Title.

HV6653.C74 W35   2000
364.16′2′0974461—dc21   00-058224

To the memory of Billy Cresta

Contents

Foreword

WHEN I WAS ASKED to read *Final Confession* for the purpose of writing this foreword, my first inclination was to say no.

I don't read much in the way of true-crime chronicles, and I can't stand those biographies or pseudoautobiographies of criminals and mobsters that have filled the shelves of our bookstores lately. Most of these books attempt to make the criminal—the Salvatore "Sammy the Bull" Gravano or the John Gotti—seem shrewd and intelligent, which I find hard to believe if they are either in Witness Protection or in jail or have been so unsuccessful at practicing illicit activities that someone can write a book about them. I also find these books unreadable because of what I call *The Godfather* syndrome, which essentially boils down to the idea that our collective perception of the Mafia is that it's like an extension of the Corleone family—we see mafiosi as handsome, Machiavellian, tragic heroes who spend a lot of time talking about honor and hosting lavish weddings and who occasionally (but with wistful regret) do the odd bad thing to horses and guys named Carlo. The criminals I had contact with in my youth weren't like that. They were usually dumb guys or, if in the mob, far more like the Al Pacino in *Donnie Brasco* than the Al Pacino in *The Godfather: Part II*, which is to say they were schlubs who dressed badly, were always short of money, and had never read a book without pictures.

There has been, to this point, only one exception to the rule, only one book that walked the line between our understandable fascination with the criminal underworld and our specious inclination to aggrandize it, one book that got it right-and that book was Nicholas Pileggi's *Wiseguy,* the story of low-level mobster Henry Hill and his friends, which became the basis for the Martin Scorsese film *Goodfellas.* What *Wiseguy* did was tell its story without melodrama or sentimentality, never once trying to paint Henry Hill as anything but what he was—a consummate hustler who, in the end, sold out everyone he knew in order to continue living the good life while the United States government picked up the tab. More than simply a story of one hustler-turned-stoolie, *Wiseguy* chronicled three decades of the major New York crime families through the eyes of one lowly soldier and brought a time, a place, and a lifestyle vividly to life.

Final Confession, I discovered to my delight, does something similar, not through the eyes of a mob underling, but through those of an independent thief, a man named Phil Cresta; a man whom most people have never heard of, which is how he liked it; a man who was behind some of Boston's more infamous robberies of the sixties and before; a man who went to his grave so silently that many of those crimes are still listed on the books as unsolved. Through Phil Cresta, Brian Wallace and Billy Crowley don't merely show us the inner workings of a thief's mind, however; they take us on a rollicking tour of the Boston underworld, from Cresta's cramped upbringing in the North End of the 1930s and 1940s, through JFK's inauguration and the Impossible Dream season of the Red Sox.

This was an underworld overseen in New England by the Patriarca family of Rhode Island, but Boston was effectively run by two notoriously hot-tempered clans—the Italian Angiulo gang and the Irish Winter Hill Gang headed up by Howie Winter and James "Whitey" Bulger. Phil Cresta moved in this world—easily at some times, precariously at others because he refused to pay tribute to its overlords. All the while, he diligently practiced his trade, approaching it the way all skilled craftsmen do, keeping up on the very latest innovations, creating his own innovations when those available didn't suffice, breathing his job every waking moment to the degree that it seemed far more a calling than a choice. The primary difference between Phil and other well-known, dedicated craftsmen was that Phil's craft was illegal.

If it wasn't nailed down, Phil Cresta stole it. He stole jewels, rare coins, watches, and cash. He cut the heads off parking meters and flew to Chicago with them, where he had keys made so that he could return to Boston and open them at will, eventually stealing, from this one operation, a hundred thousand dollars during 1961 and 1962, so baffling the City of Boston that they gave up trying to catch him and eventually replaced all the meters with new locks. He stole from a heavily guarded jewelers' expo, mob-protected diamond dealers, a Brink's truck, and once from the basement of a Boston police station. He even stole the food he served in the diner he once owned: the special of the day was dictated by what Phil and his partner clipped off Boston's docks that morning.

There is something utterly fascinating about a man so dedicated, so determined, so *nutty* when it came to the concept of not paying for, well, anything at all. Phil Cresta sucks you in and emerges from these pages as a kind of lock-picking, armored-car-robbing savant. He was many things—meticulous, shrewd, unassuming, sociopathic at times, and undeniably magnificent at his chosen profession.

In Brian Wallace's and Billy Crowley's hands, we are taken into Phil Cresta's world, into the dimly lit streets of a Boston before *Cheers,* a Boston of back-alley deals and smoky bars where, from his motel-room headquarters in Kenmore Square, Phil Cresta planned the robbery of impregnable safes, the heists of rolling fortresses with heavily armed guards, the bribing of judges, the creation of a vast network of "ears" who worked the city streets and reported to Phil any potentials for danger or for profit. After years of working solo, Phil, with his two oddball partners, spent a decade treating Boston like his personal piñata, hitting it time and time again until it spilled its precious loot and Phil could scoop it off the floor.

Along the way, he accrued the wealth of untold millions as well as a few enemies, and throughout *Final Confession* we watch as Cresta deftly maneuvers his way between treacherous "allies" like the icy Jerry Angiulo; a weaselly psychopath named Red Kelley; and Phil's archenemy, a career thug and alcoholic named Ben Tilley. Rounding out the cast is Phil's nemesis on the other side of the law, a cop with whom he engages in often hilarious battles of one-upmanship involving, among other things, the cop's beloved car. These battles were part of a kind of war that ultimately would cost Phil and his partners everything, including their freedom to taste fresh air.

You don't have to like Phil Cresta; I'm not sure I do. But within these pages you will often marvel at his ingenuity, his relentless guile, his bold, calculated daring. You will marvel too at Brian Wallace and Billy Crowley's often breathless narrative as it takes you at light speed through a Boston, and an America, that is fast fading from our mind's eye—a city of endless nights where men carrying bags full of drilling equipment, wearing uniforms that didn't belong to them, went out through dank alleys to start *their* days—and steal, steal, steal—while the rest of the city slept.

DENNIS LEHANE

PROLOGUE
Open Cases Now Closed

FIRST MET BILLY CROWLEY on March 17, 1999, on South Boston's high holiday, St. Patrick's Day. Billy is a retired Boston police detective who worked the city's streets for eight years. While undercover one day in East Boston, Billy attempted to break up a fight and was punched in the head. He began to suffer severe headaches, and a series of tests determined that he had a brain injury from that blow to his head. Reluctantly, Billy Crowley retired.

We met that March morning in the Cranberry Cafe on East Broadway in Southie. As I walked in the door I knew immediately which of the dozens of patrons was Billy. City kids like me learn how to spot a cop.

We talked for a few minutes, and I asked why he wanted to meet me. Crowley said he always read my syndicated column, "Brian's Beat," and he was a fan of mine. He told me that he had the rights to a fascinating story and he wanted to collaborate with me on a book. I asked him what the story was about.

He handed me a large manila envelope. "Have you ever heard the name Phil Cresta?" he asked. I told him I had not. He laughed and said that few people had—and for good reason.

"Phil Cresta," Billy Crowley said, "was a genius who outwitted the feds and the local police for most of his life while stealing over ten million dollars."

If Billy's purpose was to get my attention, he had succeeded. At that point he reached across the table and slid a thick pile of photocopies from the envelope, which I hadn't yet opened. "I brought these for you, to prove my stories are real." He fanned out the papers so that I could see what they were: copies of stories from the *Boston Globe* and the *Boston Herald,* with banner headlines that caught my interest. I sipped my coffee and took a few minutes to scan through such headlines as:

$119,000 DISAPPEARS AS GUARDS SIP COFFEE

RARE COINS IN $200,000 THEFT SAID TO WEIGH
HALF A TON

$25 MILLION X-WAY HAUL A DUD

HIGHWAYMEN GET $150,000 GEMS

LONER STEALS ARMORED CAR—GUARDS INSIDE
BROOKLINE STORE

WEST ROXBURY DAYLIGHT STICKUP

ANOTHER ARMORED CAR HOLDUP—2 GUARDS SHOT

MACHINE GUN BANDITS GET $68,000

FBI SEEKS HOODED TRIO IN LATEST
ARMORED CAR HOLDUP

SLEW OF ARMORED CAR HOLDUPS MAY BRING
ABOUT NEW LAWS

ARMORED TRUCK HIJACKED ON CANAL
STREET—OYSTER HOUSE DINERS UNAWARE

My interest piqued, I ordered another cup of coffee and read a few of the stories themselves. They were about well-planned jobs, but no perpetrators were named.

"What do these stories have to do with this Cresta guy?" I asked Crowley, already getting the feeling I knew the answer.

"Phil pulled all those jobs," he said with a straight face.

"How come I never heard of this guy?"

Billy just smiled and said, "I know, that's the best part!"

He pulled some papers from the bottom of the pile. There were fifty or sixty internal memos signed by J. Edgar Hoover and his successor asking their field agents why they couldn't capture Phil. They were dated between 1969 and 1974. "Even when they *knew* he'd done a job—like that Brink's heist—he gave them quite a chase." He showed me one of those top-ten-fugitives lists. Phil Cresta's name was there.

I was more than a little intrigued by all this. "I know about most if not all of the wise guys in the Boston area—from Whitey Bulger to Jerry Angiulo to Howie Winter. I know about all the bank-robbing townies in Charlestown. I can't believe I never even *heard* Phil Cresta's name before today."

Billy said, "Phil was better known in Chicago than he was in Boston—but not as a crook." Then he reminded me that most of the headlines about Cresta's "more noteworthy" crimes had occurred between 1961 and 1969, when I was in school. He laughed and said, "Besides, some of his best scores never made the papers."

"Yeah, but enough of them were printed," I said as I scanned more of the stories. I told Crowley I'd do a little research myself on this Phil Cresta thing, then let him know my decision.

I WENT TO the main branch of the Boston Public Library in Copley Square and dug up information over the next three days. I put aside other work; Cresta took over my thoughts.

I talked to a few cops who were mentioned in the newspaper stories. They said they knew Phil Cresta. When I told them Cresta had pulled many of the unsolved robberies they had worked on, they were stunned. At the time, Boston had two kinds of police: Boston cops patrolled the city itself, and the MDC (Metropolitan District Commission) cops had jurisdiction both in the city and in the cities around Boston that make up the metropolitan area. (Today the MDC police have been merged with state police.) Pretty soon both kinds of cops, mostly retired, started telephoning me. Did Cresta do this job? That one? I told them all the same thing: buy the book. For I had already decided to go ahead with the project.

Besides using Crowley's notes, which were detailed enough to include conversations Phil wanted recounted, I interviewed members of Phil Cresta's family, his friends and his enemies, good guys and bad guys, cops and robbers. I went over FBI documents, over police reports and police FIOs (field interrogation observations), and I scanned newspapers from Boston, Chicago, New York, and Kansas City. But this book would never had been written and the story never told if it wasn't for the perseverance of Billy Crowley.

Billy is a lifelong friend of Bobby Cresta, one of Phil's younger brothers. Crowley had briefly met Phil in their Medford neighborhood when Crowley was twelve years old. This was shortly after the Crestas moved from the North End to Medford, after Phil and Bobby's father died. Phil lived in Medford, near his family, after he was released from Norfolk prison in 1948. But Billy Crowley never had dealings with Phil until after the Cresta team was long out of business. For, as was often true in Boston-Irish families, Billy had had the choice of becoming either a wise guy or a cop. He chose to be a cop, one of Cresta's "enemies."

Years later, in the twilight of Phil Cresta's life, Billy Crowley, retired from the force, offered to share his South Boston apartment with a then-hard-up Phil. Night after night, the aging wise guy talked about his exploits, recalling conversations from his early days in the North End and documenting what he could. He said he wanted his story told after he died, but he asked that the real names of his two wives and one mistress, his seven children, his two partners, and the one movie star he worked with be kept secret. They had either been bystanders or under pressure to cooperate or had paid their time and deserved to go on with their lives unimpeded by publicity. As Cresta talked of his successes in the 1960s and of the famous 1968 Brink's robbery, the ex-cop Billy Crowley took copious notes.

Crime, betrayal, murder, and intrigue filled the life of Phil Cresta. The FBI's Boston chief described him in a memo to J. Edgar Hoover as one of the best burglars and lock pickers on the East Coast. That December 12, 1969, memo says that "Subject is known to have participated in many burglaries, as well as armed robberies." But that FBI agent, like most people, had no true idea how active Cresta really was. Cresta masterminded not only the Brink's robbery of December 1968, but more than five hundred other crimes that remain unsolved on police records. There is nowhere near enough room in this book to tell of them all. But thanks to Billy Crowley and my corroborating research, the story Phil Cresta told about some of these crimes is now being made public.

Phil Cresta started robbing before the crimes related in this book occurred. His robberies of jewelers, furriers, and armored car companies in the Boston area and elsewhere happened during the 1960s, and he was finally tried in 1974. During his career, he injured and killed when he felt he had to; he bought politicians, bribed judges, and got sentences fixed; he toyed with city, state, and federal law enforcement for over thirty years—yet his generosity and compassion were legendary. Here are parts of his story.

Final Confession

I
The Parker House Heist

HE PARKER HOUSE HOTEL opened in the fall of 1855 and since then has housed an array of famous guests, including Charles Dickens, Ulysses S. Grant, and John Wilkes Booth. Booth used the shooting range in the hotel's basement to hone his skills eight days before he assassinated Abraham Lincoln. The Parker House's basement vault also became the site of one of Boston's most ingenious jewel robberies.

The year was 1965. It was early October and the Red Sox had long since put away their gloves and were sitting home, like everyone else, watching Sandy Koufax and the Los Angeles Dodgers beat Harmon Killebrew and the Minnesota Twins in a seven-game World Series. Early October in Boston is a teasing time of year, tossing out samples of summer and winter from opposite hands while painting the landscape with wonderfully colored foliage.

Phil Cresta's only interest was in the green of money. While shopping in Filene's Basement one day, he ran into an old acquaintance, Louie Cohen, a well-known Boston diamond merchant known on the street as Louie Diamonds. He had one foot in the jewelry business and the other in the wise-guy business.

Phil didn't like Louie Diamonds personally, but he liked the leads he got from him. Louie knew when big-time diamond merchants were in, or coming to, Boston. He knew where they were staying and where they did their business.

That day, Louie told Phil about a huge jewelry convention and exhibit coming to Boston: the Diamond Extravaganza would be at the Parker House in six days. It was going to be a three-day show with some of the richest jewelers in the country participating. Phil didn't need to be told that this just might be the big break he'd been hoping for.

Knowing he'd need help, Phil called Augie Circella in Chicago. Augie had married Phil's older sister, Mari, who was a professional dancer, a little over a year before. He had also made enough money working for Frank "The Enforcer" Nitti in the late 1940s and 1950s to open up the Follies, the most successful burlesque house in Chicago. The Follies was the place where everyone in the Chicago mob hung out, including Tony Accardo and Joe Ferriola, the two top guys in the city. To say the least, Augie Circella was "well connected," as everyone in the Windy City knew, and he had often told Phil to call him if he needed help.

Until this time, though, Phil had rarely taken Circella up on his offer. Still, Phil was relieved when Augie sounded pleased to hear from his thirty-seven-year-old brother-in-law again. Phil got down to business.

"Augie, there's a huge diamond show coming to Boston and I need your help." "Sounds great, Phil," Augie said, "but whadda ya need from me?" "Diamonds," Phil replied, "lots of diamonds." Augie asked, "Since when are you in the diamond business?" "Since I got wind of this Diamond Extravaganza," Phil said. Augie began to laugh and, after hearing more details, told him to come to Chicago in two days. He would set Phil up with some people.

When Phil returned from Chicago he called his two partners in crime, Tony and Angelo (whose real names are not given in this book), and asked them to meet him at McGrail's, a bar on Boston's Kilmarnock Street where Phil liked to hang out. After a few beers Angelo asked, "Whadda ya gut, Phil?" Phil told him all about the Parker House diamond show. Both partners listened intently, then Tony asked, "What do *you* know about diamonds?" "They're worth a lot of money," Phil responded lightheartedly. "Well, I guess that's enough," Tony replied, laughing. "You're too easy," Angelo said, looking at Tony and shaking his head. "All right, now both you knuckleheads shut up," Phil said, and he began to outline his plan.

Two elderly registered jewelers who also worked for the Accardo mob in Chicago were bringing their diamonds from Chicago to Boston. They would rent a booth in the show.

"What's that gut to do with us?" Angelo inquired. "I'm getting to that," Phil answered. And then to the diminutive Tony, who was munching on a hot dog, he said, "Tony, are you claustrophobic?" Tony hesitated and then blushed. "Come on, Phil, you know I'm married. You know I'm not like that." "No, no, no. I mean are you afraid of being closed in, like in an elevator or an airplane?" "Of course not," Tony replied, ignoring Angelo's laughter. And then, puzzled, Tony asked, "What's that gut to do with the price of tea in China?" Angelo laughed again. "Where do you get those ridiculous sayings?"

"Come on, come on. This is important," Phil said, trying to get them to settle down. "You asking me if I get scared in an elevator, Phil?" "Well, kind of," Phil answered. And then he added, "What I really need to know is if you can be locked in a small space without going crazy." "He's already crazy," Angelo replied in jest. "Tell him to shut up, Phil," Tony said in the tone of a little kid. Phil just shot Angelo one of those keep-your-mouth-shut looks. Then he turned from Angelo to Tony and said, "Well?" "I guess it depends on how small a space and for how long," Tony answered honestly. "Fair enough," Phil said. "Let's go across the street and I'll show you how small a space."

Phil paid the bar tab, and they walked across the street to the Fenway Motor Inn on Boylston Street, where Phil had been living since he'd separated from his wife in 1963. In the middle of the floor stood a large black storage box about three feet high and two feet wide. Since it was standing on end, its lid seemed like a small door. "That's how small an area," Phil told Tony, whose face grew pale. "That's pretty small, Phil," Tony whispered. "Get in and try it for size," Phil instructed.

Tony backed up as if the box were going to bite him. "Shit, this ain't funny, Phil." "It isn't meant to be funny," Phil responded. He showed his partners how the outside lock was a dummy, glued in place to look as though the trunk were locked. He then opened the trunk's lid and showed them an inside latch that would allow a person inside to open or close the trunk.

Angelo was just standing there staring. Finally he said, "Phil, what does all of this have to do with a diamond job?"

"If dipstick here will get in the box, I'll explain it to you." Phil stepped aside.

Tony took a few deep breaths and crouched to enter the box. It was a very tight squeeze even for Tony, who was five feet three inches, and weighed no more than 110 pounds. "How's it fit?" Phil asked. "Like a friggin coffin," Tony replied. "Relax now," Phil said soothingly, "I'm just doing this for a few seconds." He again pointed out the door's inside latch and closed the front of the trunk.

Angelo looked at Phil as if he'd lost his marbles.

After about thirty seconds, Phil reopened the trunk and Tony jumped out. "Phil, that's fucking scary in there," Tony said. "Is it too scary for a half million dollars?" Phil asked. "A what?" Angelo barked. "You heard me, a half million dollars." "For that kind of money I guess I could do it. But what about air?" Tony asked. "You'll have your own air tank," Phil assured him. "How long do I have to stay *in* there?" Tony asked next, surveying the black box. "Forty minutes . . . an hour tops," Phil said. "For a half mil, I could do that." Tony smiled for the first time since he'd seen the trunk.

THE DAY BEFORE the show was to open, Phil picked up the two Chicago diamond merchants at Logan International Airport in East Boston. He waited with them until they picked up their trunk, which was only a little smaller than the one in Phil's room at the Fenway Motor Inn. Then he drove them to the Parker House, dropped them off, and left.

They checked into the hotel and signed in to get their booth assignment in the exhibit area, which was in the hotel's lobby. They called Phil from a pay phone on Tremont Street, as he had instructed, and told him where their booth was located.

The Diamond and Jewelry Extravaganza went off without a hitch for the first two of its three scheduled days. Many of the world's top diamond and jewelry brokers—practically a Who's Who of the diamond trade—did good business there.

The two guys from Chicago, who actually were registered diamond merchants, did business too. On the first night, when the show closed at nine, they, like the other exhibitors, put their merchandise into a trunk with their logo on the outside, signed a slip detailing what was in the trunk, and watched as a Boston police officer and the exhibit's security people locked all the jewels in the Parker House's basement vault.

The next morning they were the first to arrive. The vault, which was on a time lock, was opened at seven A.M. They showed their IDs, signed another paper, and waited until their jewels were wheeled out. To take possession of their trunk, they showed their IDs again and signed another paper, which verified that this was their trunk. Only then were they able to take the merchandise to their booth. The security overseeing the safety of the jewels was considered top-notch: Parker House security, Boston police officers, and a private security company.

Phil, Tony, and Angelo visited late on the second day to get a feel for the scene. Phil nodded to his two jeweler friends, but kept right on walking past their exhibit. Then they went upstairs to a room the team had rented under a fictitious name. At 8:30 on that second night of the show, the Parker House was jammed with buyers and sellers. Nobody noticed two men, dressed as security men hired by one of the three outfits working the show, transporting a black trunk into the diamond and jewelry show. The three-by-two-foot trunk looked like any of the other trunks that now crowded the Parker House basement and showroom.

But none of the other trunks, at least none that Phil Cresta knew about, contained a living, breathing human being.

At 8:45 P.M. the Chicago jewelers began to pack their wares into their own black trunk. Within five minutes they were ready, and the two-by-two-foot trunk with their jewels was taken away by the same two Parker House security men who had brought in the slightly larger trunk. At 9:15, the show already officially closed for the evening, police and security hired by the hotel began to escort the dealers to their cars or to the vault. The two Chicago businessmen filled out all the paperwork and watched as "their" trunk with their logo on it was wheeled down the elevator and into the back of the vault. By 10:15 all the other jewelers had placed their valuables in the vault and it was closed for the night. It would not be opened until 7:00 A.M., when the time-release lock was tripped.

Inside the vault since nine or so, Tony waited. He heard voices and movement for what seemed like an eternity, but in fact it was only about an hour. At approximately 10:30 P.M., when there were no more voices, he undid the inside latch and stepped out of his self-described coffin. He had a portable oxygen tank and mask in one hand and a small flashlight in the other. It took Tony a few minutes to adjust to his surroundings, but once he did, he went to work.

Phil had had the two Chicago jewelers write down which of the trunks contained the most valuable jewels. Tony took that single white paper with the instructions out of his pocket and went to work. The logos on the outsides of the trunks made Tony's job easy. With a solid ten-inch door between him and the rest of the world, he could have listened to the radio to pass the time, but Phil had allowed him only the flashlight, the oxygen tank and mask . . . and an Italian sub, without which Tony had refused to go into the vault. Phil had conceded on the sandwich, but made Tony promise that everything he took into that vault would come out with him.

Tony finished picking the locks of the trunks, collected the jewelry, stretched out on the floor, and waited for morning. At

6:50 A.M. he climbed back into the trunk, locked it with the lock Phil had fashioned, and waited. When he began to hear voices, he stayed as still as possible. Finally the vault was opened. The trunk was wheeled a short way, then given a ride in an elevator. Minutes later Tony heard Phil's unmistakable voice.

The small thief undid the inside latch, opened the lid, and Phil's worried face was the first thing he saw. "Are you all right?" Phil asked. "I could use some breakfast," Tony responded. "He's fine," Angelo joked as he looked past Tony to the loot inside the trunk.

The two Chicago jewelers were in the hotel room, too. Their eyes glazed over as they handled the precious diamonds and emeralds. "They behaved like little children at Christmas," Phil said when he told the story to Crowley. "All the jewelers could say was, 'Unbelievable!'"

After a few minutes of drooling over the merchandise, Phil told his accomplices, "Okay, guys, what are we looking at?"

"Close to a million," the older of the two said.

Phil looked at the younger jeweler, who was pushing seventy, and asked, "What do *you* think?"

"I concur wholeheartedly," he said seriously. "This is very valuable property and extremely marketable."

From the bathroom, Phil wheeled in their original two-by-two trunk and said, "Well, gentlemen, it's time to scream bloody murder."

By the time the two Chicago jewelry merchants took the elevator back to the lobby, pandemonium had already broken loose. Police seemed to be everywhere in the lobby and people were screaming at cops, at hotel officials, and at anyone else in a position of authority.

The man who'd organized this international show was standing near the front desk in a daze. Well-known jewelry brokers were yelling obscenities at him, but he was far beyond hearing them.

By the time the two elderly merchants from Chicago had their chance to report that they'd been hit for $250,000, three much younger men were walking down Tremont Street, each carrying a gym bag in his right hand. But instead of heading into the nearby YMCA, they hailed a cab and went to a bar called McGrail's, in the shadow of Fenway Park, a short walk from Kenmore Square.

A week later, Phil received a call at McGrail's from a guy who told the bartender his name was Augie. "Kid, they're all talking about you here in Chicago." Phil laughed. Very seriously Augie said, "I mean it, even the boss, Tony Accardo, asked me about you. You've made a lot of friends out here, especially those two old jewelry guys." Phil asked, "Yeah? How're they doing?" "How're they *doing*? Thanks to you they're both retiring, for crissake." Augie laughed. "They got a twofer. They hit the insurance company for a quarter of a mil on the diamonds they 'lost' at the show, and they fenced the ice you guys snatched for another half a mil, that's how they're doing. . . . I got my share. . . . Did they take care of you and your guys all right?" Augie asked, concerned. "We did fine, Augie. I have no complaints, and thanks for the help," Phil said. "Kid, whatever you need from now on, you call your brother-in-law Augie, all right?" Phil laughed and answered, "All right, Augie. And take care of my sister." Phil chuckled again when he thought of Tony scrunched inside the box, with his Italian spuckie in his back pocket.

The non-insurance take on that job came to $550,000. It was split six ways. But the heist cost the various insurance companies a lot more than that, once all the victims' claims were processed. "Those jewelry bastards were bigger thieves than we were," Phil said in admiration. "They all saw a good thing and jumped on the bandwagon. If we hit a merchant for seventy-five thousand, he told his insurance company he'd lost a hundred and fifty thousand."

The great Parker House diamond robbery was not publicized. The hotel made sure it stayed out of the papers. Despite much effort, the crime has not, until now, been solved. Boston police and insurance company investigators didn't have a clue how anyone could steal valuable jewels from a locked safe. Or how the jewels could be fenced without surfacing in Boston. That's because they were not yet well-enough acquainted with Phil Cresta Jr.

2
Schools for Thought

T WAS OVERCAST AND STORMY when Phil Cresta was born on March 2, 1928, which may have been a portent of things to come. He was the third child of Philip Cresta Sr., a first-generation Italian, and a woman who in this story will be called Ruth. Ruth Cresta had been born in Southie, on Farragut Road. The couple lived in the North End of Boston in the shadow of Paul Revere's house, just off Boston's famous Freedom Trail. At the time, Boston was teeming with immigrants eager to succeed.

Though the area called South Boston, or Southie, was the territory of the Irish newcomers, the North End held thousands of Italians. Philip Cresta Jr. and his five siblings—Mike and Mari, who were older than Phil, and Rose, Billy, and Bobby— grew up on those narrow streets of the North End. Peddlers hawked their goods on Hanover and Prince streets as the Italian boys and girls played the games of their ancestors and of America. The neighborhood could have been the site of a nice childhood with fond memories for Philip Cresta to gaze back upon. But none of the Cresta children have fond memories. Freedom for young Philip Cresta became any time he could spend outside his family's small home.

Philip Cresta Sr., seen as a truck driver to the world outside his family, was his sadistic, ignorant self at home. His main pleasures in life seemed to be cheating on his wife or—when he *was* at home and not carousing—inflicting physical and mental punishment on his wife and offspring. The children's formative years were spent watching their mother—who was only four feet eleven inches tall—being constantly beaten and kicked by their father. Not only did he abuse his petite wife, he made all his children watch and listen as their mother screamed for mercy. The family, along with Mike, the father's younger brother, lived in a tiny shed that had been converted into a two-story house. It had a coal stove in the kitchen and very little furniture. In this rodent-infested so-called home, Philip Cresta Sr. abused, tormented, and tortured his six children and his wife, Ruth. According to Phil's brothers and sisters, it was Phil who bore the brunt of these physical and psychological attacks.

While Phil Cresta Sr. might not have treasured his family, it was clear that he never met a piece of junk he didn't like. If something, anything, wasn't tied down, he considered it his, from napkins to paper clips to trash lying in the street. "Finders keepers, losers weepers" was a song that the kids in the North End sang, but the things that Cresta Sr. took were things that other people had thrown away, not lost.

He did so cleverly. In the floor of his personal car, near the gas pedal, he cut a trapdoor replete with hinges and springs. If he happened to see an object in the street that he wanted, be it an old shoe or a magazine, he would park over it, open the trapdoor, reach down, and seize the object. The Cresta house was filled to the brim with items of no earthly value except in the mind of Phil Cresta Sr.

When the dilapidated old house began running out of room for what Cresta Sr. treasured, he removed the floorboards or stuck his worthless pieces into the walls. This was the house of horrors that Phil and his siblings grew up in. Once something came into the Cresta house, it never left—especially tools.

Cresta Sr. was mechanically inclined, and he loved his tools a good deal more than he loved his kids. One day Phil, who was thirteen years old, returned home from school to find his father in a rage because one of his prized tools was missing. After beating Phil, his father handed him a shovel and said, "Dig." Phil was accustomed to the beatings, but this was new. He looked at his father and said, "What?" "You heard me," his father screamed, "I want you to dig your own grave. And when you're finished I'm going to kill you." Ruth, hearing this, ran upstairs and sent one of her daughters to her brother-in-law's house, a block away.

Mike Cresta, who moved in and out of the family's house at will, rushed over and confronted his brother as the boy continued digging. Mike was usually no savior, but he sometimes had more sense of decency than his brother. When Phil Sr. finally relented, he said to his son, "If there's ever another tool missing from this house, nobody will be able to save you from this grave."

On other occasions—and they were numerous—Cresta Sr. would take a child upstairs to one of the bedrooms. Once there, he would take the youngster's hands and place them in two holes precut in an interior wall. When the hands were through the opening, he would go into the adjoining room and place handcuffs on them, then laugh like hell at the child's predicament. Once the child was shackled, he would return downstairs or go out for hours at a time, leaving the child handcuffed. This was his idea of entertainment. No one else had keys to unlock the handcuffs or the courage to face Phil Sr.'s wrath.

Although Ruth Cresta tried her best, she was no match for her sadistic husband. The Cresta children loved their mother and cried in unison on those many occasions when their father would beat her senseless or fling her down the stairs.

Everyone around Phil Jr. knew how much he hated authority. That trait stayed with him until the day he died. It doesn't take a psychologist to figure out that his hatred of authority stemmed from how his father treated him and his family. Young Phil Cresta also had no love for athletics, or for school. He went only because the law stipulated that he must, and he planned to drop out as soon as the law allowed.

The constant beatings by his father toughened him far beyond his age. He never looked for a fight, but he never backed down from one either. He was, according to those who grew up with him, quiet and almost shy. His younger sister, Rose, recalled, "I never heard Phil say a bad word about anybody. My father beat him more than any of us; maybe that's why he became so daring."

As the Cresta kids grew older, their father became more sadistic, with the help of his brother Mike. With an electric cord, the Cresta brothers would take turns whipping the kids. Phil's older sister, Mari, remembered one occasion: "Once, for some reason, Uncle Mike reached into his back pocket and pulled out a long knife. He grabbed Phil from behind and placed the blade of the knife on his neck, screaming that he was going to kill him. But my mother grabbed Phil from Mike's grasp and disaster was averted." She went on. "We were all scared to death of my father and my uncle. My mother did not want Uncle Mike living with us, but my father insisted. It was a terrible time."

One of Phil's younger brothers, Bobby, noted, "We were constantly being beaten, Phil more than anyone, and with the beatings came the rantings and the ravings and the screaming that were almost as bad as the physical abuse. I don't think I ever saw my father happy. He was always pissed off, always ready to strike one of us. I didn't think things *could* get any worse, but then, whenever Uncle Mike came to live with us, they did. My father never gave us any credit for anything or showed us any encouragement. He always tried to tear us down, both physically and mentally."

After the United States entered World War II Phil Cresta Jr. volunteered for the army, even though he was much too young. He was rejected but encouraged to join a Civil Defense unit. His assignment was to go around the North End neighborhood to make certain that everyone's lights were out after curfew. Phil liked the job and the sense of doing something worthwhile, but it was hard for him to spend hours patrolling the city to make sure everyone maintained blackout instructions, and then come home to see what his father was doing. Phil Sr., never one to abide by anybody else's rules, had devised special black curtains and window shades that gave the appearance from the outside that all the lights were shut off, which they weren't. He taunted his son for his role in the Civil Defense.

As Phil began to become independent, he showed a bent for acquisitiveness not unlike his father's. One day while on his Civil Defense rounds, Phil saw a couple of ration booklets and stole them. He was caught, but because this was Phil's first offense, he was placed on probation.

A few months later he was arrested again, this time for stealing tires with some of his friends. One of those arrested with Phil was the son of a Medford police sergeant. The Medford cop offered each set of parents to "make this thing go away." The parents of the other boys were grateful for the offer, but Phil Cresta Sr. insisted on teaching his second son a lesson. It was one lesson that Phil never forgot—or forgave. At sixteen years of age Phil Cresta Jr. was taken out of one prison—his home—and placed in another, where he would spend the next two years. This new home was the Massachusetts Reformatory at Concord. The other boys went free.

One month after Phil was released from Concord, he was convicted of assault and battery. No longer a juvenile, he was sentenced to two more years, this time at Norfolk Prison.

Six months into that sentence, Phil's family received a letter stating that their son had been drafted into the army, but once the army heard where Phil was living at the time, he was categorized as undesirable. It's hard not to wonder what Phil's future might have been if he had been drafted six months earlier or had the chance to enter the army with the clean slate the policeman had suggested.

On September 5, 1947, while at Norfolk, Phil received word that his father, while driving his beloved specialized car, had died from a massive heart attack. Phil felt no sadness at his father's death, only resentment toward the man he blamed for putting him in Concord.

Ruth, everyone was sure, would now be much happier. Her tormentor was gone. But shortly after burying her husband, she suffered a nervous breakdown from which she never fully recovered. She and the younger children moved to Medford, where she was tended by her teenage daughter, Rose, who also finished raising the younger boys. Mari had left home some time before, and was not coming back. She teamed up with Orson Bean for a while, then went out on her own as a dancer.

When Phil came out of Norfolk at twenty years of age, he had no parents to speak of. Within a few months, on July 4, 1948, he married a woman who in this book will be called Dorothy. The couple rented an apartment at 20 Headland Way in Medford, near where Phil's mother was living with his sister Rose. Phil and Dorothy began to raise a family. Ostensibly now a car salesman, Phil put his heart into his real line of work, which had been learned, at government expense, from older crooks. He may never have been much of a student in school, but his Norfolk friends had noticed how quick a study he was, especially with picking locks. Phil's proficiency in this "elective subject" at Norfolk had brought him such admiration that he finally realized he was good at something other than taking a beating. Now free and with a family to provide for, Phil decided to put his new skill to use.

BOSTON'S CRIMINAL ELEMENT has always been considered a poor stepsister to the more organized and deadly crime syndicates in Chicago and New York, but it was no less deadly. Al Capone, Frank Nitti, Lucky Luciano, Meyer Lansky, Dutch Schultz, Mad Dog Coll, and Frank Costello were famous Mafia figures who led dangerous and glamorous lives elsewhere. Movies and newspapers could not get enough of the cigar-chewing, police-baiting gangsters who flaunted their wealth and seemed invincible.

While everyone in Boston knew the name Capone, only a handful of people, mostly in South Boston, knew of Frankie Wallace. On December 2, 1931, Wallace, leader of the Gustin

Gang of South Boston, had been invited to a meeting in the office of Joseph Lombardo, in the Testa Building in the North End. Wallace was accompanied by his top two lieutenants, Barney Walsh and Tim Coffey. The South Boston gangsters walked up the three flights of stairs to Lombardo's importing company and knocked on the door. Within seconds Wallace and Walsh were dead at the hands of seven or eight of Lombardo's men. Coffey hid in a broom closet until the cops arrived, but he refused to testify against Lombardo, whose gangland stock had risen after the daring daylight massacre that eliminated his only rivals. At the time of the Testa Building massacre Joe Lombardo was thirty-six years old.

For the next twenty-four years he and a fight promoter named Phil Buccola (also known as Filippo Bruccola) ran the loosely organized crime syndicate in Boston. Buccola was of the old school and often gave second and third chances to those who went against him. His successors, Patriarca and Angiulo, who began to take over in the 1950s, were less forgiving.

In the early 1950s Phil Cresta, then in his mid-twenties, was busy breaking and entering, laundering money, and working at other small-time endeavors to pay the bills his growing family incurred. He wanted, however, to do a lot more than just pay his bills. He wanted respect and wealth, and he was convinced that neither would be attained by carrying a lunch pail. He began to associate with Jerry Angiulo.

Jerry—nine years older than Phil, whom Phil knew from his early days in the North End—had been just twelve years old when the bullet-ridden bodies of Frankie Wallace and Barney Walsh were carried down the stairs of the Testa Building on Hanover Street. It was a lesson that young Angiulo never forgot. As the long careers of Joe Lombardo and Phil Buccola were coming to an end, a newer, tougher, more educated breed of criminal was rising to power. Angiulo—one of this breed—knew that Cresta had guts, and that he was hungry to get ahead. This would make him a perfect soldier for Angiulo's burgeoning crime empire, which he ran out of Boston's North End.

Working for Angiulo was Cresta's night job, you could say. During the day, Phil played a respectable, law-abiding citizen in various ways. For example, he ran a small West End diner called Lucy's Snack Bar. Owning a diner can be profitable, depending on how it's run and how many customers walk through the door. There was no restaurant in Boston, however, making as much money as Lucy's Snack Bar.

Most businesses, when they open, figure what their overhead will be—things such as rent, equipment, furniture, and electricity. Then they figure what they'll need to take in, to turn a profit. Most businesses. Phil Cresta and his partner, a low-level Angiulo operator named Bones, ran things differently. They had no overhead. Everything in the restaurant came from one of Phil's five-finger discounts, that is, everything was stolen. Even the rent was free; the storefront was owned by Bones's brother.

Each morning Phil and Bones would get up at sunrise and steal whatever they needed for the restaurant that day. Whatever meat or fish they stole at Faneuil Hall Marketplace or Boston's docks became the special of the day. The meat and fish taken care of, they would proceed to five-finger discounts on bread, soft drinks, milk, coffee, sugar, and whatever else the restaurant required. Their prices, as you may have guessed, were the best in Boston.

Angiulo got his cut, and everybody was happy. At Lucy's Snack Bar, a person could buy more than a meal. There were bargains on suits, sneakers, blouses, cashmere jackets—whatever the local wise guys had hijacked the night before. It was one-stop shopping at Lucy's. Phil continued running the diner until 1955.

Under Lombardo and Buccola, Angiulo had been a low-level numbers runner. With his outstanding organizational skills, though, he soon took over bookmaking in Boston. In the late 1950s, booking was profitable but still fragmented. Bookies didn't share their winnings. That changed as Angiulo gained power.

According to Phil Cresta, during the time Angiulo was con-
solidating bookmaking, Phil and three or four of his buddies, all
of whom were on Angiulo's payroll, were given a list of local
bookies to hit. They'd go into the bars or clubs where an intimidated bookie worked and take his betting slips. The very next
day, after the Suffolk Downs pari-mutuel number had been published in the newspaper, the same four or five guys would return
and tell the bookie they'd hit that pari-mutuel with *him*. They
would then produce one of the bookie's own slips, from those
taken the day before, as proof. Many of the bookies at first refused to pay, but they soon changed their minds.

"Me or one of my buddies would stick a gun down the
bookie's throat and tell him he either paid up or he died," Cresta
stated. Once a bookie was brought into line, he was told that
one of Angiulo's men would be in once a week to see that things
"like this" didn't happen again. It wasn't long before it was accepted that if a guy wanted to book in Boston he had to give a
cut to Jerry Angiulo, whose lack of patience was becoming famous. Many of those who refused didn't last longer than their
second chance.

Phil's early efforts at lock picking were not completely successful. In 1957 Phil was seen picking a lock to a house. The witness called police, who charged Cresta with breaking and entering, possession of a firearm, and assault with intent to kill.
(They claimed he tried to shoot them; Phil said that never happened.) Before his case went to trial, the high-priced lawyers
working for Angiulo had the charges reduced to entering a
home by means of subterfuge. Phil was sentenced to serve two
and a half years in the old Charlestown state prison, but later
was transferred to the newer state prison at Walpole. It was at
Walpole that Phil found a way to acquire the wealth he sought.

Phil hated prison, but he learned a lot there. He made friends
with Joe "The Animal" Barboza, Vinny "The Butcher" Flemmi,
and John Robichaud, all of whom would later become famous
for their viciousness. Phil also got to know the guys who'd

pulled off the daring Brink's robbery in 1950 that became the subject of several books, television shows, and movies. He listened to the stories of the bank jobs and the murders that The Animal had been involved with. Phil decided that their style was not for him. Their fame, and where it got them, gave Phil warning: a guy in his kind of work was better off staying in the shadows. So he decided to get better at being unobtrusive.

By the time Cresta returned to Boston's streets in 1959, there weren't many locks he couldn't pick or alarms he couldn't disable successfully. Phil had also become adept at making perfect molds of keys, a talent that had many uses. He began working his new skills.

At some point around this time he also made an enemy who vowed to bring him down, a sergeant in the police department of Arlington, a bedroom community about six miles outside Boston. Nobody knows, or at least nobody is saying, why Sergeant Jim Doherty hated Phil Cresta so much.

Doherty did his utmost to make Phil's life miserable and, to a degree, he succeeded. It became routine for Doherty to drive into Boston, pick Phil up, not charge him with any crime, beat him up, and leave him bloodied. *Miranda,* of course, had not yet come to court. The only Miranda Doherty knew of was Carmen Miranda, the woman who danced with bananas on her head. Doherty knew he had no police authority in Boston, but he harassed Cresta there anyway.

Phil retaliated with psychological warfare. Every time a severe rain- or snowstorm hit the Boston area, Cresta would drive to Arlington, pick the lock of Doherty's car, roll down all the windows, and then return to Boston. After Sergeant Doherty's shift was finished, he'd find his car's interior completely drenched. He must have felt as if a permanent rain cloud were following him. For, despite his efforts to hide his car, Phil always managed to find it and go through his ritual.

Sergeant Doherty wasn't the only cop who knew that Phil Cresta was more than a car salesman, but few were able to discover exactly what he did for his "real" job, now that the diner was long closed. Phil received some unwanted publicity when on November 12, 1959, a worker in the Everett dump found the body of Joseph "Angie" DeMarco. A well-known North End criminal, DeMarco was found lying faceup, with six bullets in his head. His body was covered with wooden crates and rubble. "He definitely wasn't killed in Everett," Lieutenant Henry Fitzgerald of the Everett Police Department told the *Boston Herald*. "His body was dumped here by his attackers." DeMarco had last been seen at an after-hours joint in Boston called the Coliseum, which was owned by the Mafia. The last person he was seen talking to was Phil Cresta.

Middlesex District Attorney John Droney was aware of the public's fascination with the Mafia and did not let go of the story until he'd milked it dry. He called the DeMarco slaying a gangland execution, and assured reporters that he was not going to stand by and watch Middlesex County become a dumping ground for "racketeers, dope peddlers, loan sharks, and other hoodlums." DeMarco's background was publicized: he had spent the better part of his forty-two years in prison. In 1943 he had been sentenced to fifteen to twenty years for manslaughter; he was released in 1955. Three years later he was arrested and sent away briefly for carrying a concealed weapon. He was released in November 1958, but was back in jail in March 1959, this time after a wild auto chase. The grand jury proceedings on the DeMarco killing became more of a media show than an inquiry.

When the grand jury convened in Middlesex County Superior Court in Cambridge, they called six witnesses: Jerry Angiulo; Larry Baione, who would later become an underboss in the Angiulo syndicate; Phil Waggenheim, who was a notorious contract killer; Henry Noyes, a well-known Mafia member; Peter Jordan, the former mayor of Revere; and a young upstart named Phil Cresta Jr. It was pretty heady company for the former North End kid.

Years later Cresta would say callously, "Angie DeMarco was a piece of shit, a low-life scumbag who couldn't be trusted. He'd started robbing Angiulo's 'protected' bookies after leaving jail in 1959. It made us look bad—and that made him dead. DeMarco was also a fool. He knew he was playing with fire and he got burned."

It is not clear from Cresta's tales who actually shot DeMarco, though Cresta certainly wouldn't have had any problem putting bullets into DeMarco's brain if he'd been given the contract. Cresta had no pity for the district attorney's office, either, who never got their indictment for DeMarco's murder. "They knew they'd never solve that DeMarco hit. The number of people who wanted to see DeMarco dead could fill Boston Garden."

Though Droney's public indignation did not bring about an indictment, Phil Cresta did get in trouble because of the investigation. He had to show up at the courthouse daily, as did the other gangsters who had been subpoenaed with him. One day as he waited in the corridor Phil met one of his old friends from his younger days at the Concord reformatory, who was now a felon. The two went across the street to a deli and talked about their days at Concord and life since. Little did Phil know that his old nemesis, Sergeant Doherty, was sitting in a back booth.

After Phil and his buddy left, Doherty went straight to Phil's parole officer, turned him in for associating with a felon, and insisted on punishment. So, though Phil had recently been seen on television every night in the company of the known felons subpoenaed by Droney, Cresta was returned to prison for violation of parole. He did not stay there long.

By this time, Phil had a small army on his payroll: informants, hoods, elected and appointed officials. To him, crime was a game, and whoever had enough money, connections, or influence usually won. One of Phil's payees worked in Governor Foster Furcolo's office, and he gave Phil a get-out-of-jail-free card after he'd served only three weeks.

It just so happened that the day Phil left jail, it was raining. Hard. Phil decided to pay a debt. Instead of going to his favorite bar, he headed for Arlington. The next morning, after a night of steady rain, Sergeant Doherty discovered his car windows wide open and about a foot of rainwater on the car floor. He complained bitterly about Cresta's release to a guy in the governor's office. The man listened to Doherty's claims that Phil Cresta was responsible for everything except the bombing of Pearl Harbor, thanked Doherty for all the information, then called Phil to tell him what the sergeant had just said about him.

3

Massachusetts Tightens Its Pockets

PHIL DIDN'T LIKE ANGIULO. In Phil's words, "Jerry Angiulo was a greedy bastard who liked to have his ass kissed." By the time January 1961 rolled around, Phil figured he'd made enough money for Angiulo and it was time to make some for himself. He was still doing some muscle work for Angiulo, but being a strong arm was never his forte. Phil had been working on an idea for quite some time. All he needed was the right day to set his plan in motion.

"When I woke up on the morning of Kennedy's inauguration, I knew that was the day. The weather had to be some kind of omen. Not only was there a couple of feet of snow on the ground, but this was the one day when everyone, at least everyone in Boston, would be home watching Kennedy. It was perfect."

Phil left the house wearing a large trench coat and a mask, which could be pulled down over his face to ward off both the weather and nosy witnesses. He also carried a large black suitcase. Inside was a hacksaw. Phil was the only person on downtown Boston's Washington Street that day, which gave him an eerie feeling. "I knew there wouldn't be a lot of people on the street, but it was like I was in the Twilight Zone or something. There was nobody around, nobody. All the time I'm walking down Washington Street, I can hear radios broadcasting Kennedy's being sworn in, and his inauguration speech."

If someone had been watching the area that day, that person would have seen a trench-coated man stop at a parking meter, open his suitcase, and take out a hacksaw. He then very quickly sawed through the pole, just below the meter, as he kept an eye out for possible witnesses, snowplows, or police vehicles. There were none. Once the top of the parking meter was free, the man placed it in his suitcase and continued his stroll through downtown Boston.

After he had cut the heads off three parking meters, Phil headed back to the warmth of his favorite North End social club on Hanover Street. "I was frozen by the time I got to the North End, but I knew I had what I'd come for, which made the trip a little easier," Phil said. "As I walked into the club, there were about fifteen wise guys hanging in front of the TV, watching the Kennedy stuff. They looked at me like I was crazy to be out in that kind of weather, and when I opened the suitcase, they *really* thought I was crazy." Phil laughed.

The puzzled onlookers watched in amazement as Cresta brazenly dropped the three parking meter heads on a card table. The puzzlement quickly turned to scorn. "Hey, big fucking score, Cresta, you gutta have at least a double sawbuck in there," one guy yelled out as everyone laughed with the speaker. "Hey, Phil, ya get caught with that and you do life with no ticket," a well-known mob figure screamed. "No ticket, ya get it?" In the parlance of Walpole State Prison, where most of the guys in that room had spent some time, a ticket was more formally known as parole.

"I stayed in that zoo just long enough to get warm and then I loaded the three meters back into the suitcase and screwed," Phil said. "Where ya going, Cresta, on ya honeymoon?" "What ya gut, a new sex toy?" some of the goons called out as Phil closed the door behind him. They may have all thought that Phil had lost his marbles, but the laughter soon turned to jealousy when Phil Cresta became Boston's most wanted scofflaw.

The day after John Fitzgerald Kennedy was sworn in as President of the United States, Phil Cresta took a cab from his home in Lynn, where he was living at that time with his wife Dorothy and his four children, to Logan International Airport in East Boston. He had in his possession one black suitcase. With his newspaper, suitcase, and boarding pass for a flight to Chicago, he looked like any normal passenger. But while other passengers' suitcases contained clothes and personal items, Phil Cresta's contained items that belonged to the City of Boston. By this time, though his sister had not yet married Augie Circella, Phil had some very good friends in Chicago's syndicate, a hugely profitable corporation grown out of the efforts of people like Al Capone, Frank Nitti, and Tony Accardo. Nobody in Boston's mob could hold a candle to Chicago, and nobody could "smoke" (duplicate) keys like the Chicago guys.

While serving time, Phil had become captivated with cons who were called "picks" by the other cons. Picks weren't the biggest or the toughest prisoners; in fact, they looked like accountants or businessmen. But they impressed Phil with their expertise and with the fact that they didn't tend to get rubbed out like the mob's heavies did. Cresta was close to six feet tall and his weight, though it fluctuated, averaged about 190 pounds. He was as tough as any con in prison, but though he didn't graduate from high school, he was intelligent enough to see that learning to pick locks was a win-win situation. He decided in prison to become the best pickman in Boston.

As Phil later said, "I could've been muscle for anybody in the United States, but those guys, like Barboza and DeMarco, always wind up with a bullet behind their ear, and that wasn't going to happen to me."

When he had left prison in 1959, Phil used his prison friends to get the necessary introductions to their pick counterparts in

Chicago. It was a match made in heaven, and this trip in 1961 would not be the last time Phil traveled from Boston to Chicago.

When Phil got off the plane in the Windy City, he headed for the Chicago locksmith who would help to make him a rich man. He asked the locksmith to make three keys, one to fit each type of meter he'd brought with him. The next day Phil was back in Boston with his new keys.

Within a week he was clearing $250 per day. And he did not get caught. Phil Cresta had done his homework.

Conveniently enough, Phil had made friends with a woman who worked as secretary to Bill Doyle, Boston's assistant parking commissioner. Phil knew that, sooner or later, he'd need an "ear" to the man who'd lead the investigation when someone discovered how massive the amounts of money were that Phil planned to siphon from meters.

Phil started out with the Beacon Hill area of Boston, which surrounds the State House. "I was a little too cautious at first. I thought everyone was looking at me every time I opened up a meter, but in reality I was invisible. Nobody gave a second glance to a guy dressed as a parking attendant unloading change from the meters. After the first week, it got too easy; there was no challenge, but the money was damn good," Phil said. The city's traffic department had no idea what was happening, and the wise-guy population was no longer laughing at Phil Cresta.

"Angiulo and his soldiers wanted a piece of my action, but I just smiled and kept making easy money. Anything that was easy was attractive to Angiulo. He wanted a piece of everything, but I wasn't some frightened little bookie and he knew it. If they wanted my keys they were going to have to take them from my dead body—and they didn't have the balls to deal with that." So for the next seventeen months, Phil Cresta was a one-man crime wave, stealing over a hundred thousand dollars from the City of Boston.

Finally, in May of 1962, the Boston traffic commissioner, Tom Carty, after looking at revenue shortfalls, called for an in-house investigation. "They thought it was an inside job, so it took them another two months to determine that someone was clipping them from *outside* the department," Phil commented. He found out from his lady friend in the commissioner's office that the investigation had come up empty and that the commissioner had decided to change all the parking meters to an Ace lock system, which was said to be theftproof. "She told me it would take three months after the bids were sent out before there'd be any changes in the existing meters. That was all I had to hear," Phil said, chuckling. The next day, it seemed, Phil Cresta had a change of heart.

"I went down to the North End club and began to meet secretly with some of the wise guys who were always after me for a key. Separately, I told each man that I'd give him his own key for fifteen hundred dollars. But part of the deal was they couldn't tell anyone else, or I'd have to sell them a key, too. I sold twelve keys for fifteen hundred each, and all twelve of them thought I was the greatest guy in the world to give them a piece of my score. A couple of months later, the keys were as useless as tits on a bull. I walked out of that score with over a hundred grand and twelve new friends—no, make that eleven new friends and one archenemy."

The archenemy's name was Ben Tilley.

In Phil's opinion, Tilley was a small-time hood who liked to hang around big-time gangsters. His claim to fame was that he had been an early suspect in the famous Brink's robbery of 1950. (The feds dropped him from their list of suspects, then found the crooks who'd really pulled the job.) "Tilley had about as much to do with that Brink's job as my mother did. Pulling that score took balls, and Tilley was short two of those. That little fuck went around telling anyone who'd listen that *he* was the one who got away," Phil said. "Nobody got away."

The one thing Tilley did have was a string of good informants who led him to some pretty good scores, although he never actually did the jobs. Tilley would case them and then hire some muscle to actually pull them off. "Tilley was a little pervert who got his jollies by watching. I never liked Tilley," Phil said, "and one of the happiest days of my life was when I sold him that bogus key for fifteen hundred dollars."

About a week after Phil sold Tilley the key, Tilley got arrested on Beacon Street by two Boston cops. "The asshole was hitting parking meters in a three-piece suit!" Phil said derisively. "He deserved to get busted." Tilley was arraigned for possession of burglarious tools and for petty larceny. He pleaded not guilty in Boston Municipal Court and was released on his own recognizance. A couple of months later he was found guilty on all counts.

Tilley was furious, but instead of taking the pinch and paying the fine, he appealed it on the grounds that a key, in and of itself, was not a burglarious tool. Tilley lost round after round until finally his case was heard by the Massachusetts Supreme Judicial Court. The justices ruled that a key does not in and of itself constitute a burglarious tool. They also ruled, however, that if that same key was used in the performance of a crime, then it was, in fact, a burglarious tool. And Tilley had, in fact, used it for larceny.

The case cost Tilley six figures. He turned his hatred on Phil Cresta and told a number of wise guys that Cresta had set him up. Though nothing came of their enmity at the time, both would suffer for it in years to come.

4

The Team Forms

FTER THE PARKING METER SCAM and a few other jobs that he pulled off solo, Phil achieved newfound respect in the ranks of the Boston underworld. He was well liked and well connected, but he was still no fan of Jerry Angiulo. Though a number of people talked incessantly to Phil about "being made" (initiated into Angiulo's branch of La Cosa Nostra), Phil wasn't sure he wanted to go that route. He listened, though.

"I never closed one door before another one opened," Phil noted years later. "At that time nobody was beating down my door with work, so I went along with the made-guy routine for a while. I was between a rock and a hard place. I knew that if I went with Angiulo and became a made man, I'd have the benefit of their protection and muscle, which was considerable. But I would also have to give them a piece of everything I stole, and I didn't like giving Angiulo anything.

"If I went out on my own, I knew I'd have to keep one eye on the law and the other on Angiulo's stooges, who didn't take too kindly to independents working their area. I knew Angiulo was pissed at me for the parking meter thing. He told a few people close to me that I should've given him more respect. What he meant was I should've given him a *cut*.

"Make no mistake about it, everything has to do with money. Money is respect. If you brought in a lot of money, you gained a lot of respect. If you didn't, you were at the bottom of the totem pole. We used to say, 'If you earn money, you're funny; if you're broke, you're a joke.'"

A FEW MONTHS after Ben Tilley got pinched with the parking meter key, Phil was standing at the bar in McGrail's, where lawyers, cops, Red Sox players, visiting-team baseball players, judges, newspapermen, crooks, and blue-collar workers all gathered to have a few beers and share stories. It was summer 1962. Someone mentioned Tilley's name and a big guy at the end of the bar jerked his head around and looked up. He was obviously listening in on the conversation and trying to be discreet about it. His interest caught Phil's attention. "A lot of guys in this business have big mouths and they usually bring themselves down by opening them at the wrong time," Phil commented. "This guy caught no one's attention but mine, and *that* got me interested in him."

Phil waited until most of the others had left and then introduced himself. "I know who you are," the big guy said to Phil. Phil bought him a drink and they talked. His name will be given here only as Angelo. He had grown up in Medford and he stood over six feet three inches, weighing in at about 240 pounds. He told Phil that he'd been doing some work for Tilley and was always interested in what was being said about his boss. Then Angelo said he'd never been arrested.

"He was kind of ashamed to tell me," Phil remembered, "but I told him it was good he had no record. If the cops don't know ya, then they can't suspect ya." This made Angelo feel better about his virgin status. According to Phil, he was strictly small-time, but had a great deal of potential. "I liked him right from the get-go," Phil said.

"Whadda ya hear on Tilley?" Phil asked Angelo cautiously.

"I hear he's blaming you for his pinch," Angelo said, looking Phil straight in the eyes.

"Are *you?*"

"Hey, I owe Tilley shit. He's a big boy; if he don't know how to steal, then he shouldn't be in the business."

"I really liked this kid," Phil recounted. "There was no bullshit about him. If you asked him a question, you got an answer—no song and dance—and I liked that." Still, Phil checked him out. Angelo's reputation turned out to be solid. As Phil put it, "The word on the street was that Angelo was somebody you didn't mess with."

A few days later Angelo was back in McGrail's. Phil Cresta went there too—mostly just to listen, but that night he did some more talking.

Angelo had heard that Cresta was an independent who worked alone, so couldn't believe his luck when Phil asked if he'd be interested in working together. Angelo later stated, "I could tell he was a straight-up guy—just the opposite of Tilley—and I really liked that. I couldn't believe all the shit Tilley was pulling. His arrest was strictly nickel-and-dime, and he made a federal case out of it, almost literally. When Phil asked me if I'd be interested in doing some work with him, I almost shit. I said yes before he had a chance to change his mind." Angelo then suggested including his best friend, who also did some work for Tilley.

"I really didn't want to meet anyone's friend, but I liked this Angelo kid, so I took a chance," Phil said. "I was sitting in McGrail's and the Sox were playing a doubleheader. The place was packed. I had my back to the wall, which was something I did whenever I was in public. I never let anyone get behind me, anywhere, anytime. I'd seen too many guys get hit from behind. It wasn't going to happen to me," Phil explained. "I was talking to a few Boston dicks when I spotted Angelo coming in. It looked like he was alone, so I motioned him over with a jerk of my head. He froze. Then he turned around and walked out. I had no idea what was going on. All I could think of, as I followed him out, was how ghost-white his face had turned."

Phil pushed through the Sox fans and made his way out to the street. "What's the matter?" he asked Angelo, who was apparently alone.

Angelo blurted, "Phil, those two guys you were talking to are cops!"

"I know," Phil said.

"One of those motherfuckers busted a friend of mine three years ago."

"Well, I can guarantee they won't bust *you*." Phil smiled.

"How the fuck can you do that, Phil? They're cops, for crissake."

"I own 'em."

"Honest to God?" Phil heard a voice from behind him say. Startled, Phil turned quickly and saw Tony for the first time. He was only five-three and would barely tip the scales at 110 pounds, but he had managed to remain undetected, which gained Phil's immediate respect. Later, Phil said of Tony, "He had big black glasses. They looked like he'd taken the bottoms off of two Coke bottles and put frames around them. He wasn't at all what I'd expected." Tony was from Revere, Angelo told Phil, but had always hung out with kids from the North End.

Of the time they met, Phil said, laughing, "When the guy said 'Honest to God' he blessed himself!" It reminded me of when we were little kids in the North End and someone would challenge whatever you said by saying, 'Mother's honor?' Then you had to raise your right hand and say 'Mother's honor' back to him. If you couldn't say 'Mother's honor,' everyone knew you were lying. I don't even know why, but that day I said to Tony, 'Mother's honor.' All three of us started to laugh hysterically."

That was the start of a three-man team that would become legendary in New England throughout the 1960s. They were a most unlikely threesome.

Phil was quiet, introspective, always plotting the next move. He never shared himself or any details of his life with any of them. They learned, though, that, like his father, he had a temper.

Angelo was an imposing physical presence whose menacing look was enough to scare anyone. Like Phil, Angelo was quiet and a perfectionist who never tired of going over details. He had a steady temperament.

And Tony. "The son of a bitch never shut up," joked Phil. "He had a habit of saying the wrong thing at the wrong time, and then apologizing over and over until he had to be physically threatened to make him shut up. I once told him he had foot-in-the-mouth disease, and Angelo said, 'Don't tell him that; he'll be at Mass General tomorrow demanding a checkup.' We would be clocking jobs, and there were times when Tony spoke nonstop for over two hours," Phil said in amazement. "It would get so bad, Angelo and I would have to completely shut him out—but he'd keep on talking anyway."

While Phil and Angelo looked like wise guys, Tony looked the exact opposite, which worked in their favor on many occasions. "Not only could he talk," Phil said, "the son of a bitch could eat. And he never stopped talking about food. He'd say, 'Hey, Phil, how about this for a sangwich?' and then he'd describe his idea for a new kind of sandwich for the next half hour. Once he told me, 'Phil, I could make you a sangwich that would make your dick stiff.'"

That was the team: three men nobody knew. Three men who would steal millions of dollars in just six and a half years. Three men—one from the North End, one from Medford, and one from Revere—who would have died for each other and often came close to doing so. Their three-man crime wave eventually had everyone from J. Edgar Hoover to Brink's, Incorporated, trying in exasperation to catch them.

IN SOME WAYS Phil Cresta was unlike any of the other wise guys who hung around the North End. First of all, he didn't consider himself a wise guy, and he certainly never gambled. A lot of the North End wise guys walked around with the thousand-dollar suits and four pounds of jewelry. Phil Cresta thought that jewelry was something to steal, not wear. Because he shunned the limelight, most police officers didn't know Phil Cresta from Phil Rizzuto. That was just the way Cresta wanted it. In today's jargon Phil would be called a control freak. Back then he was often called a taskmaster.

He went over every detail of every plan until he knew what he'd be doing step by step. When he teamed up with Angelo and Tony, he'd have them go over details until they could recite in their sleep where they were to be, and at what time exactly, because it was planning and good decision making that kept them alive and out of jail.

While Phil was planning the parking meter scam, he watched parking attendants for hours. He noted what they wore, how they opened the meters, all their mannerisms. When he went to Chicago to have the duplicate keys made, he asked the gang's locksmith if the Accardo mob had a tailor. People who heard the question assumed Phil wanted to pick up a few new suits while he was in the Windy City. He was given the name and address of a guy the Chicago syndicate used. "Can this guy be trusted?" Phil asked one of Accardo's hit men. "Yeah, I promise he won't tell a soul that you wear a forty-four long," the guy said, laughing. "I don't want a suit," Phil responded, "I don't wear them. I need someone to make me a uniform." He was driven to the tailor in downtown Chicago.

Phil handed the tailor a picture of a Boston parking meter attendant and asked if he could make that uniform. The tailor studied the photo and said, "I can match everything except the patches." Phil produced two pristine patches that a certain woman in the Boston traffic commissioner's office had given to him. "Are these all right?" he asked. "They're perfect," the tailor answered, full of new respect. This was the start of a long friendship and working relationship between Cresta and the

Chicago tailor, who received a nice Christmas bonus from Boston from then on.

The tailor kept Phil's, Angelo's, and Tony's sizes on file. Phil would fly to Chicago and have whatever uniform he needed made while he visited his sister, or he would send the tailor a photo in the mail with specific instructions. All three uniforms would be sent to Phil by mail.

"Blending in was half the battle," Phil said. "My guy in Chicago was the best. He would even put phony name tags on the uniforms that we wore. We felt invincible, and that helped us to do what we had to do. We had every kind of armored guard uniform in existence. We had Brink's uniforms and hats, Skelly uniforms and hats, Armored Car Carrier Corporation uniforms and hats. We also had painters' uniforms or mechanics' uniforms, UPS uniforms—you name it, we had it. When we pulled a job in broad daylight, it didn't matter what we wore, as long as we had masks that concealed our faces. We never wore anything twice, because it would give the feds an MO [method of operation]. Most guys get caught because they forget to take care of the little things. I vowed that would never happen to us."

How they got to and from a crime scene was just as important to Phil as what they did once there. "We would get trucks from different rental companies and have them professionally painted with a bogus company name on the side. Once the job was done, we'd have them repainted the color they were when we rented them." Many times, when they returned a truck or van, the owner would remark how clean the truck looked, never realizing that it had a brand-new paint job.

The same thing held true for cars. Tony and Angelo were two of the best car thieves in the business. When they spotted the car they wanted, they would break into it and take off in less than a minute. "Stealing the car wasn't the hard part, it was *where* you stole it that mattered," Phil noted. They never had a stolen car for more than one day. That was an absolute rule.

"The last thing we needed," Phil pointed out, "was to have the car we were riding in on the stolen car list."

Logan Airport's long-term parking lot was an ideal source of cars. The night before a score was to go down, Tony and Angelo would drive over to the airport and park their car near the long-term lot. It was amazing to Phil how naive people could be. "People would actually put a note on the dashboard near the front window saying when they'd be returning from their trip. It was like taking candy from a baby." Angelo and Tony would search for a car with such a note. As soon as they found one it was theirs, as long as the car's inspection sticker was valid. Long-term parking was one twenty-dollar fee, whether your car sat for five or twenty days—so there were no tickets. Tony or Angelo, whoever was driving, would pay twenty dollars and be buzzing through the tunnel between the airport and Boston proper before you could say "stolen car."

Then they'd wash the car and inspect it. They looked at the headlights, the brake lights, the directional lights, and anything else that a cop or a state trooper might pull them over for. Once confident that the car was in decent shape, they would park it at the Fenway Motor Inn lot until the job began. When the job was completed, Tony would drive the car back to Logan and put it back where he'd found it or in a spot nearby. He'd walk out of the lot and drive home with Angelo, who would have followed him.

Nobody ever reported a stolen car because of them, and the owners were often pleasantly surprised that their cars were so clean when they returned. Except for the people who were the team's victims, it was a win-win situation.

5
A Key for Your Thoughts

N SOME WAYS Boston is a small town, and everyone knows who's doing what. By August 1963 Cresta's team was pulling off respectable smaller jobs and not getting caught. "You had to be on your toes all the time," Phil said. "No matter how many friends you had or how many cops you paid off, there was always one guy who didn't like you or one cop who didn't get enough. I was constantly watching my back, constantly paying off people to be quiet. It only takes one pissed-off guy to bring you down. Most of the guys who ended up in Walpole never knew who ratted them out. It was expensive. We had to provide our own muscle just to keep people off our backs. But in a tough business, you gotta do what you gotta do."

Phil, Tony, and Angelo worked at developing a string of "ears" throughout Boston. "You can never have enough ears," Phil stated. "I might have had only two eyes, but I had a couple of hundred ears working for me by the mid-sixties."

These hired ears, not unlike the ones on people's heads, came in different styles. One ear might share information on one good score he'd been planning for years but never had the courage to pull off himself. Another ear might work in a bank or at an armored car facility or in some other business where money changed hands and either wanted more money or simply talked too much. Still another might have a vendetta against a certain individual or company. Everyone knows that the best way to get back at someone is through the pocketbook.

A friendly bartender or barber was one of the best kind of ears; people told them things without being aware they were doing so. Pretty women were great ears too. Then there were the professional ears, or "moles," who made a living out of dealing in information. "I liked working with reliable moles because they knew the importance of keeping their own mouths shut, even though they made a living out of other people opening theirs," Phil explained. A good mole could make a fine living without worrying about going to prison or getting shot, as long as he knew who he was dealing with.

Being an ear was a very competitive business and, as in any other, buyers who paid the most usually got the best results. Everyone knew that Angiulo, now clearly an underboss to Patriarca, could pay the highest price for ears, but a lot of people on the street were afraid to hook up with the mob. This drove them to listen for Phil, Angelo, and Tony. "That was fine with us," Phil said, laughing. "We always paid top dollar for good information. When word got around that we could deliver—and the return was good—we had more info on potential jobs than we could handle. It was simple: you had to spend money to make money. We treated people with respect—not like Angiulo, who intimidated and insulted people—and the good ears always came back to us."

One of Phil's favorite ears was a barber who still owns a shop on Commonwealth Avenue, in Kenmore Square. Phil would hang out there and act as if he were waiting for a haircut. He'd listen to some of the stories and watch the ball players, who stayed at the nearby Kenmore Hotel, come in for haircuts. Mickey Mantle, Whitey Ford, Billy Martin were among the players who came in whenever they were in town, playing the Red Sox. It wasn't surprising to see Mickey Mantle and Billy Martin in the barbershop one morning and then at McGrail's, getting last call that night. The bartender at McGrail's was Phil's other favorite ear. "People tend to tell a friendly bartender or barber a lot more than they tell anyone else. Every bartender and barber who worked in Kenmore Square was on our payroll," Phil explained.

Kenmore Square was now Phil's center of operation. It was away from Angiulo's North End operations, and since Phil had separated from his wife, Dorothy, earlier in 1963, he'd been living rent-free at the Fenway Motor Inn, across the street from McGrail's. The motel was owned by the legendary Boston exdentist and bookmaker Doc Sagansky, who was a close friend of Phil's. Since the mobster didn't charge for the two rooms Phil kept there, whenever he scored big, Phil compensated Sagansky in return.

At this time, there were several banks around Kenmore Square. One day after a Sox game a bartender at McGrail's mentioned to Phil that a guard had been coming into the bar after the bank closed, and he regularly stayed until last call. Phil stored the information away and asked the bartender, who was on Phil's payroll, to point the guy out the next time he came in. About a week later, Phil and Angelo were in the bar, and the bartender kept looking toward Phil to get his attention. When the bartender had it, he motioned his head toward a guy sitting alone at the end of the bar. The guy wore a bank guard's uniform.

Phil told Angelo he had some business to attend to and moved to the stool next to the bank guard. Phil started talking about the Red Sox, a subject everyone in Boston had an opinion about. Within an hour he had this guard thinking he was his new best friend.

The guard, it turned out, had no family and was bitter that life had passed him by. He made little money at his job, and it was obvious that he liked to drink. Phil began buying him top-shelf whiskey, meeting him nightly, and listening to his tales of woe. Within a week Phil had the guard in his pocket.

One night the guard got really drunk. When last call came,

Phil invited him to sleep it off at one his rooms at the Fenway Motor Inn. He had two, he pointed out, and they were conveniently located right across the street. The guard was reluctant at first. Phil told him he'd set the alarm so the guard would be on time for work. When Cresta added that there was unlimited booze at the inn, the setup was synched. A half hour after entering Phil's room, the guard was out cold.

Phil telephoned Angelo, who came over. Together they went through the guard's belongings. "The guy had a key ring hooked onto his belt, so we took the keys off one by one. When we had them all, we took them next door to the room I used for a workshop and made duplicates," Phil said. He set the alarm for the guard as he'd told him he would, returned all the keys to the key ring, and spent the night in his second room. Two nights later the guy was back at McGrail's, falling all over himself, thanking Phil for his kindness and hospitality. After giving the man half a dozen drinks, Phil remarked that the guard carried a lot of keys on his ring and asked what they were all for. "Oh, some are for my house and some are for work," the guy replied nonchalantly. Phil called Angelo.

Several hours later, around three-thirty in the morning, they headed over to a certain Kenmore Square bank. "There's no way they'd give that drunk any important keys," Angelo insisted as Phil tried one in the bank's back door, then a second. The tumblers clicked. Phil turned to Angelo and responded, "That drunk just got us into this bank." Phil and Angelo looked at each other, laughed, relocked the door, and walked away.

Within a week, Phil's team knew everything they needed to know about the bank's layout. "Getting into a bank isn't that hard, all you have to do is break the window. It's what you do once you're in that determines whether you go from there to Hawaii or Walpole," Phil said philosophically.

They waited for a night when the Red Sox would be away and the weather rainy. That night came in late August 1963.

Tony drove the car, which he parked behind the bank, to wait for the getaway. Phil and Angelo, dressed as industrial cleaning men, carried their equipment down a long alley. They dumped that equipment at the bank's back door. Within seconds Phil had disabled the alarm, and they were inside, thanks to the duplicate key they had made. They headed directly toward the vault, knowing that it would take at least seven minutes before anyone would come to check on the disabled alarm. Having made several earlier trips to case the bank, they were as familiar with its layout as they were with their own homes. They did not turn on any lights, for Phil considered that too risky.

Within thirty seconds of entering, Phil was kneeling in front of the vault. Since there were no windows in the room, he turned on a little flashlight that gave him just enough light to see the numbers. In less than a minute Phil had the lock picked and he was inside the ancient vault. "I can't believe how much banks spend on alarms and how little they spend on vault locks," Phil later commented. They were in and out of the bank in less than three minutes.

"We scared the shit out of Tony when we came back out so quick," Phil said, laughing. "What's wrong, what's wrong?" he kept asking. "Nothing. Just drive—and take your time. We're in no hurry. Just take it easy," Phil said to reassure his nervous partner. The next day the bank reported that $75,000 was stolen from the vault by professional thieves. "We appreciated the compliment," Phil said, "but we got only fifty-five thousand that night. It seems we weren't the only crooks in that bank." The bank president inflated the amount stolen, to get more insurance money. He was not caught.

As planned, the guard they got the key from never knew he was in any way connected to the robbery. He was questioned on five different occasions, but he had nothing to tell. Phil, who was never questioned about that heist, made it a habit to pick up the guard's bar tab from that night on. Keeping a source safe was a matter of pride.

6

Expensive Cup of Java

ROM 1962 THROUGH 1964 the team made a living—not a great one, but they managed to get by. As they began to rob higher-level marks, they found themselves spending more time clocking and pulling jobs and, eventually, no time at legitimate jobs. They kept the appearance of holding down legal jobs, however. Phil paid a car dealer to make it look as if he worked for the man. This gave Phil an alibi when jobs were pulled, and gave the car dealer extra money.

As Phil put it, "People think that robbing's easy. But we worked hard every day at it, from morning until night. When we planned a hit, we left nothing to chance. There's always the possibility that something will happen during job to make you change plans. The difference between a successful robber and a robber who goes to jail is planning for the unexpected."

By late 1964 they were still pulling small-time scores but always looking for the one score that would take them to the next level. Angelo and Tony were anxious for that big score, but Phil warned them not to force things. Their days of eating at the Ritz-Carlton would come, and in the meantime, they certainly weren't starving.

Phil said of those days, "I knew our break would come if we continued to work carefully and look for opportunities."

When planning a score Phil took everything into account, especially the weather. As he had with his parking meter theft and with the Kenmore Square heist, Phil continued to use the weather to his advantage. A case in point is the famous Quincy armored car robbery.

In Phil's words, "We were out clocking armored cars in Braintree one day in November, when we happened to see a guard come out of a supermarket carrying a moneybag. He walked straight to an unmarked station wagon, threw the moneybag in the backseat, and got into the front passenger seat. He nodded to the driver, who looked all around and then took off. But it was what they did next that really caught our attention." Phil laughed when he related this story. "It seemed too good to be true," he said. "Mistakes like that were what we lived for. We immediately dropped the other plans we had and began to put all our time and effort into casing that job."

The first day they spotted the guards was Saturday, November 14, 1964. The team watched them leave the Braintree supermarket, make two more stops, and then stop for coffee and lunch at the Wheel House Diner, at 453 Hancock Street in Quincy. Against all policy, they left the money in the car—untended.

To make sure they broke policy consistently, Phil, Tony, and Angelo followed them in different cars for six more Saturdays. One week Phil drove. The next week Tony drove, and the next Angelo. The guards never looked around to see if they were being tailed, but it still paid to be safe. The team fine-tuned their plans en route. Finally, after seven freezing trips, the team decided it was time to take them down. They planned for January 2, 1965, but then Phil told Angelo and Tony to hold off.

They were irritated. They reminded Phil how easy a mark this was. "Easy I like; perfect I like better," Phil told them. "We need to wait for a little cooperation." Tony and Angelo complained about waiting that week and the following Saturday too. But on Saturday, January 16, 1965, exactly nine weeks after they'd first spotted the guard in Braintree, Phil got his cooperation.

It began snowing in the early morning hours, and while every other guy in Boston was thinking about the AFL all-star game in which Patriots linebacker Nick Buonoconti would run back a seventeen-yard fumble for a touchdown, Phil Cresta was thinking about two guards and a diner in Quincy.

"It's on," he said to Angelo. Angelo just grinned. He knew exactly what he had to do, so he got the car. With a smiling Tony in the backseat, Phil got into the front. They drove to a parking lot in Quincy, where Phil picked the lock of a nondescript 1963 Buick.

Phil drove Tony in the stolen Buick to the spot they had chosen, about thirty yards from the diner. They parked. Angelo drove the other car to their predetermined rendezvous point, a mile and a half from the diner. Phil and Tony watched people entering the diner from the front seat of the Buick. "There's always nervous tension at a time like that," Phil noted, "but we felt very good about the situation. We just weren't sure of the take." About twenty-five minutes later, the station wagon carrying the two guards pulled into the parking lot. Phil watched the guards lock the car and head inside for a hot cup of coffee and a lunch they would never forget.

Phil got out of the driver's seat. Tony slid over and picked up the binoculars, with which in a minute or two he would begin casing the area around the diner. Phil had a hat pulled almost completely over his face, a heavy coat, fake glasses, and winter gloves. To any person walking or riding by he looked as if he was just another guy trying to keep warm, to shield himself from the elements. As he got near the station wagon he quickly looked at the diner window where the two guards always sat. Though the window was ten feet from the station wagon, it was, as Phil had hoped, completely frosted over.

Phil could have picked the lock in seconds, but he didn't. Like an amateur, he simply broke the vent window and opened the front door. As he did, he spotted a cardboard box about the size of a case of beer on the front seat. He grabbed it and walked back down to the end of the driveway, where Tony was waiting. The robbery took less than thirty seconds.

Once in the car, Phil had a hard time containing his excitement. He knew by the number of bags and manila envelopes in the cardboard box that this score was going to be profitable. "How'd we do, how'd we do?" Tony kept asking as he drove them away. Phil didn't reply. The two met up with Angelo and ditched the stolen Buick.

Meanwhile, the two guards, laughing, left the diner and headed for their station wagon. They quickly froze in their tracks—and not because of the weather. Then they ran back into the diner screaming, "Call the police! Somebody stole our deposits!"

Within minutes, the Norfolk Downs section of Quincy was awash with police cars. Quincy Police, working with FBI agents from the Boston bureau, told the press that the actual amount of money stolen was $119,047.19. Guards Joseph Whitfield and James E. Carroll of the Skelly Detective Agency had just been "Crested."

AS PHIL, TONY, AND ANGELO drove along Route 3 to Cape Cod, Angelo asked, "Any problems, Phil?"

"Naw, piece of cake," Phil responded, laughing. He had finished looking over the take.

"Speaking of cake, I'm kinda hungry," Tony said.

Angelo and Phil just shook their heads, amazed at how anyone could be hungry at a time like this.

"How much?" Angelo anxiously inquired.

"Over a hundred large." Phil waited for a reaction.

"Wow! I thought these guys were small-time." Angelo reached over to look in the bag. "I would've been happy with twenty or twenty-five large."

Phil slapped his hand. "Take it easy, we'll count it more closely when we get to the Cape."

Angelo was quiet for a few minutes, but as they were passing Norwell he asked, "Did you pick it okay?"

"I didn't use a pick," Phil shot back.

"How'd ya open it up?"

"The old-fashioned way." Phil, the best lock man on the East Coast, smiled. "I broke the fucking window."

Phil could tell from the looks on their faces that they needed an explanation. "I knew the guards couldn't see shit because the window was frozen over and the snow was coming down pretty good. Ya with me?"

They both nodded like students at Christopher Columbus High in the North End.

"I didn't want to give the cops nothing to go on—no MO—especially with Tilley still out there. Okay so far?"

Again they both nodded. They knew how angry Tilley still was that Phil had "stolen" his gang. Keeping Tilley thinking the Cresta team wasn't making a lot of money was wise.

Professor Phil went on slowly. "I wanted them to think this was a small-time hood who got lucky, so I decided to bust the window and open the door just like we did when we were kids on Hanover Street."

Angelo was shaking his head in admiration.

Tony said, "Yeah, Phil, but we never scored no hundred large on Hanover Street."

Then all three sat back, lesson over, and drove in silence until Plymouth, where Tony announced, "*Now* I get it! That's why you waited two extra weeks? You were waiting for the snow?"

"Light dawns on Marblehead," Phil responded, and he and Angelo laughed the rest of the way to the Bourne Bridge and Cape Cod.

7
Holiday Weekend Activity

Y THE TIME 1965 rolled around, the Cresta crew was on the edge of "living large." Besides the Quincy armored car heist, they had hit another Kenmore Square bank for $40,000, working on a tip from a woman employed in the bank, who was dating Angelo. As with the bank guard, she never knew that she had given out crucial information to her boyfriend, who was just a plain mechanic—or so she thought. It got to the point where Phil's crew was getting too many leads, and as a result, they were able to choose their jobs.

"We were sitting pretty good in the mid-sixties. We had a lot of money stored away, and the word on the street was that we were stand-up guys who could be trusted. I always worried about Angiulo, because we weren't giving him a dime, which pissed him off. But he never bothered us," Phil said. "For a guy in my business, it's always important to be dealing from strength. We were on top in the sixties and everyone knew it. We had juice even though we weren't made men. You always rob from strength; never rob when you're down, that's when you get caught. We paid what we had to pay for information, and we never got burned. You do what you have to do, you pay what you have to pay, and you go on to the next job. Simple as that."

The barbershop where Phil hung out is located on the bottom floor of a five-story apartment building on Commonwealth Avenue. Phil was in the shop one day in April 1965 when a well-dressed man entered and asked Phil if he was next. Phil shook his head. The well-dressed man got in the chair and gave the barber precise instructions on how to cut his hair. When he left, Phil asked his barber friend, Frank, who the rich guy was. His name was Percy Rideout, Frank said, and he was a coin and stamp collector. "What's he doing here?" Phil asked, his curiosity piqued. "He lives upstairs, on the third floor," Frank replied. "How often does he come in for a haircut?" Phil asked. "Too friggin often," the barber replied, not hiding his disdain. "He says the same friggin thing every time he comes in this friggin place. I guess he thinks I'm retarded or something. Those rich people, they're all assholes."

"Do you get a lot of rich people in here?" Phil asked.

"Naw, thank God. He's about the only one."

Phil left the barbershop and walked down Commonwealth Avenue to Copley Square. He went into the public library there, to do a little research on this Mr. Percy Rideout. What he found started his juices flowing.

"This guy Rideout was the real deal," Phil said. "Just about every publication on stamps, coins, or rare documents had a quote from this guy or at least used his name somewhere in the article."

Phil left the library, called Tony and Angelo, and asked them to meet him at McGrail's. He told them about his run-in with Rideout and about his research at the library. They both listened intently. "What do you think?" Phil asked. "Let's go for it," Angelo said. Tony, a little hesitant, said, "Honestly, Phil, it seems like a lot of work just to get some stamps. Can't we just buy them at the post office?" After they explained to Tony that they weren't going to steal *current* postage stamps, he felt a lot better. From that night on, Percy Rideout's habits were under intense scrutiny, although Rideout never had a clue.

"There was no way of knowing exactly what Rideout had in his apartment and his office, which were on the second and third floors of the building," Phil explained. "Though Rideout was clearly one of the top collectors of stamps, coins, and historical documents in the United States, nobody had ever estimated how much he or his collection was worth. We didn't know if we were looking at two mil or only a hundred thousand dollars," Phil said, "but we knew it was big."

Phil, Angelo, and Tony tailed Rideout for over a month. They learned his habits, his hangouts, his friends—and when he got his weekly haircut, which ultimately proved to be more important than all the other tips combined. Rideout was a creature of habit, and every Wednesday at one o'clock he sat in that barber's chair and issued the same instructions to Frank. "Not too much off the top, just even the sides and trim the back." Cresta and his partners took turns being in the barbershop when Rideout came in so that he wouldn't recognize them. "But," as Phil observed, "that guy was so caught up in himself, Mickey Mantle, Whitey Ford, and Roger Maris could all have been sitting there for a haircut and he wouldn't have noticed."

One Wednesday afternoon Phil took a call from an excited Angelo. "I just left the barbershop," he sputtered. "Rideout told Frank he wouldn't be in next week because he's going to Maine on a fishing trip." The break they'd sought had finally come. They put everything into motion for the Memorial Day weekend, just a few days away.

Rideout's building had two elevators, one for residents, the other a service elevator for deliveries. On Saturday, May 29, Phil placed an Out of Order sign on the service elevator. Phil, Angelo, and Tony were dressed as painters, complete with those white masks for keeping out dust and fumes—and for preventing curious residents from getting a good look at their faces. Their white uniforms had even been painstakingly soiled with three different paint colors. Phil was again acting on his observation that normal people didn't pay much attention to workmen going about their duties; they had their own problems to think about. Rich people paid absolutely *no* attention whatsoever, as long as the workmen seemed ordinary.

"The place was deserted as we put the sign on the elevator and headed up to Rideout's apartment. We even had a work order with Rideout's forged signature, in case anyone questioned us," Phil explained.

Phil picked the lock easily, and they entered the apartment. They were stunned by the size of the safes.

"There were two huge safes in one room and another one in the downstairs room," Phil said. "Anyone with that many huge safes has a lot of stuff he doesn't want other people to get their hands on. From the minute we saw those safes I knew this was going to be a good score." But Phil's exuberance was dampened when he got a close look at the top-of-the-line locks on Rideout's safes: he'd never seen any locks like them. "We've got trouble, Ange," Phil said. "These boxes won't be easy."

Phil spent the next two hours trying to crack the safes. Nothing worked. Angelo and Tony were downstairs in Rideout's office. When they came back, Phil told them it was no-go. "Let's blow 'em," Angelo suggested. "What, are you, crazy?" Tony responded. "We're in an apartment building in the middle of Kenmore Square and you want to blow three safes?" Angelo shot back, "I'm not walking out of here empty-handed." "Let's think this thing over," Phil said, trying to calm them down. After discussing alternatives, they decided to blow the upstairs safes.

They brought four mattresses from Rideout's bedroom and put them next to the larger safe, which was six feet high and four feet wide, and brand-new. Phil told Angelo and Tony to go downstairs and wait, with the truck ready, in case it was needed for a quick escape. Then he measured the charge, attached a long fuse, and taped it to the top two hinges. The charge had to be perfect—if too little, nothing would happen; if too much, the police and firemen would be all over the place. Phil taped the four mattresses around the safe. Then he waited until he heard the truck being started. He lit the fuse, ran into the bathroom, jumped into the bathtub, and waited. In case the blast turned out to be bigger than expected, he didn't want to be too close. "The wait seemed to take forever," Phil remembered.

Finally there was the sound of a mild explosion. Phil went into the den to see if it had worked, for he'd been expecting a much louder blow. The four mattresses had cushioned the sound.

"Those mattresses were pretty well shot, but they'd done the job. I waited for about ten minutes. No cavalry came, so I looked out the back window and told Angelo and Tony to come up," Phil said. "When ya gonna blow it?" Tony asked. Phil smiled and led them into the den, where the two safes were. "Holy shit, Phil, that was good. We didn't even hear nothing," Tony commented. "Cut those hinges like butter," Angelo marveled, as he examined Phil's work.

They emptied out the contents of the large safe, and Tony seemed disappointed. "What's wrong?" Phil asked. "Phil, are you sure this stuff is worth money? It all looks pretty old, if you ask me." "That's the whole point, numbskull," Angelo piped up. "This stuff is valuable *because* it's so old." "I don't get it," Tony replied, frowning, but he continued to take box after box out of the huge safe.

The stuff that baffled Tony sat in more than 250 boxes, each about eighteen inches by four inches, containing valuable coins. There were also 130 albums of rare stamps taken out of the smaller safe, which Phil blew later that day. They had never done a job like this before. The coins weighed more than half a ton, and it took six trips on the service elevator to get everything into the U-Haul truck they'd painted on both sides to say CARDOZZA & SONS PAINTING.

It took them all day and half the night to empty the two safes and transport the contents to a garage in Everett. Two days later, Monday, May 31, the building superintendent discovered the break-in, but it wasn't until June 2, when Rideout returned, that the robbery was reported to the Boston Police. The *Boston Globe*'s front-page headline on Friday, June 4, 1965, read: FAMED

COIN COLLECTION LOOTED HERE. The *Globe* reported that the Back Bay collection of Percy Rideout was considered one of the most prized in the world. The *Herald* stated that Rideout thought the robbery similar to ones pulled by some thieves who had been hitting the largest coin collectors across Europe. After Rideout inventoried his collection it was announced that the Memorial Day robbery was the largest of its kind in history. The *Herald Traveler*'s front page that same day was headlined: RARE COIN COLLECTION VALUED AT $200,000 WIPED OUT. Rideout told police that the thieves' only mistake was that they'd overlooked albums of early American historical material valued at between $100,000 and $150,000. They had been sitting under two photo albums.

Boston policemen assigned to the crime could find no marks indicating that the apartment door had been forced. So, the *Globe* reported, authorities believed the thieves had been well acquainted with Rideout's movements and had used a master key to enter both the second- and third-floor apartments. Authorities were correct about the gang's careful clocking of Rideout, but wrong about their means of entry. Phil's excellent lock picking left little trace of his work.

The team stored all the loot in a garage in Everett that belonged to Phil's friend Jackie the Wolf, a former loan shark, scalper, and bookie who knew Phil from the North End. "Jackie had gotten in real deep and was almost whacked," Phil related. "Sometime before that heist, he'd come crying to me that Angiulo was going to whack him if he didn't pay. I asked him how much he owed. It was $5,500, and he didn't have two nickels to rub together." Phil had intervened with Angiulo on Jackie's behalf and saved Jackie's life. Then he'd made Jackie promise to get out of the business. To say Jackie owed Phil would be an understatement.

Jackie had been married a month when Phil, Angelo, and Tony lined his garage with the stamps, coins, and valuable documents. He was worried about having hot property in his garage: what if his wife found it? Phil told him not to worry; it would be moved in two or three days. But Cresta couldn't get a fence.

It was such unique—and hot—loot that nobody wanted to touch it.

On Friday, with news of the robbery in the papers, Phil met Angelo and Tony at the motor inn. He explained that he'd had no success fencing the material. Tony argued that if they hadn't been able to fence it in the last couple of days, what were they going to do now that the story was on the front page of every newspaper in Boston? Angelo wanted to hold on to the goods until things cooled down. Phil recalled, "I knew Jackie was already having a heart attack; the last thing he needed was for me to tell him to keep the stuff in his garage for a few more months. So we decided to use some of our contacts to see if there was any interest for what we had."

Two days later Tony called Phil to say that he had a guy interested in fencing the loot. He neglected to mention that the fence was his old boss, Ben Tilley.

After Tony told him that Phil was trying to unload the Rideout stuff for the right price, Tilley called a guy named Paul Nester, who just happened to be married to Percy Rideout's daughter. Tilley said he could get his hands on all the property that had been stolen; his asking price was $50,000. Nester agreed to discuss the matter with Percy Rideout and get back to Tilley.

But when Nester told Rideout about his conversation with Tilley, the collector hit the roof and called the police. Detective Charlie Hutchinson and another detective who will be identified here as Joe Leonard were assigned to the case. As soon as they heard Nester's story, they brought Tilley in for questioning.

Tilley told them that someone had phoned him and asked him to be an intermediary. He said he'd been instructed to contact Rideout and make him an offer. Detective Leonard asked Tilley who'd called him. Tilley said he didn't know. Although the detectives knew he was lying, there was nothing they could do.

Rideout told police he'd never pay thieves for his own property. "I don't care about the money," Rideout said, "but I'll never give those bastards a dime. Never."

Nester, on his own, called Tilley and offered $30,000 for the goods. Tilley took the proposal to Tony. Phil refused it and went into a rage when he heard that Tilley was the go-between. As soon as he heard Tilley was involved, he ended the negotiations. Rather than deal with Tilley, Phil called Augie Circella in Chicago. In the meantime, Jackie the Wolf was howling nervously at the moon, as the media jumped all over the "coin robbery of the century."

Augie Circella was now married to Phil's sister Mari. A professional dancer, she had met him when dancing at the Follies Burlesque Theater that Circella owned. Circella, of course, was the man who would help Phil with the Parker House heist later that same year.

Circella called Phil three days later to say he had an interested party, familiar with Rideout's work, who would buy the entire lot for $100,000. Phil was floored. "A hundred large, Augie? You sure?" Phil asked in disbelief. "Not enough, kid?" Augie replied smoothly. You want me to go back and squeeze 'em?" "No, no, Augie. Those numbers are just fine," Phil said, knowing full well what methods Augie used to squeeze people. He hadn't expected more than $50,000. "Think you can get the stuff out here?" Augie asked. "For a hundred large, I'll walk it there," Phil answered, laughing.

The next day Phil, Angelo, and Tony each rented a brand-new Lincoln Continental. They parked two of them in South Boston, and headed toward Jackie's garage in Everett in the third. Jackie the Wolf, at Phil's insistence, had moved his car out of his garage and parked it on the next block.

Jackie walked home that day just in time to see a large black Lincoln Continental turning onto his street. Phil was driving, Angelo was riding shotgun, and Tony was in the backseat. Phil pulled the car into Jackie's garage and they went to work. They took every removable panel off the car. They took out the backseat, placed stamps and coins in the car's panels and behind the backseat, and then reassembled the car. All the particularly valuable items were hidden inside the car's frame. When they finished with that car, they drove it to a warehouse in South Boston, parked it, and returned with an identical Lincoln Continental. To the casual observer—or to any nosy Everett neighbor—it looked as if the same car that pulled out of the garage an hour earlier had returned: same people, same car. They made three trips to the garage in three different cars, then drove the cars to Chicago.

All the way to the Windy City, they kept within eyesight of each other just in case of trouble along the way. There was none. They returned to Boston two days later, a lot richer. They returned the rental cars at Logan Airport, then headed over to Everett once again. This time Phil drove his own Bonneville into Jackie the Wolf's driveway. When they left, the Wolf was also a richer man, to the tune of $5,000—which he used to pay off Angiullo.

Phil, Angelo, and Tony took separate vacations after the Rideout score. Tony and Angelo both used the time to see family in Italy. Phil went to visit his sister in Chicago for a month or so.

Tilley, one of Boston's Finest's favorite robbery suspects, was never again questioned about the Rideout robbery. Rideout continued his weekly Wednesday haircuts, never knowing that they were responsible in any way for the theft. Jackie the Wolf started gambling again and got himself into another jam. This time Phil Cresta did not intervene. Jackie the Wolf disappeared in 1969. His body has never been recovered.

Not much bothered Phil after the successful Rideout job, but he was deeply irritated that Tilley knew they'd pulled it. Phil decided to lie low for a while to see what the fallout would be and whether or not there would be a "Tilley factor." Phil wasn't pleased that Tony had been stupid enough to bring Tilley in as a go-between, but he'd known that Tony would never be mistaken for a Harvard graduate. "Tony is Tony," Phil later explained. "What you see is what you get. He could make a dynamite 'sangwich' and drive a getaway car, but he wasn't going to be a contestant on *Jeopardy!*"

While "vacationing" in Chicago, Phil kept a close eye on the

Boston papers. The Rideout case, after that first media barrage, seemed to slip from the radar screen. In mid-July 1965 Phil decided that the heat had cooled enough for him to return home. He took in some Red Sox games, but was getting itchy for some action of his own. Within a week of his return to Boston, both Angelo and Tony were also back. "We were like the Three Stooges, just hanging around, driving each other crazy," Phil recalled. "We had some serious money in the bank, but life wasn't always about money. There's no way I can describe the feeling you get when you take down an armored car for half a mil or open a vault and see all that soon-to-be green staring you in the face. It's like it's us against them."

8
The Checks Cancel Out

N JULY 26, 1965, one of the team's best informants came calling at McGrail's. Phil said later that he remembered the exact date Cushman came with the news on this potential target because July 26 became an unofficial holiday to the Cresta team only a year later. The informant's name was Cushman and he was a small-timer from South Boston. He had done a few years at Walpole and was well liked by both cops and robbers.

"Cushman should've been a comedian," Phil said. "He was a big red-faced Irishman who weighed about 250 pounds. He always had a grin on his face, as if he found everything in life funny. Cushman reminded me of an oversized leprechaun," Phil said, laughing, "and he always had about ten new jokes. He was the only guy I knew who could tell Jerry Angiulo Italian jokes and make him laugh.

"One day," Phil recalled, "Cushman walked into the European Restaurant on Hanover Street in the North End and spotted Angiulo having dinner with some of Patriarca's mob from Providence. Cushman walked over to the table and asked, 'Hey, Jerry, what happened when the Italian stopped paying his garbage bill?' Angiulo squinted and shrugged. Cushman looked him straight in the eye and said, 'They stopped delivering.' Everybody looked at Angiulo to see his reaction, but there was none. Cushman then inquired, 'Jerry, did you hear about the Italian who locked himself out of his car on Hanover Street?' Angiulo just glared. 'It took him three hours to get his family out.' Angiulo smiled; the others didn't. 'One last one and then I gotta go,' Cushman assured him. 'Why do they bury Italians with their asses sticking out of the ground?' Nobody stirred. 'So their relatives will have somewhere to park their bicycles when they come to the cemetery.' Angiulo began to laugh, and with this cue so did the others, although most of them didn't appreciate Cushman's humor. As Cushman walked away Angiulo said, 'That guy kills me.' One of Patriarca's men, of Italian descent and unappreciative of Cushman's jokes, growled, 'I'd like to kill *him*.' With this, the whole table erupted in laughter.

"I don't know of anyone in the world who could pull a stunt like that, except Cushman," Phil marveled. "He'd tell Irish jokes to Irish cops, Catholic jokes to priests. Nobody was spared, and 'most everyone loved him. That was why he was one of the best ears we had on the street. He was able to get close to many people without raising any antennas."

But Cushman scared Tony, who felt that anyone crazy enough to tell Angiulo those kinds of jokes was too crazy for him. Angelo explained away Tony's fear of the Irishman by simply saying, "Tony just didn't get the punch lines."

Whether you loved him or hated him, Cushman was a welcome sight as he marched into McGrail's that day. Now that the heat was off in regard to the Rideout job, the team was looking for a new lead and Cushman had a reputation for giving information on high-paying scores. There was nothing remotely funny about Cushman when it came to information. He could play the clown, and that's all some people saw. But those people were deceived. Cushman was a shrewd businessman.

And business was the reason he was sitting with the Cresta crew that July afternoon. After the obligatory jokes and some pleasantries, Phil asked what he had. "Sit down," Cushman said to Tony, who responded by asking why. "Just sit the fuck down, that's why," Cushman barked. Tony grabbed a chair and sat at the end of the booth rather than next to the Irishman. He looked at Cushman through suspicious eyes and asked, "Are you happy now?" Cushman didn't reply. "Come on, stop stalling. What's the score worth?" Angelo asked. Cushman looked around to see if anyone was listening, and whispered, "Fifty million." "Dollars?" Tony blurted out. "No. Fucking cannolis, you dipshit," Cushman spat out. "Is this some kind of a joke?" Phil asked. "Serious business," Cushman replied, smiling now. "Fifty mil," Phil whispered. "What are we taking down—Fort Knox?" Angelo blanched, and then said, "I think that's a little out of our league." "Even if all that loot is in an armored truck that travels through Boston?" Cushman asked, beaming now.

"We'll meet you at the Fenway Motor Inn, room nine, in ten minutes," Phil said. And he got up to leave, leading the way.

The very next day Phil, Angelo, and Tony clocked the armored truck that Cushman identified as the one carrying up to $50 million. It was driven by two guards. They would stop at all the banks in downtown Boston and pick up six or more moneybags at each bank. The Cresta crew followed that armored truck every day for three weeks; the routine never varied. It seemed too good to be true.

They met up to four times a week with Cushman, who was all business, no jokes. They knew a score this big would set them up for life. Phil wanted to make sure every issue was considered before they even thought about the robbery itself.

A week before the robbery was scheduled to take place, Cushman showed up at the Fenway Motor Inn and announced that he had some good news and some bad news. Angelo said, "What's the deal, jokeman?" "One of the guards who drives on the route is going on vacation next week." Phil moaned, then said that they didn't need to change plans. "We'll just wait a week till he comes back," Angelo said. All this time Cushman stood there, not saying a word. Finally he announced, "Whoa, whoa, take it easy. Do you want to hear the good news now?"

They all stared at him. "This armored truck company is so cheap they're not replacing him." He let what he had said sink in. Phil looked at Angelo and they both looked at Tony. *"Get the fuck outta here, Cushman,"* Tony yelled. "You telling me these guys are letting one guard carry fifty million dollars?" Smugly Cushman responded, "That's what I'm telling you."

"Well then, we've got ourselves a ball game," Phil said, breaking the silence.

The next Monday morning, after the three of them had breakfast at the Hayes Bickford's in South Station, they headed toward the Bank of Boston on Water Street and waited for the armored truck to make its daily delivery. Sure enough, just as Cushman had told them it would, the truck had only one guard inside. The guard had to make four trips into the bank, twice the number he and his partner normally made. The Cresta team couldn't believe what they were seeing. They met that night with Cushman and Phil asked, "Are you sure they're moving that much money?" "Absolutely," a grinning Cushman responded. Phil looked around and announced, "We take him on Saturday." Nobody responded; there was nothing more to say.

The group had one final strategy session, without Cushman, on Friday, August 20, 1965. All was now ready. They left the Fenway Motor Inn at 5:30 on Saturday morning, August 21, and headed toward North Station.

At 6:50 an armored truck owned by Armored Car Carrier Corporation headed west on Causeway Street, then took a left up the ramp onto the Southeast Expressway. Traffic was light that morning as the driver, working alone, headed south, oblivious to the light blue car that followed closely behind him. As the truck approached the High Street off ramp, the driver felt a small jolt, for the front right bumper of the blue car had struck the rear left bumper of the armored truck. The driver of the truck, seeing that the High Street off ramp was less than fifteen feet away, headed down the ramp and pulled over to exchange papers with the driver of the blue car.

As he started to get out of the truck, the driver was confronted by two masked men who produced guns and forced him back into the cab of the truck. "What do you want?" the frightened driver asked the gunmen. "Money," one said. "I don't have any," the driver pleaded. "We heard different," one of the gunmen replied.

The smaller of the two bandits then jumped into the passenger side of the truck. As soon as he was in, he pointed his gun at the driver's head and asked if he knew where the Columbia Point project was. The driver did. He was told to proceed slowly to the Columbia Point Housing Development on the border of South Boston and Dorchester. The other bandit drove the blue car and followed the truck. At one point during the ten-minute trip the driver looked in his rearview mirror. He was told if he did that one more time, it would be the last thing he ever did. The robber in the armored truck kept his mask on during the entire trip and crouched down to avoid detection by anyone driving by. At seven on a Saturday morning, traffic headed out of Boston, as they were headed, was extremely light.

The armored truck and the blue car trailing it left the expressway at the Columbia Station exit, went around the rotary, and down Mt. Vernon Street into the Columbia Point project. The two vehicles proceeded to the very end of the street before turning into a vacant lot—a "greenie," as it is called in Boston. A man was sitting behind the wheel of a car parked there. Once the truck pulled to a stop the driver was tied with baling wire, gagged, blindfolded, and then retied to the truck's steering wheel by the person who had ridden with him. One robber then began to transfer the sixty-four bags from the truck to the car parked in the greenie. Wearing surgical gloves, he and the other two bandits made the transfer in less than five minutes. It was not yet seven-thirty in the morning when the bandits finished their task and drove away.

The driver waited for about fifteen minutes, and then began to bang his head on the horn. At first there were only angry demands from nearby residents that the noise stop. After twenty-five minutes, though, a woman walked from her apartment across the street to the armored truck. She untied the driver and then ran back home and called the police.

Detectives John Halliday and Joseph Montalo of the MDC (Metropolitan District Commission) police were assigned to call the local banks and tell them that there had been a holdup. Halliday asked the driver how much the thieves had gotten. "Nothing," he answered. Halliday, confused, asked if the truck had been carrying any money. "No, sir," the guard replied. "Just canceled checks."

Within thirty minutes of the robbery, the greenie was overrun with the media. The MDC police held a press conference at noon in their South Boston barracks, located only half a mile from the robbery. They described how the truck was stolen; how the driver was bound, blindfolded, and gagged; and how the robbers cleaned out the truck and were gone in less than five minutes. A reporter asked how much was taken. The answer: "Nothing." Dumbfounded, the reporter asked, "What *was* taken, then?" "Sixty-four bags of canceled checks," Detective Halliday responded. The room erupted in laughter.

Phil Cresta, back at the Fenway Motor Inn, saw nothing even remotely funny about this news.

Once they had transferred the sixty-four bags that they'd believed contained money, the team left the stolen blue car and jumped into the car that Angelo had driven to a predetermined transfer location. They were giddy with excitement as they drove down Columbia Road and then headed for the Fenway Motor Inn. Phil had never seen so many moneybags in one truck, and he was trying to gauge how much money they had stolen. "Cushman was right on the money, it looks like," Tony said. "Angelo was very quiet on the ride back to the Fenway," Phil recalled. "I knew something was bothering him, but I was too caught up in the moment to focus on his problems."

They rolled into the parking lot at the motor inn a little after eight o'clock. "We backed the car up to my room and took one bag out of the trunk. They emptied the contents of the bag onto the lone bed in the room and their hearts dropped. "Get another one," Phil barked to Tony. Same thing: canceled checks, no money. By the time they had emptied a dozen moneybags on the bed, it was clear that there would be no big payday, at least not that day. Phil was livid. Tony was babbling. Angelo said, "I knew it. There's no way they were gonna let one man guard fifty mil, no way. We should kill that fucking mick Cushman."

At noon they turned on the television to catch the news. The cops and the reporters were laughing at them. Phil could hardly bear it. "Nobody knows about this ever, do you hear me?" he screamed. Phil looked at Tony and said, "If Tilley finds out about this, we might as well get out of town. Do you understand, Tony?" Tony shrugged and never looked up.

"What about Cushman? What do we do about him?" Angelo asked. "Not a thing," Phil said. "You don't think Cushman will want to take any credit for the stupidest robbery in history, do you? In this business if you got no muscle, you better have good sources. Cushman will be through in this town if word gets out he put this fiasco together," Phil said.

It got even more embarrassing. The *Boston Evening Globe's* front-page story on August 21 read, "Downtown Boston this morning had history's greatest armored car theft . . . of canceled checks." The story went on to say, "The robbery, which took one hour in broad daylight, netted the bandits between \$25–\$50 million in canceled checks." The *Boston Herald Traveler* was much nastier. Its front-page story read, "A pair of bandits, who must have spent their early years transmuting gold into lead, bungled yesterday as they tried to pull off what could have been history's largest armored car theft. . . . The only trouble was that the checks were cancelled and scarcely worth the price of an admission to *The Lavender Hill Mob*. . . . The bandits may be feeling frustrated right now, but so do the bookkeepers, who will probably have to put in a good deal of overtime in the next few days straightening out the records. One last note . . . The *Herald* can't confirm it, but there are those who claim that the bandits' convertible was an Edsel, a discontinued model, easily trace-able. With their luck, it figures."

"If I'd had Cushman in front of me then, I probably would've whacked him," Phil recalled. "I knew Angelo was out looking for him, even though I asked him to let it go." Tony and Angelo took all the bank bags to the incinerator near City Hospital and burned them. "We went from the penthouse to the outhouse in a matter of minutes," Phil said. "It sure was humiliating. I'm just glad nobody knew who pulled the job."

Cushman disappeared for a couple of months until things died down. Phil told Tony and Angelo not to dwell on what could have been, and to think about their next score. But that was hard for even Phil to do. Finally he got word from an inter-mediary that Cushman wanted to talk. The two of them met at Castle Island in Southie. Cushman insisted they meet at a crowded place because he thought he was going to get whacked.

There were no jokes that day, just apologies. He was like a scared child, whimpering and apologizing. He said he'd gotten some bum information. Phil agreed. Cushman then asked Phil about Angelo, and was told he should stay away from Angelo for the rest of his life, or Angelo would shorten that life consider-ably. Cushman agreed. Phil made it very clear that if he ever mentioned the canceled-check robbery to anyone, Cresta would kill him. Cushman thanked Phil and left. "I never saw Cushman after that day," Phil noted.

"Angelo was pretty shook up by the fiasco. He stayed in his house for a couple of weeks, which was unlike him," Phil said. Finally Angelo called Phil at McGrail's. "He sounded depressed, so I told him we were having a big surprise birthday party at McGrail's for Tony," Phil recalled. At first Angelo feigned indif-ference, but Phil told him how disappointed Tony would be if he was AWOL. Angelo grudgingly agreed to stop by.

When he showed up at McGrail's he was astounded to hear everyone start singing "Happy Birthday" to him as he walked in the door. "What the hell's going on, Phil?" Angelo asked as the regulars continued to serenade him. "We're having a birthday party. What's it look like?" Phil said, laughing. "You told me it was *Tony's* birthday," Angelo yelled over the singing. "Well, I guess we're even because I told Tony it was *yours.*" Phil smiled. "What the fuck are you up to?" Angelo asked angrily. "Lighten up, Ange, I just wanted us to do some celebrating together, that's all." "*Celebrate!*" Angelo yelled sarcastically. "We look like a bunch of no-talent clowns and you want to celebrate? Celebrate *what?*" "Celebrate that we're all alive, celebrate that nobody's going to jail, and celebrate that nobody knows we had anything to do with that canceled-check robbery. Is that enough for you?" Phil angrily shot back. Angelo hung his head and after a few seconds he said shyly, "I'm sorry, Phil. I guess I've been acting like an asshole. You're right. I got nothing to bitch about." Phil smiled and said, "Well, come on, let's drink up. And happy birthday."

That was the last time the canceled-check robbery was ever brought up.

9
Kansas City, Here We Come

ESPITE THE CANCELED-CHECKS FIASCO, the team was doing well. After the Parker House heist, Phil decided that, though there was nothing that matched the adrenaline rush of opening a vault or popping an armored car, for the time being he liked being a jewel thief. "It was like being Cary Grant in *To Catch a Thief*," he later remarked.

After the Rideout job in May 1965 and the Parker House heist in October of that year, Phil Cresta began to have a bigger name with the wise guys in Chicago than he did in Boston. That was just the way he wanted it. Between January and Halloween 1965 the team had made over three-quarters of a million dollars.

Bank robberies and armored car hits drew a lot of media attention, though, and that, in turn, drew the interest of people like Angiulo and Tilley. Phil didn't want that. If Angiulo ever learned that Phil had made over three-quarters of a million dollars in ten months right under his nose, there would have been trouble. The best thing about the Parker House job, Phil decided, was its absence of publicity. The hotel and the insurance companies had taken the hit and kept their mouths shut because they didn't want to invite copycat robberies. So, for a

while, he and his team concentrated on crimes with little publicity.

Thanks to their recent big scores, the Cresta team was able to
buy higher-placed ears. Although they kept their street informants, Phil, Angelo, and Tony began to move in new circles. After his Parker House tip paid off, Louie Diamonds, in Boston,
became one of their most regular ears for some time. Mari's
husband, Augie Circella, in Chicago, was also turning out to be
an invaluable connection. These and other new informants
acted as go-betweens, so the Cresta team rarely met face-to-face
with the people now selling them information.

If the team liked a potential job Louie or Circella told them
about, they went forward. If they didn't, they looked elsewhere.
It was nice to be able to pick and choose.

Many of the Circella sources were guys making six figures but
who had gambling or investment "problems" and needed quick
cash. One of these indirect six-figure informants led them,
through Circella, to Kansas City. Phil soon had an airplane pilot
on his payroll.

The pilot had done a lot of work for the Chicago mob. A former TWA pilot, he had gotten in over his head with loan sharks
and was forever compromised by the Chicago wise guys. He
now chartered legitimate planes, but often for illegitimate pur-
poses. Sometimes he would fly such people as Sam Giancana
and Gussie Alex to Vegas or Hollywood. The man jumped at the
chance to make money with this new Boston team.

But it was a lot different for the Cresta crew to fly to Kansas
City instead of driving around Boston to pull a score; Tony had
never been on a plane and he was scared. When Phil told him
they we were flying to the Midwest for a job, he asked, "Aren't
there enough jobs in Boston?" "Not like this one," Phil told him.
Tony went along—kicking and screaming, but he went.

On their first flight from Logan in November 1965, Phil and
Angelo each brought only a shaving kit. Tony arrived with
enough food to feed an army. Knowing that food was his comfort, Phil and Angelo chuckled, but not to Tony's face. By the

time the plane touched down in Kansas City, Tony was the pilot's buddy, sitting next to him in the cockpit, feeding him his special "sangwiches," and asking a million questions. He loved every minute of the flight, except the takeoff and landing. They never again had to coax Tony to fly.

Their first job outside New England was just before Thanksgiving 1965 and involved furs. Augie Circella, through his connections, had become very friendly with the Civella family, who ran everything in Kansas City. The Kansas City mob owned the Tropicana Hotel and they told Augie about a fur dealer who stayed there twice a year and who carried particularly precious furs with him. "We had never done anything with furs," Phil explained, "but Augie assured me they were even easier than diamonds to unload. Plus, he told us, it was wise to make friends with the Civella family, with whom we'd be splitting the take. So we went for it."

The furrier's partner had the bad habit of losing money on the ponies. He was in debt to the Kansas City mob for over $100,000 and the meter was running. The Civella family didn't want to steal anything from a hotel they owned, so Augie had offered to bring in Phil for the job. It was a simple "pick and haul" job, according to Augie. No hardware, no violence, just pick the lock and take the furs. The victim and his partner would collect insurance, part of which would pay back the Civellas. Phil would fence the furs and split that take with Augie.

Phil was assured that the loot would be in the furrier's hotel room. The guy they were hitting was known to love spending time with the ladies when he was at the Tropicana. This was taken into consideration when Phil planned the score.

The first night in Kansas City, Tony staked out the furrier's room, waiting at the end of the hall. When the guy came out, Tony followed him down to the lobby and into the lounge. The guy weighed about 280 pounds. He was wearing a leisure suit and a toupee that hadn't set him back much money. He certainly had an eye for the ladies, but given his looks, the only lady he was likely to take to his room that night would be one who charged for her services. Phil, Angelo, and Tony watched with amusement as the poor guy tried unsuccessfully to pick up one woman after another. Phil recalled, "The guy struck out more than Reggie Jackson on a very bad day."

That night, after the lounge closed, Phil called Augie in Chicago. "Something wrong?" Augie whispered when he heard Phil's voice. "It's late, Phil. You scared me." Phil humorously related the events of the evening to Augie, who laughed uproariously. Phil asked Augie if he had a woman who would knock the furrier's socks off just by walking into the lounge. "You want a pro?" Augie asked. "No, no prostitutes. I need a real looker, someone appealing but not cheap." There were a few seconds of silence and then Augie said, "I got exactly what you need. I'll call you tomorrow with the details."

The Accardo family, who ran Chicago at that time, was heavily involved in the movie business. They had vast holdings and many friends in Hollywood. After Augie spoke with Phil, he called Sid Korshak, who looked after the mob's interests in Hollywood, and told him what they needed. A wink of an eye from Korshak could make or break a starlet's career.

As promised, Augie telephoned Phil at nine the next morning. "We're all set, Phil. She'll be landing at three-thirty." "Where's she coming from?" Phil inquired. "Hollywood, where else?" was Augie's response.

"What does she look like?" Phil asked. "How will I know her?"

Augie began to chuckle and said reassuringly, "Don't worry, Phil. You'll know her when you see her."

Phil grabbed Angelo and Tony and told them they had to go to the Kansas City airport for a "package." They went to a bar in the airport and waited, with Tony peppering Phil about what kind of package he was expecting. Phil told him to be patient. At three-thirty Phil and the other two men headed over to the gate where the flight was scheduled to arrive. Most of the passengers alighted from the plane. Tony kept pestering Phil, who was starting to get a little worried. The furrier would be leaving the Tropicana the next day, so they had to strike that night.

Phil looked back at the Arrivals board just to make sure he had the right flight. Then he heard Tony say, "Holy shit!" Phil wheeled around and almost had a heart attack. One of the most beautiful women he'd ever seen was walking into the waiting area. Every eye in the airport turned toward her.

"Phil! Phil! Look at that! Look at that!" Tony exclaimed. "That's our package," Phil replied. "Don't you wish," Tony said.

Phil waved and the beautiful young woman smiled and walked over to him. "Are you Joey Zito?" she asked, using one of Phil's aliases. "That's me," Phil responded. "Welcome to Kansas City." Tony suddenly had trouble finding his voice and Angelo just stared. "Do you have any luggage?" Phil asked. "Do you know any ladies who travel anywhere *without* luggage?" she answered teasingly. Tony and Angelo almost killed each other getting her suitcases.

Phil reminisced later about her. "She was the most incredible woman I've ever seen, and I've seen some lookers. She looked like Marilyn Monroe at her best, and it was amazing how everyone stopped what they were doing, to watch her walk through the airport. Not just men, either. Every woman she passed stopped and stared. She had an innocent sensuality that would've given a eunuch a hard-on."

On their way from the airport to the hotel, they filled her in on some of what was going on. They gave her a picture of the furrier, which had been supplied to the Civella family by the victim's partner. "This is the guy," Phil told her. "You don't have to sleep with him, just keep him occupied for an hour or so. I don't think that's going to be a problem for you," he finished, laughing.

Phil dropped her off outside the hotel, after explaining how important it was that they not be seen with her. She understood and went inside to check in.

Upstairs, they met in her room. Phil told her that, when she saw her mark enter the lounge, the clock was running and she needed to keep him there for at least an hour. And when she saw Phil come back into the lounge, they'd need at least ten more minutes. Then her work would be finished.

He told her not to worry about a thing, all she had to do was play her part and they'd do the rest. He reminded her that Tony would be sitting at the bar, looking after her the whole time in case something went wrong. She asked Phil how they knew the furrier would go into the lounge. "We know more about this guy than his wife does," Phil remarked in a tone that halted more questions about his sources.

"She was no dummy," Phil said. "That night she was simply an actress playing a part. She knew it was an important role, at least as far as influence was concerned. She was so cool beneath that bombshell body. And, man, was she good-looking!"

Phil arrived in the lobby first. He sat in a big overstuffed chair and began to read a newspaper. Angelo arrived five minutes later, sat down, and began to peruse a magazine. Tony already had a seat at the bar, where he seemed to be watching a game show on television. At six o'clock the elevator door opened. Phil and Angelo almost had heart failure.

"She was wearing a tight white dress with a slit up the side. There was cleavage for days, and she had a pair of legs that would've made Betty Grable jealous. She was absolutely breathtaking. And she was a pro. She walked by Angelo and me, and she never gave us so much as a glance. Everybody in the lobby stopped when she stepped out of that elevator. The desk man stopped registering guests. The doorman came in and stood inside the door rather than outside. The shoeshine man stopped shining his shoes. The guests, all of them, just stopped dead in their tracks. That night she could've stopped a watch."

She made her way into the darkened lounge and sat in a booth near the back of the room. Twenty minutes later, Mr. Leisure Suit popped out of the elevator and headed directly for the lounge. The game clock was on.

Phil and Angelo were in the elevator before the furrier even got to the lounge. They went to Phil's room first, and put on the uniforms of hotel maintenance workers. They loaded two dollies, which they'd borrowed from the hotel lobby, with two large black trunks each, and took the stairs down a flight to the furrier's floor. Phil had been given the key by the Civellas.

They loaded some very expensive furs into the first two trunks and were ready to leave the room in twenty minutes. The hard part would be lugging the heavy trunks down four flights of stairs—Phil had decided not to use either elevator. If they used the service elevator, he figured, and a hotel employee got on, that person might recognize them as imposters. And two maintenance men using the guest elevator would create suspicion. So they used their muscles and took the two trunks down the back stairs and out to a waiting van, which the Civellas had also supplied.

After they put them in the van, though, Phil decided they'd taken enough. There were only about twenty furs left in the room and going back didn't seem worth the risk. They left the other two trunks in the victim's room, glad to have finished the job in half the time they'd estimated.

Phil and Angelo went back up to their own room, packed their belongings, and changed out of uniform. Angelo went directly outside to where they had moved the van after placing the two trunks inside. Phil headed for the hotel lounge. The plan was for Tony, when he saw Phil, to leave the bar, check out at the front desk, and wait in the van with Angelo until Phil joined them.

Phil entered the lounge, sat down at a table, and ordered a drink. He looked around and saw Tony at the bar, but Tony didn't leave. The Hollywood starlet was sitting by herself in a booth in the back. The furrier, oblivious to her, was dancing with a fat lady. Both were wiggling their bodies around without a hint of rhythm. Phil, astonished, to say the least, tried again to get Tony's attention. But Tony wasn't taking his eyes off the young starlet.

Finally, after ten minutes or so, Tony saw Phil sitting there giving him a dirty look. He quickly paid his tab, gave his dream girl one last look, and headed out to the front desk to check out.

Phil ordered another drink and asked the waitress to send one over to the beautiful lady sitting in the back. After it had been served, he walked over to her. "Lonely?" he asked. She smiled a smile that would one day melt the hearts of millions of moviegoers, then motioned for Phil to sit down. "He never even looked at me," she said in disbelief. "He spotted that *thing* he's dancing with and never took his eyes off her." Phil and the starlet glanced at the dance floor, where the two figures—one in a leisure suit and the other in a muumuu—were dancing. The thief and his decoy started to laugh hysterically.

"So much for taste," Phil said finally. The starlet leaned over and whispered, "Now, who would *you* have chosen, me or her?" "Listen, I gotta go," Phil said, fearing that if he didn't leave then, he wouldn't be able to tear himself away. "Am I done, then?" she asked. "Check's in the mail—and I really wish I *could* stay." Phil frowned. "Yeah, me too," she agreed. "Now I got a whole night to kill—in Kansas City, of all places." Then she smiled and asked, "Will you call me again? This is the best job, I've ever had." "I sure hope so," Phil answered. He meant every word.

Tony and Angelo greeted him when he got out to the van. They drove through the night and arrived in Chicago the next morning. Through the whole trip, Phil found himself wishing he'd been able to stay in Kansas City.

Augie took the furs and told the Cresta team they could stay at his apartment until the furs were sold. "Was the girl all right?" Augie asked. When Tony described her, Augie said, "And nobody got *nothing* from her?" Tony smiled and said, "I have something to dream about for the rest of my life, and that's enough." "That fur guy never even *looked* at her?" Augie asked in disbelief. "Not even a look-see," Tony answered. "What about you, Phil? You're a ladies' man. Did you take a shot at her?" Augie smiled. "She was out of my league, Augie, strictly out of my league."

Augie sold the furs within a day and gave Phil $150,000 in cash, which Phil split with Angelo and Tony. "Do we pay the broad?" Augie asked. "Give her five thousand," Phil responded. "Five large!" Augie spit out the sum in dismay. "For crissake, Phil, she didn't *do* nothing." Phil reiterated, "Five large, Augie, and it's not negotiable. She did exactly what we asked her to do.

It's not her fault the guy likes fat broads." "I suppose it comes from my end?" Augie said, sulking. "Naw. Tell the Civellas to pay it. For expenses incurred," Phil said, laughing.

The starlet got her money. The next time Phil saw her she was in a movie at the Music Hall in Boston. She looked as great on the big screen as she had in the Kansas City hotel lounge. Because he was fond of her, Cresta asked that her name not be included when this story was told.

10
Breakdowns

HANKS TO AUGIE, Phil was now getting leads on jobs all over the country. He liked the freedom of working outside Boston. When they went to St. Louis or Kansas City, they didn't have to keep looking over their shoulders for the cops because nobody knew them there. He also liked it that neither Angiulo nor Tilley had any pull on them outside their territory. Some of these faraway jobs were more successful than others, but the Cresta team never got caught. Tony and Angelo, however, grew tired of being away from home. By the Christmas season of 1965 they were in New York. Beautiful as Manhattan was at that time of year, it wasn't Boston.

"We were making good money, but I could tell Tony was growing restless," Phil recalled. "He'd lost his edge, and that worried me. But when Tony stopped eating, I knew things were really bad." While casing a job in Manhattan, Phil told Angelo that Tony didn't seem to want to be there. Angelo's response was, "Neither do I. I miss my family." That was when Phil knew it was time to take his team home. He had broken off his own marriage two years before, and had practically no contact with his ex-wife and six children. But Angelo and Tony were close to their wives and kids. So Phil suggested they complete this last planned job, then return to Boston.

"Honest to God?" Angelo asked, stealing one of Tony's lines. "Mother's honor," Phil said, and they both chuckled. They went out to dinner that night and painted the town to celebrate. Afterward, Tony and Angelo were smiling from ear to ear when the taxi pulled up to their hotel. Phil looked at Tony and said, "Tomorrow, Tony, it's bada-bing bada-bang, and we're home." Tony laughed and said, "You gut it, Phil."

The next day they did some sightseeing and Christmas shopping. That night they were ready for business. Augie had given them a lead on a big-time New York jewelry salesmen. The guy lived in Connecticut but had an apartment in New York City provided by the Gambino family. Once or twice a week he would drive from Connecticut to the Big Apple, pick up a shipment of uncut diamonds, and deliver them to New Jersey. The diamond salesman paid the Gambino family protection money, so nobody from New York would touch the guy. But as Phil noted, the Cresta team wasn't from New York.

Phil, Angelo, and Tony waited outside the New York address they'd been given by Augie. At eleven P.M. the jewelry salesman climbed into his Cadillac and headed for New Jersey. "He was a Don Knotts look-alike," Phil recalled. "He weighed about a hundred and ten pounds soaking wet. I knew we wouldn't have any problem with him, once he picked up the diamonds." Phil was right; it wasn't the jewelry salesman they had problems with.

They had followed him for about thirty miles, through a few darkened towns, when Phil felt the car begin to vibrate. The vibration became worse every time Tony pushed the accelerator to over seventy miles per hour. They were beginning to lose the guy, and once that happened, the caper would be over.

Phil, already into his pre-job hyper mood, was livid. "Where did you guys get this car?" he asked. "La Guardia," Tony answered. "Did you check it out?" Phil inquired. "Yeah, Phil, we did what we always do," Angelo shot back. "But we didn't get a friggin tune-up, if that's what you're asking." "Sorry, Ange," Phil said. "But with this piece of shit, we're going to lose the guy *and* a big payday." Nobody said anything. They didn't have to.

A few miles later the car sputtered and died, and so did their chances for the big score. "*Now* what do we do?" Phil asked as the car slowed to a halt. "Let's find a gas station," Tony said. "Yeah, like there's gonna be an all-night gas station right around the corner," Phil said sarcastically.

Phil told Tony to stay with the car and he would scout around. He began walking, and as he rounded the bend, he started to laugh. There was a gas station. He ran back to the car and told Tony and Angelo. They laughed together. "See, Phil? I know what I'm talking about," Tony said. Angelo added, "If there's a half-eaten Italian spuckie in there, I'll *know* we're in the Twilight Zone."

As they got closer they could see that the gas station was closed. Phil got out of the car and told Tony and Angelo to push it the last 150 yards, by which time he'd be inside the station waiting for them. Phil picked the ancient lock and was rummaging around when he heard Tony and Angelo arrive. He opened the bay doors, and they pushed the dead car into one of the bays. "We were really in the boonies, so we weren't too worried about getting caught," Phil commented.

Phil, who was a good mechanic, borrowed a few tools and found the problem almost immediately, then searched the garage for parts to repair it. Tony and Angelo decided to take a look around, to kill time.

As Phil was finishing the repair, Tony came running up behind him. "*Phil, Phil, you gutta see this!*" he yelled. "Why don't you yell a little louder? There's still a few people all the way to New York who didn't hear you," Phil said. The rebuke didn't bother Tony a bit. "Look at these, Phil," he said, shoving a handful of pens into Phil's greasy hand. Phil was duly unimpressed. "Great, Tony, you found a couple of nice pens. Meanwhile we just blew a hundred thousand dollars." "Not a *couple*, Phil." Tony smiled. "Thousands."

When Phil finished with the car he went to the back storage room with his pals. It was filled with boxes of pens.

Phil opened one of the boxes, which had the name OMAS written on the front. Phil, like Tony, had never heard of the brand before. Nonetheless, they piled box upon box into their car and headed for Boston. "We barely had enough room to breathe," Phil recalled, chuckling. "Tony, of course, complained the entire trip."

Once there, they went straight to a safe-storage area that Phil had rented on West First Street in South Boston, and unloaded the pens. The next day they met at McGrail's and Phil called Louie Diamonds.

"Phil, where have you been? Everyone's been asking about you," Louie said. "I'm sure," Phil replied, knowing only too well that "everyone" was Jerry Angiulo. "What kind of precious jewels do you have for me?" Louie asked. "No glass, Louie, but I do have something I thought you could help me unload." Phil didn't go into detail about how he'd stolen the pens, he just told Louie what kind they were and how many he had. Louie was disappointed, but promised Phil he'd get back to him within a day or two.

Phil's phone rang at eight the next morning. An excited Louie Diamonds asked, "Phil, you say the name of the pens is OMAS, right?" "Yeah, that's the name. Can we get anything for them?" "Twenty bucks," Louie said. "Twenty bucks for what, for the whole lot?" Phil asked. "No. Twenty bucks *apiece*," Louie said, laughing. It took Phil a few seconds to get over his initial dismay, and then it took him a few more seconds to compute the value of the pens. "The whole shipment?" he asked Louie. "Kit and caboodle, that's two hundred thousand dollars."

"I know, I know! And my cut is ten percent," Louie quickly added. He told Phil to drop off the pens at an address on Bromfield Street, in downtown Boston. "What about the money?" Phil inquired. "I'll have half of it for you upon delivery," Louie said, then he hung up the phone. Phil called Angelo and Tony and instructed them to meet him in Southie at the storage place.

They were waiting when Phil parked his newly rented Ryder truck on West First Street. "Whadda ya gut, Phil, ya gut a buyer?" Tony anxiously asked. "Yeah, he's on Bromfield Street," Phil answered with a straight face. "What's the price?" Angelo asked. "Twenty bucks," Phil said. "Twenty bucks! Screw Bromfield Street, I'm not lugging all these boxes all the way over there. Let's donate 'em to St. Augustine's on E Street. Maybe we can buy our way into heaven," Angelo said in jest. Hardly able to contain himself, Phil finally commented, "I don't know, guys, maybe a hundred and eighty large won't get us into heaven, but it sure is going to make our life on earth a lot more enjoyable."

They didn't get it, and continued to mumble and bitch about the stupid pens. Finally Angelo looked over at Phil, who had a big grin on his face. *"A hundred eighty large!"* he yelled. "Phil, you've gutta be shittin' me. Someone's gonna give us a hundred and eighty large for these friggin pens?" Phil just nodded as he and Angelo looked over at Tony, who was busy stacking the boxes of pens. "Tony, can you imagine how many Italian spuckies sixty thousand dollars will buy?" Phil said. Tony spun around and said, "Nobody in their right mind would pay that much for friggin pens."

Phil pointed out that if someone was willing to pay them twenty dollars apiece, then someone else must be willing to pay forty or fifty bucks or more. (Italian-made OMAS pens today sell for hundreds of dollars apiece.) It was way too much for Tony to take in. "Rich people, I don't get 'em." Tony shrugged. "Whadda ya mean you don't get 'em, Tony?" Angelo asked, laughing. "You're *one* of 'em." "Let's go eat," was Tony's response. "You buying, rich man?" Phil asked. "Not till I see the money. I still think you're full of shit," Tony replied.

As it turned out, Phil was right on the mark. They delivered the pens to the back door of the place on Bromfield Street. Then they met Louie Diamonds in his office that night. Louie counted out a hundred crisp thousand-dollar bills and gave them to Phil. Tony, seeing the money, still couldn't believe what was happening. A couple of days later they met in Louie Cohen's office again; this time he counted out another eighty crisp thousand-dollar bills.

Phil received a call from Augie in Chicago. "What happened?" he asked. "My guy in New York tells me the pigeon never got hit." "He's right, Augie, it never went down." "Did ya get a bum steer?" Augie was probing for details. "No, no, the setup was perfect. We just didn't want to take down one of Gambino's guys—too risky. We backed off at the last minute," Phil lied. "Yeah, maybe you're right." Augie laughed. "It hasn't been a very good week for the Gambinos. They just got served papers and someone stole some of their property from a fence in New Jersey."

Phil went stone silent.

"Ya didn't clip some fancy pens while you were in New York, did ya?" Augie asked, laughing.

Phil froze. Then, attempting a lighthearted tone, he said, "What are you, crazy? We don't steal pens. Shit, we don't even *use* pens."

Augie told him that someone had hit one of Gambino's places in Jersey and they were less than happy about it. "Ya can't steal from the mob, right, Phil?"

"Absofuckinglutely," Phil said, and hung up. He immediately called Louie Diamonds and told him whose pens they had.

"Louie almost shit himself," Phil said, chuckling, "but he did the right thing. He told his buyer that mum was the word on the pens." There were no repercussions.

"SOMETIMES IT'S BETTER to be lucky than good," Phil pointed out. The pen robbery was a one-in-a-million shot, and Phil knew it. If the Gambino family had found out who'd stolen their merchandise, there would have been nowhere for the Cresta team to hide. Not even Augie and the Chicago people would be able to save them. So after he collected the money from the OMAS job, Phil took a vacation until the Gambinos cooled off.

He visited his sister Mari in Chicago and spent a few days upgrading his skills. The locksmith who had helped Phil with the parking meter job had turned his back room into a sort of college for enterprising young picks, vault men, and alarm men. Phil Cresta had graduated earlier, summa cum laude. But being a believer in lifelong education, whenever he traveled to Chicago he would spend hours learning how to get into the newest vaults being manufactured, how to disable state-of-the-art alarms, and how to make duplicate keys in less than a minute. It was an atmosphere Phil reveled in.

Once, he had devised what he called a miniature "smoker." With it he could heat (smoke) a regular key and make a perfect duplicate in under a minute. He kept the smoker in his glove compartment and the speed it gave his break-ins became one of his trademarks.

During this late-1965 trip to Chicago Phil designed something new. Soon after New Year's Day 1966 he returned to Boston. It took him a day or two to buy all the components for the device he had drawn. When he finished, he called Tony and Angelo and met them at Amrhein's, a well-known South Boston restaurant. Phil told them to meet him at noon.

Phil, who was usually punctual, arrived fifteen minutes late on purpose. As he pulled into the restaurant's snow-covered parking lot, he saw Tony's car at the far end. He walked across the half-filled lot to Tony's car, reached into his leather coat, and pulled out a little box that was about the size of a pack of cigarettes. He lifted the hood of Tony's car and placed the object on the engine. Shutting the hood, he went into Amrhein's to meet his two friends, whom he hadn't seen in over three weeks.

Tony was so happy to see Phil that he insisted on paying for lunch, but Phil could see a look of concern on Angelo's face. "What's wrong, Ange?" he asked. "Nothing now," Angelo replied. "It's just not like you to be late. I was worried." "Well, I had good reason for being late. Let's go for a ride later, and I'll explain."

They ate. When they left the restaurant, Angelo and Phil walked ahead while Tony paid the bill. "We'll meet you at McGrail's," Phil yelled to Tony. "Angelo and I will follow you."

"Why so secretive, Phil? What's up?" Angelo asked a short time later, when they were heading over the Broadway Bridge. The only reply he got was, "You'll see."

As the two cars turned onto Commonwealth Avenue, Tony's began to sputter and eventually died at the intersection of Commonwealth Avenue and Exeter Street. "Bingo!" Phil said.

Angelo began to get out of the car to help Tony, but Phil ordered him to stay put. Angelo and Phil watched as Tony opened the hood of the car and began to jiggle hoses and tighten plugs. After a few minutes Tony got back in his car; it started with no trouble. "Must have been a loose hose," Angelo commented. Phil said nothing.

As the two cars were approaching Kenmore Square, Tony's car again began to sputter and then died in front of Waterman's Funeral Home. This time Phil could not contain himself when he saw Tony, now very annoyed, jump out of his car and kick it. "Phil, what the hell is going on?" Angelo asked. Phil reached into his pocket and pulled out a small device that was no larger than a cigarette lighter. He handed it to Angelo.

"What's this?" Angelo asked. "This," Phil said, "is what's stopping Tony's car." Angelo looked down at the device and then looked at Tony, who again was searching under his hood. "Get the hook," Angelo said, meaning he didn't believe Phil. Phil just laughed and told him, "Grab that knucklehead before he does something crazy to that car."

Angelo jumped out and told Tony to try starting the car again, which he did. This time he made it the three blocks to Kilmarnock Street.

Angelo was so excited that he bounded into McGrail's, ordered a round for them, and grabbed a booth by the back window. Tony followed, still cursing his car. Angelo could hardly contain himself and urged Phil to tell Tony. "Easy, easy," was Phil's response.

Tony was staring at the two of them with a puzzled look. "Tell Tony what?" he asked. "Phil stalled your car today. Twice," Angelo proudly announced. "Get lost. My car just needs a tune-up," Tony answered. "When was the last time you had a tune-up?" Phil asked. Tony pondered the question for a moment and then said, "Shit, Phil, it was only two weeks ago." "See, asshole? It was Phil who stalled your car," Angelo boastfully insisted.

Tony may not have been known for his intelligence, but he knew when he was being made to look foolish. "Why you guys always fucking with me?" he asked angrily. "We're not, Tony," Phil said as he produced the little remote-control device. Tony examined it and began to laugh. "You're trying to tell me this little thing, which isn't even *in* my car, stalled it?" "That's what I'm trying to tell you," Phil answered. Then he finished his beer and invited his partners to follow him outside.

Phil led them over to Tony's car, opened the hood, and said to Tony, "See if there's anything on that engine that doesn't belong there." Taking the bait, Tony inspected his engine block. After a few minutes he remarked, "Holy shit." With his right hand he gingerly picked up an object the size of a cigarette pack, holding it away from his body, as if it were a bomb. "Don't worry, it's not gonna hurt you," Phil assured him. Angelo ran over and took it out of Tony's hand. Tony kept repeating, "Wow, wow, wow," and then added, "Phil, you're a son of a bitch." Still examining the mysterious little device, Angelo commented, "Yeah, but he is one *smart son of a bitch.*"

The three of them walked across the street to the Fenway Motor Inn and into room nine. Angelo was like a little kid in a candy store. "Phil, you know what this thing means, don't you?" he asked. "Of course I do. Why do you think I invented it?" Tony, still in the dark, asked, "Phil, why did you have to do that to *me?*" "I'm sorry, Tony, but I had to see if it would work, and then I had to see if you'd be able to find it once you opened up the hood," Phil explained. "Oh, okay, then." But he sounded un-convinced, so Phil added, "Tony, you know everything about cars. I figured if *you* couldn't find it, then nobody will be able to." Tony beamed with pride. "Thanks, Phil. Thanks for trying it on me." Phil told them the next step would be a call from Louie Diamonds, after which they would put the little gadget to work.

THE CALL FROM LOUIE came on January 10, 1966. He told Phil that a diamond merchant representing Baumgold, Incorpo-rated, a major jewelry company in New York, would be driving north the next day and had several meetings set up in Boston. One would be at Louie's office, in the Jeweler's Building at 333 Washington Street in Boston, opposite Filene's.

Phil was being extremely wary of anything to do with New York since the OMAS theft. "Does this guy have even the remot-est connection with the Gambinos?" Phil asked Louie. "This guy is strictly an independent who does buying for some of New York's largest houses," Louie answered him. "He'll be meeting with me at noon, in my office. You can take it from there. Re-member, he's coming here to buy. Don't do anything to him un-til he's completed his work. Not *anything*," Louie emphasized, "until you're sure he's driving back to New York, okay?"

The next day, a skinny little guy with Coke-bottle-thick glasses was sitting in Louie Diamonds's waiting room. At few minutes later a well-dressed short man carrying a black case walked into the office and insisted on seeing Louie Cohen im-mediately. Just as Louie came out to greet his self-important customer, the man with the glasses, having viewed the mark, rose and left the office.

He took the elevator down three floors, walked out of the Jeweler's Building, and got into a waiting car. In the car were two men, both wearing sunglasses and baseball caps. The driver, Phil Cresta, asked whether Tony had seen "him." "Yeah, I saw him and I don't like him," Tony replied. "Did he put the make on you?" Angelo asked. "That stuck-up little son of a bitch only wanted Louie. Elizabeth Taylor could've been in that room and he wouldn't have noticed," Tony said angrily. Phil and Angelo responded at the same time, "Good."

Thirty-five minutes later the well-dressed diamond merchant from New York strode out the building's front door and walked along Washington Street, with Angelo close behind. He went into three nearby jewelry stores. Each visit lasted about an hour. After the third stop, he headed back toward Diamonds's office building, but kept walking in the direction of the subway stop by Filene's. Phil motioned Angelo to stay with him, started the car, and took a right onto Franklin Street.

Phil knew the guy would never travel by subway; he was too good for that. He also noticed that there were two unoccupied taxis parked right there, which the jeweler never even looked at. "So I quickly figured he had to have his own car parked somewhere downtown. Since Washington Street is one-way and there weren't a whole lot of parking lots on Washington, I went around the block and took a right onto Summer."

As Phil turned onto Summer Street Tony spotted the jeweler, with Angelo behind him. They had lucked out. "It's always important to know the lay of the land," Phil said. "If something like that had happened to us in Kansas City or St. Louis, we would've been up shit's creek, but this was where I grew up; I know Boston. I was working in a comfort zone I liked." As the New York jeweler headed into a parking lot on Summer, Angelo quickly jumped into the back of the car Phil was driving, a car that had, of course, been freshly lifted from Logan Airport.

They followed the jeweler as he got on the Massachusetts Turnpike and headed to Newton. He made a couple of stops in Chestnut Hill, in the shadow of Boston College, and around seven that evening he went into a restaurant in Brighton, carrying the black case with him. Tony was going crazy because he hadn't eaten for at least four hours. "He wanted to go into the same restaurant that our mark was in and get takeout," Phil said in disbelief. Angelo sent him elsewhere to get some pizza, which they'd eat in the car as they waited for the salesman to finish his dinner.

While Tony was getting the pizzas, Phil walked across Market Street and into the restaurant's parking lot, opened the hood of the car with the blue New York license plates, and placed something on the car's engine. An hour later the diamond merchant left the restaurant with the black case held firmly in his right hand. He started the car and headed home to the New York.

But a funny thing happened as he drove toward the turnpike; he had just passed the Brighton courthouse when his car gave a groan and abruptly stopped. Darkness was descending as the angry salesman jumped out of his car and began to walk up Chestnut Hill Avenue. "Now what's he doing?" Tony asked. "Probably going to a gas station," Phil answered. He sent Angelo to follow the man, who had taken the heavy black case with him.

Ten minutes later the New Yorker was back with a mechanic and a tow truck. The mechanic got in the car and tried unsuccessfully to start it. Then he hooked it up to his tow truck. The salesman, who was still holding on to the black case, got in the truck's passenger side and they drove off. Phil waited a few seconds and then followed the truck two blocks up the street to a gas station. Angelo was standing on the sidewalk as Phil parked.

There were two brothers running the full-service station that night. One signaled the other—the tow truck driver—to bring the stalled car into the garage and pull it into one of the bays, then he went back into the office, where he could see if anyone pulled in wanting gas. Angelo followed him and began asking directions to Somerville. But he only pretended to listen to the answer. The information he was really interested in came from the attendant's brother, who was now telling the angry man from New York that it would be at least twenty-five minutes before he could even look at his car.

"Don't worry. We'll get it going, but it's going to take a little time. We're open till nine, but we'll stay till we get it fixed," he told the driver. The disgruntled New Yorker asked where he could get a coffee. The mechanic pointed to a mom-and-pop store right next door. "Don't worry, your car's not going anywhere," he joked. The New Yorker saw nothing humorous in the situation.

The well-dressed little man said he'd be back in ten minutes. He walked over to the car and opened the trunk. Angelo couldn't believe their good fortune as the guy put the heavy black case in the trunk before going for his coffee.

The mechanic went back to the car he was working on before the tow call, his head under the hood.

Before Angelo, who had wandered into the garage area, could say "diamonds," Phil slipped into the station. He went right to the trunk, opened it, reached in, and grabbed the black case. It took thirty seconds at most. Then, passing the case to Angelo, Phil headed toward the front end of the car where he opened the hood, reached in, grabbed his electronic device, gently closed the hood, and left. The mechanic never looked up.

Tony was in the driver's seat waiting for them. Angelo got in front and Phil climbed into the back. They headed back to McGrail's. It would turn out to be the most expensive cup of coffee the New Yorker had ever ordered—around $150,000. The police, the gas station attendants, not to mention the diamond salesman, were all baffled.

THE "STALLER"—Tony's name for the little device—would be used in four more robberies. All thanks to Louie Diamonds, all successful, all unsolved. One of the Boston TV stations labeled the next such theft the work of the "Highwaymen Robbers" because it occurred while jewelry salesmen were driving on the highway. The name stuck for all but this first of the staller robberies.

The next three of the four so-called highwaymen robberies alarmed every jewelry salesman driving in and around Boston, for they all occurred within a month. They angered local police departments, who didn't have a clue as to why the cars were breaking down at night, in the most desolate locations, and were always pounced upon within minutes of becoming disabled. There were never any witnesses other than the jewelry salesmen themselves, who were never injured and who saw only the masks of the men who robbed them. No clues were left behind, but each highwaymen robbery had the same MO.

The driver who had diamonds or other precious jewels in his possession would feel his car begin to sputter, and then it would stall. As soon as the car came to a dead stop, two men, both wearing masks, were on top of the driver. On each occasion, one of the gunmen instructed the driver to turn off the car engine.

In each but the last robbery, one of the thieves would open the hood of the car to make it look to any passing motorists as if the auto had broken down. That is, at least, what police theorized. In fact, what Phil was doing as Angelo helped himself to the jewels was reaching into the engine block and retrieving the staller. Phil knew that most people were not going to stop on a deserted road in the middle of the night to help anyone.

Three of the four subsequent diamond salesmen were also from New York, and all four told the police that the robbery was over almost before it started. Two of the men had driven their own cars from New York and were using them at the time of the robberies. The third salesman was driving a rental car when he was hit; the last, who wasn't hit till May, was again driving his own car.

Police at first theorized that the robbers had put sand or sugar in the cars, but MDC police lieutenant Neil Cadigan dismissed that notion. Though he couldn't explain how the robbers had achieved the stall-outs, Cadigan told reporters that sugar or sand might have caused each car to stall in similar ways. But how could the robbers have determined when and where the cars would stall? Sand or sugar didn't give such exact results. The police were back to square one, as the highwaymen grew rich feeding off New York diamond merchants.

The three subsequent staller robberies that the Cresta crew pulled in January and February of 1966 went like clockwork. The

team couldn't have been hotter. The cops were going crazy trying to catch them, and Angiulo's guys were trying to figure out
who was pulling all those major scores in their territory. Angiulo
also started getting heat from Gambino because some of the
larger New York diamond merchants went to Gambino for protection after the third highwaymen robbery. Gambino was tied
into the diamond business in a large way and the highwaymen
robbers were hurting his pocketbook. Gambino warned Angiulo
that he'd better find out who was behind the diamond robberies
or there would be trouble between them, which was the last
thing Angiulo wanted.

Things were getting way too hot for the highwaymen robbers
by late February 1966. It was also getting too easy, which worried
Phil. They'd done four such heists now, and he felt they were
losing their edge. He'd seen too many good crooks become
greedy and end up either dead or in jail. The staller was worth
its weight in gold, but Phil knew it was time to retire it before it
retired them. There was just too much heat on from all sides.
Plus, Phil had heard that Angiulo had summoned Louie Diamonds for an interrogation. Louie would be under a lot of pressure to come up with names, and Phil knew that a weak man
like Diamonds would need incentive to stand up to Angiulo's
pressure.

After the third highwaymen robbery (the fourth staller heist)
in February 1966, Phil called Louie Diamonds and asked to
meet him at Castle Island in South Boston. "Louie thought we
were gonna whack him," Phil recalled. "I could see how nervous
he was, so I told him straight up that we were out of the diamond business, and that *he* would be out of business perma-
nently if anyone ever found out who the highwaymen were."
Louie was obviously feeling a great deal of pressure from
Angiulo, and now from Cresta. Phil reminded Cohen of the fact
that he had made a good buck by supplying information. "If *we*
go down hard, Louie, *you* go down hard too," Phil warned.

Louie asked what to say to Angiulo. Phil smiled and said,
"Tell him that you aren't sure, but you heard the name Ben Til-

ley tossed around. You don't know any more than that. That'll get you off the hook."

As Phil left Castle Island he took a right onto Farragut Road, where his mother had been born. He was not thinking about any of his family, though, as he went on to McGrail's to meet his partners. He explained to Tony and Angelo that they were out of the diamond business for good. Counting the first score in Brighton, which was never connected to the highwaymen, they had pulled four diamond robberies in the span of a month. The take, after Louie deducted his cut, was $870,000, which was split among the three of them. They had been fortunate and Phil told his two buddies to sit back and enjoy it for a while. And that is exactly what Phil Cresta did . . . for two days.

II
Cresta Tries It Alone

N FEBRUARY 25, 1966, Phil went to Brookline Bank to make a very large deposit in one of his many safe-deposit boxes. Since he was a man who preferred to come early and check out his surroundings, especially the means of egress, he arrived that morning around eight-fifteen. As was the case when he was planning jobs, Phil had learned that when he carried money to deposit somewhere, there was no such thing as being too careful. He parked his Bonneville and entered a small restaurant on Harvard Street to have breakfast, kill time before the bank opened at nine, and make sure no one was following him.

No one was. But as he was finishing his coffee, he noticed a Skelly armored truck parking directly across from the restaurant. Phil watched in amazement as both guards left the armored truck, locked but with its engine running, and carried moneybags into the New England Food Fair. He paid for his breakfast and went outside in order to observe the guards' movements more effectively. They stayed in the supermarket for about ten minutes, which astonished Phil. When the two came out, they both carried bags that, Phil suspected, contained the receipts from the day before. Phil watched closely as the taller and older of the two guards reached down, grabbed a key from his belt, and opened the back door of the truck.

Phil remembered standing there watching the armored truck disappear. "I had a hundred twenty-five thousand dollars in my gym bag, which I was just about to bring into the bank and put in my safe-deposit box. I should've walked away and kept on walking, but I couldn't. I had just watched two armored truck guards break every rule in the book. Most people wouldn't have noticed a thing, but I am not most people."

Phil deposited his money and went home, but he couldn't get those Skelly guards out of his mind. The next morning, as the truck pulled up outside the New England Food Fair, Phil stood directly across the street at the bus stop. Dressed in a security guard's uniform, he carried a lunch box and thermos. The apparent security guard looked as if he were waiting for a bus to take him to work. But he was already at work.

Phil observed the same two Skelly guards get out of the armored truck. The driver checked to make sure his door was locked and then he went to the back of the truck and grabbed three moneybags. Phil could not see the other guard, but he soon joined the driver and reached in and took out two moneybags. They both headed into the supermarket. From where Phil stood, he could see smoke coming from the truck's tailpipe. Once again it took them about ten minutes before they reappeared and put new bags into the back of the armored truck. As they were doing this, the apparent security guard who had seemed to be waiting for a bus crossed Harvard Street, walked directly behind the truck, and disappeared around the corner.

Phil explained that he had needed to make sure they didn't have another guard in back, as some companies did. "I assumed those cheap bastards who owned Skelly's would never spring for three guards, but you know what they say about people who assume. In my line of work, if your assumption is wrong, it can be the last time you assume *anything*."

For the next six working days that same "security guard" was standing at the bus stop with his lunch box and thermos. Every day he watched as the same two guards went through the same routine. But the curious security guard never got on a bus.

Phil didn't tell Angelo and Tony about the Skelly truck. He had just encouraged them to take some time off and he wasn't about to draw them back to work. Moreover, he had devised a plan for a one-man show. A show that would use one of the three Skelly uniforms that his Chicago tailor had made for him.

Phil did ask Angelo and Tony to meet him in the back parking lot of the Joseph P. Kennedy Memorial Hospital in Brighton on Thursday morning at 8:45. "Angelo got all upset when I asked him to meet me there," Phil recalled. "He thought I was going in there to die or something." Phil assured his friend that he was fine, but he needed them to be on time. And by the way, Phil asked Angelo, could they make a stop at Logan Airport and steal a car for their meeting at the hospital? "Are we doing a job?" Angelo asked. "Not really," said Phil, "but I want to be on the safe side."

On Thursday, March 3, 1966, nobody paid any attention as the same security guard, with lunch box and thermos in hand, stood at the bus stop across from the New England Food Fair. He had become part of the scenery. Today he wore a light blue jacket over his uniform and he had a hat under his right arm. He kept looking at his watch, which was perfectly normal for anyone waiting for a bus. But that wasn't what Phil was waiting for. The seven previous times he had clocked this route, the two guards were always at the supermarket by 8:20. He was starting to worry when they didn't appear by 8:30.

He was ready to leave and head over to the Kennedy Hospital when he saw the armored truck with the name SKELLY DETEC-TIVE AGENCY turn onto Harvard Street and stop in front of the New England Food Fair.

Two guards, one of whom Phil hadn't seen before, got out of the truck, locked both front doors, and took out five moneybags through the back door of the truck. The larger and older guard locked the back door and checked to make sure the truck was secure. The engine was left running.

Phil hesitated about going through with the job because he hated unanticipated change. But once both guards, carrying the bags of money, headed into the supermarket to pick up the receipts from the day before, he decided to proceed as planned. The urge to try such an easy job was irresistible. The bus appeared, and all the people standing at the Harvard Street bus stop got on. All except one.

Once the bus pulled away, the lone man quickly stripped off his light blue jacket, revealing a Skelly jacket underneath, and put on his uniform hat. He put the blue jacket, the newspaper, the lunch box, and the thermos into a trash barrel and walked up the street until he was even with the armored truck. The man quickly crossed the street, pulled a key ring from his pants pocket, and inserted first one key, then another. On the third try the front door opened. He got in, slid over to the driver's seat, put the truck in gear, and slowly drove up Harvard Street in the direction of Boston.

As Phil drove the truck into the Kennedy Hospital parking lot, he could see Angelo and Tony sitting in a parked car. It was 8:50. He drove by the stolen car, and both of them, out of habit, started to check out the armored truck. They never looked at the driver.

Phil circled them with the truck and came to a stop next to the car. They looked at the truck, looked at each other, and shrugged. Phil finally got out of the truck and knocked on the car's window on the passenger side, where Tony was sitting. He stopped breathing for a moment, then jumped out of the car when he finally realized that the guy in the Skelly uniform was Phil.

"What in God's name are you doing?" Tony hissed. "Just looking for a little help unloading some moneybags," Phil responded coolly. Both Angelo's and Tony's faces went white and Tony exclaimed, "You hit a truck by yourself?" "What are you, crazy?" Angelo added.

"Are you two gonna talk or help me?" Phil asked. It took only two minutes to transfer all the moneybags from the armored truck into the stolen car. Once finished, Angelo tossed Tony the keys and told him to drive. Phil jumped in the front, Angelo got in the back, and Tony left rubber as they peeled out of the parking lot. "I couldn't believe that knucklehead drove out of the lot like he was in the Indianapolis Five Hundred," Phil remembered. "I yelled, 'Tony, for crissake, take it easy! We don't need to get pulled over now.' Tony slowed down as we took the Mass Pike to Southie," Phil said.

On Thursday, March 3, a *Boston Evening Globe* front-page headline dubbed him THE LONER BANDIT.

The next day, in a front-page story in the *Boston Globe* a store employee said that, as the armored truck had moved off, he had been stocking a window display. He looked up and saw a man, whom he described to police as being about forty-five years old and wearing a Skelly uniform and hat, driving the truck away. The employee said, "I didn't think anything of it until I saw the two Skelly guards still in the store." He yelled to them, *"Hey, there goes your truck!"* The guards ran out of the store just as the truck turned left.

Police from Boston and Brookline were immediately called to the scene. Meanwhile, an employee of the Joseph P. Kennedy Memorial Hospital in Brighton saw a car containing three men speed out of the hospital parking lot between eight-thirty and nine-thirty. The hospital employee later told Boston police detectives that he attached little significance to the speeding car until around noontime, when he spotted a Skelly armored truck abandoned in the same lot.

Detectives Harry O'Malley and Anthony Manfra found no signs of the truck having been broken into. O'Malley told reporters that the lone robber must have had a key for the truck's front door. O'Malley stated, "The carbine was in its regular place inside the truck, but the fifty-eight thousand dollars the truck was carrying was missing."

Phil was dismayed to read that one of the store employees had spotted him in the driver's seat. He'd had his hat pulled down pretty far over his face and thought that nobody would take a second look, even if they took a first one.

It was the first armored truck job Phil had pulled in a while, and he felt the old adrenaline rush return. The money from that job was far less than they'd been getting from the jewel and fur robberies, but for Phil nothing compared with taking down an armored truck or opening a bank vault. "There's just no feeling in the world like that one," Phil said.

They picked up a clean car in Southie, transferred the money, and went down to the Cape for a few days. "I thought there'd be a lot more than fifty-eight thousand in the truck," Phil said. "But it was harder explaining why I pulled the score without Angelo and Tony than it was stealing the money. They shut up when they each received their nineteen grand, though. We always split everything three ways. Always. I promised I'd never do anything like that without them again," Phil went on. "And I kept that promise."

Because the truck's lock was undamaged, police in Brookline and Boston focused their investigations on the Skelly guards, but they were exonerated after two days of questioning. They never discovered Phil's jacket, lunch box, or thermos in the trash barrel, which was only twenty yards from where he stole the Skelly truck, which was owned by Armored Car Carrier Corporation.

In a recent deal, Phil had come by copies of copies of the master keys for almost every Armored Car Carrier truck in Massachusetts. He hadn't really trusted that they were usable and hadn't intended ever to use them. But when he saw those Skelly guards leave their truck running, unguarded, the temptation had been too strong to resist. It was the opportunity of a lifetime, Phil knew, for he had read all the armored truck companies' manuals and knew that rule number one was "Never leave a truck unguarded."

Phil later found out that it was the younger guard's first day on the job. Poor guy, he was working less than an hour when he was robbed and treated like a suspect—all before lunch. Two weeks later he quit. But Phil felt Skelly deserved what they got: they had become complacent and they paid for it.

Police had no usable leads, and the case was never solved.

PHIL KNEW ANGIULO suspected him of being one of the high-waymen robbers. He was too street-smart not to know. He knew too that if he was found out, he was, as the wise guys would say, walking around in a dead man's suit. Making so much money in Angiulo's territory without paying dues was frowned upon.

Angelo and Tony weren't much safer. Phil told them he had a plan that he hoped would take some of the heat off. He didn't trust that, even if Louie Diamonds stuck to the story Phil had suggested, Angiulo would swallow easily.

They stayed at the Hyannis Sheraton and relaxed for a few days before heading back to Boston. Phil's plan went into effect once they were back.

Tony called Ben Tilley from McGrail's and set up a meeting in a small Dorchester restaurant called Linda Mae's. Tilley was happy to see his old partner Tony, and he was even more anxious to talk about Tony's new friend and partner, the now-successful Phil Cresta. Tilley wasted no time.

"I figured you'd be driving a new Cadoo," he said, laughing.

"I'm lucky I'm eating three meals a day," Tony shot back.

"The way I hear it, you guys have been making a killing," Tilley said, obviously probing.

Tony threw out the bait. "Ben, we made one good score in the last six months, and we thought the haul would be three times what we took in."

"What about the diamond jobs?" Tilley asked. "Word on the street is that Phil either did them or knows who did."

Tony began to laugh, just as he had when he and Phil had rehearsed. "You gutta be shittin' me. You think we did the high-waymen stuff?"

"Well . . . maybe not you, but word is that Phil knows something about them," Tilley insisted.

"Ben, let me just tell you, Phil isn't as good as people think. In fact he's a pain in the ass. He spent the last three months clocking that stupid job in Brookline the other day, and what do we get but fifty-eight large. Fifty-eight large, for crissake! That's less than twenty large apiece—for three months' work," he lied. "You don't buy Cadoos with that kind of green."

Tilley was all excited, as Phil knew he would be. "You pulled that Brookline job? I knew it, I knew it!" Tilley beamed.

"Hey, I'm not bragging about that score. My brother-in-law makes more a week, and he's legit." Tony scowled.

"It was still a fine piece of work, Tony." Tilley laughed. "And fifty-eight large is fifty-eight large. I'd take that kind of money any day."

Tony then went in for the kill. "Hey, I'm not saying I can't use the money, but compared to what those highwaymen are taking down, fifty-eight large is just chump change."

Tilley responded with, "Tony, I'll be honest with you. I thought you guys were somewhere behind those scores."

"I wish." Tony shrugged.

"Ya know, I got called into the North End on the highwaymen hits," Tilley whispered.

"No way!" Tony said, as if shocked.

"Yeah. The big guy himself sat me down and grilled me about the scores," Tilley said nervously.

"Angiulo called you in? Were you scared?"

Tilley looked Tony straight in the eyes and admitted, "I was shittin' bricks, but you know how it is: if he calls, you answer." Tilley wiped sweat from his face at just the thought of the incident.

Tony whispered, "Angiulo thought you were behind the highwaymen hits?"

"Yeah," Tilley answered. "Can you imagine that? I have no idea where he got my name, but I squared it with him."

Tony asked how.

"Luckily I was out of the country when two of the jobs went down," Tilley explained.

"So he bought it?" Tony asked.

"Yeah, but the prick made me show him my passport. Can you believe that?"

"With Angiulo I'll believe anything." Tony sighed. "So you're off the hook?"

"As far as I know," Tilley said, looking around.

"Good." Tony smiled. "Maybe we can do some stuff together. I'm sick of working with Cresta, and Angelo feels the same way."

"Seriously?" Tilley was smiling now.

"Absolutely. We're both tired of Mr. Perfection and all his planning and waiting and then more planning and more waiting," Tony scoffed.

Tilley was thrilled at the prospect that his prodigal sons might be returning. He grabbed the check and paid it.

On the way to their cars, Tony said, "Who knows, Ben, maybe we can start our own highwaymen scores."

Tilley spun around and said with a scowl, "Don't even kid like that, Tony. Whoever did those jobs, they're already dead. They just don't know it yet."

By that afternoon word had spread throughout the criminal population of Boston and beyond that Phil Cresta was the loner who robbed the Brookline armored truck—just as Phil had hoped it would. The highwaymen heat was turned way down, as the robberies stopped and crime went back to normal.

Not long after Tony's meeting with Tilley, Phil, Angelo, and Tony watched the 1966 St. Patrick's Day parade in front of the Transit Cafe in South Boston with some wise guys from Southie. "It was funny," Phil said. "We'd made more than a million dollars in just over two months and we couldn't tell anybody. Everyone in Southie that St. Patrick's Day was talking about the highwaymen scores and they were all praising the robbers. I felt like jumping up on the table and yelling, 'We did them, we did them.' We would've been big heroes that day in Southie, but we would've been buried the next day. So we just sat there listening to all the gossip. It was pretty funny. Whitey Bulger, according to one Southie wise guy, was the only one smart enough to plan jobs like that. On and on the speculation and the theories went."

A Southie guy named Nee asked, "What about you, Phil? Who do you think the highwaymen are?" Angelo and Tony spun around and looked at Phil, who was cool as a cucumber. "I have no idea," Phil responded, laughing, "and I don't really give a shit as long as they stay away from armored cars." "Yeah, a loner doesn't need company, right, Phil?" Nee asked, chuckling as did everyone else in the room, all of whom were fully aware that Phil was the loner who'd stolen $58,000 two weeks before. "Hey, I didn't pull that score," Phil protested weakly. "Yeah," Nee shouted, "you probably wouldn't tell us if you were one of the highwaymen either." "I have no idea what you're talking about," Phil protested again. And again everyone laughed.

12
The No-Headlined Theft

HIL SPENT the rest of March 1966 lying low and catching up on some homework. Both the police and Angiulo wanted the highwaymen. Phil wasn't worried about the cops—there had been no extras on their team for the highway robberies, so there was no possibility of an informant. He wanted to give Angiulo time to cool down, though. Boston's boss did not like his turf being invaded.

Back in 1962, when Phil had been making a couple of hundred bucks a day from parking meters, tax free, he'd wisely invested in some property in New Hampshire, just over the Massachusetts border—a long way from the hellhole where he grew up. By New England standards, the land was miles from civilization, and he loved going there. But the farm, as he called it, ended up being used more for business than for pleasure. It was his East Coast place for studying the newest alarm systems, the newest locks and vaults. This is where Phil spent the early spring of 1966.

On that farm he had a whole workshop in which he could spend hour after hour improving his skills. Angelo noted, "Once Phil got with those locks and alarms he was in another world. He would not leave that back room until he had mastered every new lock on the market. He got a huge kick out of being able to open those new locks and alarms. And, man, he was good at it."

The isolated farmhouse also served as a shooting range. Phil, Tony, and Angelo would practice with handguns, shotguns, and rifles that they bought or stole. Practice kept them busy during the down times, and their skills sharp. For the next few weeks Phil stayed at the farm. Angelo and Tony visited often.

In mid-April Phil returned to Boston, rested and anxious to use his skills. Louie Diamonds had gotten word to him at the farm, through either Angelo or Tony, that he had some information to sell. Phil was anxious to buy.

He hadn't talked to Louie since their meeting at Castle Island. He wondered how Louie would greet him. As soon as he entered Louie's office, he relaxed. Louie seemed genuinely happy to see him. Louie told about being called to the North End to meet with the boss, and how, maybe thanks to Phil's advice and threat, Louie had been smarter than Phil had really hoped.

Louie had admitted doing business with Phil on the first diamond merchant robbed in Brighton; but since that theft hadn't been classified as a highwaymen hit, Angiulo didn't care. He believed Louie when Louie said he'd had nothing to do with the other three New York guys. But, being thorough, Angiulo sniffed Louie Diamonds out for other names. Ben Tilley was the only name Louie could come up with.

Phil was relieved that his own name hadn't come up. And more relieved when Louie informed him that nobody had mentioned the highwaymen stuff in over a month. The Angiulo investigation appeared to be over.

In the very next breath Louie said, "It's too bad you're out of business, though." "Why?" Phil asked. "Well, I just got wind of a big diamond guy who'll be in Boston next week." "Go on," Phil said, "I'm listening."

For the next half hour Louie told Phil about a diamond salesman who worked between Boston and New York and who wasn't connected in any way with the mob. "Are you sure?" Phil pressed. "The last guys, according to you, weren't connected either, and look what happened." "You're wrong, Phil. They *weren't* connected when you hit them. They went to Gambino for protection *after* a couple of jobs went down." Phil thought about it and realized that Louie was right, but he countered, "Don't you think the same thing will happen with what's-his-name?" "Walter Bain," Louie said helpfully, and then, "If you make this your last highwaymen robbery ever, what do you care what kind of heat Gambino puts on Angiulo? Fuck both of them."

"Yeah, and they'll fuck both of *us* pretty good if they *do* find out."

"I'm not saying anything, Phil, and I know you're not either. So how is anyone gonna find out?"

"I don't like to push my luck, that's all. I'm surprised we've kept it a secret this long," Phil said.

But the Bain thing was tempting. Louie was estimating the take to be in the area of half a mil. As he left the diamond broker's office, Phil told Louie, "I don't know, let me think about it."

Phil pitched the idea to Angelo and Tony that night at McGrail's. They were both skeptical. "What if Louie's just setting us up?" Tony asked Phil. "For who?" Phil replied. "Could be Angiulo. Could be Gambino. Who knows?" Tony said. "He knows he's a dead man if he sets us up," Phil argued emphatically. He pointed out that Louie was far too smart for that. "We made the guy some decent money. How much does he want this time?" Angelo wondered aloud. "More. It's always more, no matter how much he's made," Phil responded. "Yeah, I guess you're right," Tony said.

Since they weren't getting any closer to a decision, Phil suggested they check this guy Bain out, then talk again. They agreed.

Walter Bain was a forty-two-year-old diamond broker from Dedham, Massachusetts. He was a big-time broker who worked exclusively for Baumgold, Incorporated, of New York. After clocking Bain for a couple of weeks, the team decided to take him down. There were a few things that would differentiate this highwaymen robbery from the others. First, Bain traveled only in daylight. This was going to make the Bain theft a lot more difficult than the others. And Bain was shrewd. They'd clocked him on six different occasions and he never took the same route out of Boston twice. He would leave his house around nine-thirty in the morning and go to Dedham Police headquarters, where he'd have left his uncut diamonds for safekeeping the night before. He not only kept his car in his locked garage, he had a lock on his gas tank. He was a very thorough person. He was also a careful driver: he never went over the speed limit and he never changed lanes. Once he got on the Massachusetts Turnpike, he moved to the center lane and stayed there. He was doing all the right things to protect himself.

"Bain was good," Phil said, "but we were better."

They set the date to hit Bain: May 2, 1966. But before that day came, Louie Diamonds dangled another temptation in front of Phil Cresta's face.

BESIDES KNOWING when diamond merchants were in town and where they were staying, Louie Diamonds often knew where they would store their merchandise for safekeeping while in town. In those days some of the top-of-the-line jewelry sales-men, when visiting Boston, would temporarily store their mer-chandise in a local police station. What better place, right?

Wrong!

A famous diamond merchant came from New York to Boston for a show at Hynes Convention Center in late April 1966. Louie Diamonds told Phil that the salesmen was staying at the Parker House, a piece of news that brought a smile to Phil's face. Louie also told Phil that the New Yorker always kept his diamonds and other jewels somewhere in Station 1 on North Street, four blocks from the Parker House. The news, to Phil, was like one of those challenges from his days on the streets of the North End. He could almost hear the words behind Louie's informa-tion: "I dare you!"

Phil found out when the merchant was arriving, and Tony and Angelo, a picture of the salesman in hand, waited at the airport, in East Boston, for him. Phil was standing at the corner of North Street, downtown.

At the airport, the salesman hailed a taxi and went directly to the North Street police station. Tony and Angelo followed at a safe distance, through the tunnel that connects East Boston to downtown, and onto North Street. Tony spotted Phil standing on the corner and, as agreed, hit the horn three times.

As soon as he heard the three beeps, Phil turned and started toward the police station. By the time the jewelry salesman and the taxi driver began unloading three big cases and carrying them into the station, Phil was already inside, looking at some pictures of wanted men taped to the wall, some of whom he knew. To the average observer, Phil, dressed in chinos and a blue-and-gold windbreaker with an insignia on it, looked like an off-duty detective. There were three civilians filing complaints in the lobby, and a dozen or so officers coming and going. Nobody even looked in Phil's direction.

The salesman came to the desk and asked for the captain, who came out and greeted him like an old friend. The captain called a couple of young cops, who carried the three cases down a flight of stairs, followed by the captain, the jewelry salesman—and Phil Cresta.

The captain pulled a bunch of keys from his pocket and told the cops to put the cases down and go back upstairs. They passed Phil on their way up, and disappeared. The door the captain opened, about twenty feet to the left of the bottom step, had no lettering on it. Phil watched as the captain and the jewelry salesman carried the three cases into the room, then he exited the station before the men began their trek up the stairs.

Having seen all he needed, Phil walked over to the European Restaurant, where he found Tony stuffing his mouth with a huge sausage sandwich. Tony tried to ask Phil a question, but the words were inaudible. Angelo, sipping on a bottle of Schlitz, inquired, "How'd it go, Officer?" Phil looked down at his Boston

Police Emerald Society windbreaker and laughed. "You'd better take that jacket off before Angiulo's guys whack you," Angelo said, laughing. "Not only am I a cop, but an Irish one to boot," Phil said, smiling. "Yeah, you're about as Irish as Capone," Tony exclaimed. Phil stripped off his Emerald Society jacket and got down to business.

The diamond show was not scheduled to open until the next afternoon. Phil and Angelo drove to Sears and purchased a new suitcase, then back to the Fenway Motor Inn, where Phil showered and put on the same clothes that he'd worn that afternoon in the police station. This was a two-man job, and Phil decided to use Angelo only.

At 9:00 P.M. he and Angelo left the motor inn and headed downtown. In the trunk of the car lay the new piece of luggage and inside it were three red bricks. Phil and Angelo sat outside the police station for an hour, watching and waiting. It was a Friday night, which generally meant a lot of police action in downtown Boston. By 10:00 o'clock many people were plastered and just looking for trouble, which they usually found. By 10:30 that night, the North Street police station was humming, as squad cars and wagons brought in their human cargo to be processed and booked. It was mass confusion, as drunken students intermingled with pickpockets and shoplifters.

Phil liked what he saw, but still he waited. At 10:45 six young women walked into the station, apparently to report a crime. Phil knew instinctively that the time was ripe. He grabbed the suitcase with the bricks inside and headed into the station. He heard the women reporting that their car had been stolen. Nobody paid any attention to him as he headed down the stairs, took a left, and stopped in front of the unmarked door. It took Phil less than ten seconds to pick the lock. Once inside, he hit the light switch and headed for the three locked jewelry cases in the far corner of the tiny room. He picked their locks in a matter of seconds. He then took the bricks out of his suitcase and placed the contents of the three cases into it. Once all the jewelry was safely stashed, he placed a red brick in each of the jewelry cases, relocked each case, and left the room.

He quickly climbed the stairs. The women were still crying to the desk sergeant about their lost car. He walked out the door, crossed North Street, placed the suitcase in the backseat, and got into the front seat of a car that Angelo and Tony had stolen that afternoon from Logan Airport.

The next morning Phil anxiously looked in both Boston newspapers to see if there was any mention of the jewel robbery. There was none, nor would there ever be. It was too embarrassing for the Boston Police to admit that someone walked into one of their stations and carried out $750,000 worth of precious stones. The jeweler, Phil later learned, picked up his three cases the next morning and went to Hynes Convention Center, where the jewelry show was being held. He opened the first case and almost had a heart attack.

Phil was on a plane to Chicago by then. He visited his two elderly jeweler friends, who were pleased to see him and even more delighted to see the jewels. While he was there, waiting for the jewels to be fenced, Angelo and Tony were in Boston, continuing to clock Bain. Since there had been no publicity on the police station heist, they felt safe to keep the schedule they'd set up to hit Bain.

Phil stayed in Chicago with Mari for three days. On the third day he got a call from one of the jewelry merchants he'd visited when he arrived in town, who asked him to stop by their store. Phil accepted the invitation as well as the $450,000 in cash that he was handed. He flew back to Boston, where he split it with Tony and Angelo. "We split everything three ways. That was the one rule we lived by," Phil said. Tony always laughed about the police station robbery in which he didn't really play a major role. He told Angelo that Phil paid him $150,000 for eating a sausage sangwich.

"The best part about that job," Phil said, "was that we didn't have to cut in that sleaze Louie Diamonds. He had heard the rumors like everyone else, but he could never put us together with the robbery."

The salesman recouped his losses from his insurance company. Although there were rumors in some circles about the theft, nobody publicized it. The story took on legendary status and no one knew for sure how the $750,000 worth of jewels had disappeared from so "safe" a place. While many people, especially those in the jewelry business, have talked about the robbery, nobody knew how it was done or by whom—until now, that is.

13

The Highwaymen, One Last Time

N MAY 2, 1966, summerlike weather came to the Boston area. Three men emerged from a room at the Fenway Motor Inn at two A.M. They were dressed in black. Half an hour later a maroon sedan registered to someone other than its driver moved along Highland Terrace in Dedham. The sedan stopped briefly at the corner of Highland Terrace and one of the men got out. Then the car turned around and parked down the street, heading in the opposite direction. A few seconds later, the man who had alighted from the sedan walked into the driveway of 42 Highland Terrace.

The street was quiet. The man walked around the garage twice, then bent down and opened the garage door with an object he pulled from his pants pocket. Inside, he clicked on a small flashlight, barely illuminating the car in the garage. Less than thirty seconds after the flashlight went on, it went off. The man quietly closed and locked the garage door and walked back to the nearby waiting car. The scene was now set.

At approximately nine-thirty that same morning, the man who had opened the garage door some seven hours earlier still sat in the front seat of the same maroon sedan. He watched as Walter Bain kissed his wife at their front door and entered his garage from outside. The three men sitting in the parked car waited anxiously to see if the diamond broker noticed anything out of the ordinary. Their answer came a minute later. Bain drove out of his garage as usual, and headed in the direction of police headquarters.

Tony waited until Bain turned off Highland Terrace before he headed in the opposite direction. He arrived at headquarters a couple of minutes before Bain, thanks to a series of shortcuts he'd mapped out while clocking this job.

The Cresta team watched as Bain entered empty-handed and returned ten minutes later carrying what they estimated to be about $250,000 in uncut diamonds. Bain looked around cautiously, unlocked his car door, and placed the diamonds in the backseat.

"That was the key for me," Phil said. "If he'd placed the diamonds in his trunk that day, we might have just gone to breakfast." From observing the man over the previous two weeks, Phil knew Bain sometimes put his diamonds in the trunk, other times in the backseat. On that Monday, Bain put his diamonds in the backseat. That decision would cost him dearly.

Bain drove to the Charles River and onto the VFW Parkway. Not long after entering the parkway, Bain later told MDC police, his car's engine suddenly seemed to skip. He thought little of it until the skipping grew worse. When he stopped at the edge of the parkway, Bain saw a maroon sedan pull up in front of him. Two men got out and approached his car, while a third stayed behind the wheel of the sedan. The two men tried unsuccessfully to open Bain's car doors. Then the one at the driver's door pulled a gun from his pocket and aimed it at Bain's face. Bain opened the door. The gunman pushed him across the front seat. When Bain unlocked the back door the other gunman grabbed his briefcase with the diamonds. They then forced Bain's hands over his head and handcuffed him, ran back to their sedan, and headed toward Boston.

Bain jumped from his car and tried to flag down a passing motorist. But nobody would stop for a man who was handcuffed and waving like a maniac. After ten futile minutes, Bain dashed across the VFW Parkway and into West Roxbury's Veterans Hospital. There, hospital workers listened to his story and called the police. Both MDC and Boston police responded. Neither the Boston nor the MDC officers could open the unique handcuffs that bound Bain. He was taken to a Boston locksmith who, after several failed attempts, was finally able to free him. Meanwhile, Boston police found the maroon sedan believed to have been used in the robbery. It had been abandoned on the grounds of the Blue Hills Country Club in Canton.

In the *Boston Globe*'s evening edition of May 2, MDC police reported that, as in the previous highwaymen robberies, they suspected a foreign substance had been put into the gas tank to make the car stall on the parkway. As in all the other highwaymen robberies, there were no clues or witnesses, even though hundreds of cars had driven past Bain's stalled car and the maroon sedan at the time of the robbery.

The next day, however, a front-page story in the *Globe* told a different story. MDC Lieutenant Neil Cadigan told reporters that an electronic device was found on the engine of Walter Bain's car. It probably had been used to disable it. The secret was finally out, although it didn't make Walter Bain or the Baumgold company any happier. Baumgold had been hit three times by the highwaymen. Their losses far exceeded half a million dollars.

The three highwaymen were out of business after the Walter Bain robbery. "I let them have the staller," Phil explained, "because I knew it was our last highwaymen robbery. I also knew how dangerous it was to be out on the VFW Parkway during rush hour traffic with guns drawn and masks on. I told Angelo before the job that it would be in and out—no worrying about the staller, no dillydallying. When we found the door of Bain's car locked, I was afraid Bain was going to play the hero and maybe get shot. I was glad he opened the door when he saw Angelo's gun in his face. Once the door was open, I knew we'd get the loot, but in the back of my mind I was thinking about the

MDC and Boston cops who are always patrolling the parkway. I kept looking for a cop car, but we were lucky. I've always have said, 'Sometimes it's better to be lucky than good.'"

The ex-highwaymen drove directly to New Hampshire. The next day Phil, with his loaded briefcase, headed for a plane to Chicago. When he got to Logan, he saw a huge headline in the *Record American* that read, $150,000 HUB JEWEL HOLDUP. Louie Diamonds had assured Phil that Bain would be hauling more like half a mil. For a while Phil wondered if they'd taken too great a risk for so small a haul. But then he reminded himself of past reports he'd read—how the marks and their companies used one figure for the paper, another for the insurance companies, and then they had the real figure, which wasn't even close to the other two. It was all a game, and usually it was the insurance companies who were the big losers.

But not this time. Bain had been telling the truth. Chicago verified that he'd had only about $150,000 worth of diamonds. Louie Diamonds had given Phil an inflated estimate. Phil never dealt with him again.

Phil said, "It was kind of weird to be waiting for a plane and listening to everyone talk about the 'big robbery.' They all had their own opinions on this and that, and I found it very amusing to listen to the different scenarios. One guy, who couldn't stop talking about the highwaymen robbers, asked me and a few others where we thought the jewels and the highwaymen were right then. The guy didn't know it, but the jewels were about five feet away from him, tucked into a false bottom of my suitcase, and he was talking to one of the highwaymen. It was like that time in Southie at the Transit Cafe when all the wise guys were trying to figure out who the highwaymen were and we were sitting right in front of them."

14

Machine Guns at the VA

ESPITE CRESTA'S EFFORTS to keep violence to a minimum during his crimes, violence erupted on a sizzling hot Tuesday, July 26, 1966. The temperature was approaching 90 humid degrees as the staff of the VA Hospital in Jamaica Plain was going to lunch. It was exactly 12:22 P.M. when Bernard Fisher and Donald Bettano, of Armored Banking Services of Lynn, pulled their truck into a small alcove near the main lobby of the hospital. As usual on a Tuesday, the guards were bringing $68,000 cash so that the hospital could cash its employees' paychecks the next day.

Fisher, the first guard, walked toward the front entrance of the hospital as his partner, Bettano, moved toward the back door of the truck to lock it. Each had three bags of money in his hands. The men would normally go into the hospital together, drop off the six bags of cash, return to the truck, unlock the back door, and bring in more bags of cash. But this day was different.

As Bettano started to lock the back door, a blue panel truck came roaring up the hospital driveway and screeched to a halt directly behind him. According to witnesses, three men dressed in black and wearing ski masks bolted from the blue truck and began to open fire. Two of the bandits were carrying submachine guns, while the third had a handgun. Fisher, hearing the screeching tires, turned quickly and reached for his .38-caliber revolver. He was immediately cut down by bullets fired by the man with the handgun. Bettano, seeing his partner wounded on the ground, tried to finish locking the armored truck's back door. He didn't succeed. The same gunman who shot Fisher wheeled and fired, hitting Bettano somewhere near his back. He fell to the ground.

Within a matter of seconds, the same robber was standing directly over Fisher, whose gun was lying a few feet to his right. Fisher tried to get up but collapsed. The masked gunman kicked Fisher's gun about ten yards down the driveway, then reached down and took the three moneybags lying on the pavement. He said something to Fisher; then, walking backward and keeping the gun pointed directly at the guards, retreated only slightly.

The other two robbers, by that time, had put their submachine guns away, taken Bettano's three moneybags, and opened the back door with Bettano's keys. The smaller of the two moved the blue panel truck so that it was back-to-back with the armored truck, and remained at the wheel. The robber in the armored truck then began to throw the remaining bags of money into the back of the panel truck. The one who had shot the guards just stood there pointing his gun at both Fisher and Bettano.

Within a matter of seconds it was over. The man in the back of the armored truck jumped into the back of the blue panel truck and shut the doors. The driver beeped his horn once. The one standing over the wounded guards turned and jumped into the front seat, and they were gone. The blue panel truck sped along the overpass on South Huntington Avenue toward Brookline.

At the hospital, nobody moved for at least thirty seconds, until the shock of what had happened in front of their eyes wore off. Edward Sezinsky, who saw the robbery from a second-floor window, recalled, "Everything happened in seconds. There was one long burst that might have been from a machine gun, and then two shots, which sounded like they were from a handgun. I looked out the window and saw two guards lying on the ground. One was just in back of the armored truck and the other one was about fifteen yards from the hospital's front door. There was a gun lying next to the guard who was near the front entrance. I saw one bandit go over to the guard and kick the gun away. I thought he was going to shoot him for sure. One of the other robbers was already in the truck and he kept throwing bags into the blue paneled vehicle. The third guy was sitting behind the wheel just looking around. He acted as if he'd just stopped for a red light. Those guys were very cool and very professional. After the last bag was thrown from the armored truck, the driver beeped his horn, which must have been a signal, and they were gone. Talk about professionals! Nobody had time to think, and by the time anyone came to their senses, the thieves were already over the bridge. Those guys, whoever they were, really knew what they were doing."

The FBI didn't agree with that assessment, however. The banner headline in the *Boston Globe* on July 27 read, ROBBERS LEFT "SUBSTANTIAL" CLUES. Boston Police crime laboratory technicians said they'd obtained a substantial amount of physical evidence from the paneled truck, which they found abandoned less than a mile from the crime scene. All evidence, according to the *Globe*, was immediately turned over to the FBI because the crime had been committed on government property. According to the Boston Police, the pattern of the VA Hospital robbery was exactly the same as that of a $147,000 armored car robbery that had occurred only four days before in Bedford. The only difference was that there were no shots fired in Bedford.

The FBI, in that same *Globe* story, said that in both robberies a stolen panel truck was used. In both thefts three men, all dressed in black and wearing ski masks and all very professional, waited until they saw one guard leave the truck before they approached it. Two had submachine guns and one had a handgun.

The three men in Bedford matched the descriptions of the three VA Hospital robbers. In the Bedford case one of the witnesses heard one of the robbers call another "Lennie." In the VA Hospital robbery, according to an eyewitness, the name "Red" was used.

Some witnesses told the FBI and the Boston Police that a white sedan followed the panel truck out of the VA Hospital parking lot and onto South Huntington. Another report, which was featured in the *Boston Globe,* said that shortly after the robbery two men were seen getting into a sports car on VFW Parkway in West Roxbury. Other witnesses told the FBI that a car carrying three other men was parked on South Huntington Avenue and followed the robbers as they pulled onto the bridge.

Police recovered twelve shells from the VA Hospital parking lot. The hospital director, Dr. Francis Carroll, stated, "I was in my office around twelve-thirty, when I first heard what sounded like gunfire. I looked out the window and saw two men lying on the sidewalk. Two bullets thudded into the wall above our switchboard. The bullets barely missed our receptionists. Three bullets ripped through hospital windows on the ground floor, but nobody inside was injured, thank God."

In addition to the hospital personnel who witnessed the daylight robbery there were dozens of motorists who stopped to watch, as well as pedestrians and hospital visitors. Two boys from Worcester had just arrived at the hospital to visit a sick relative, and found themselves right in the middle of a shootout. One said they were no more than twenty feet from the armored truck. He told the FBI that the gunman who shot both guards did so without any warning and before either of the guards went for their guns. (He apparently didn't see Fisher's weapon on the ground.) He said he ran into the hospital to get to a telephone to call for help and was met by hospital workers. He told them not to go outside because two people had already been shot.

A woman who refused to give her name stated that she was visiting her husband on the ninth floor and looked out the window to see one guard lying facedown on the ground and the other lying on his back. At first she thought people were making a movie and the guys lying on the ground were just acting. But then she saw a blue truck move along the driveway with a machine gun sticking out the back window, and she knew it was not just a movie.

Fisher suffered a fractured leg and Bettano was treated for a single bullet wound to the hip. Neither guard had life-threatening injuries. Fisher, who was a World War II veteran, said he'd be back on the job as soon as his leg healed. Bettano, who had worked for the armored car company only three months before that July afternoon, wasn't so sure he'd go back to that line of work.

Phil Cresta shot both Bernard Fisher and Donald Bettano. He remembered events differently from the witnesses. "They're all full of shit," Cresta said when he read the newspaper accounts. "I was the first one out the door, and I saw the guard turn and go for his gun. He had the drop on Angelo, who was heading for the armored truck, so I shot him in the leg. If I wanted to kill that guy, his wife would be a widow right now." Cresta often said that he never had anything against the guys who were guarding the money. "They were just working stiffs, like us, trying to provide for their families. I understand that. They just had something I wanted, and I was determined to get it. Nothing personal. I hate it when guys try to be heroes. It's not *their* money—I don't understand all the heroics. I shot the second guard when he headed back to the armored truck. I thought he was going to lock himself in the back of the truck, so I took him out before he got there. I didn't aim for his head or even his back. I shot him in the ass. Now how cold-blooded is that?" Phil asked.

His explanation went on, obviously important to him. "We're stickup guys, not killers. We just wanted to get in, get the money, and get out. But sometimes things don't go as planned, so you have to do what you have to do. That's what we did at the VA Hospital. We've pulled hundreds of jobs and ninety percent of the time we never even had to pull a gun, but if you're going to be in this business, you'd better be willing to use it when it's needed. Every score we did was clocked and mapped to the max. We knew everything about the VA job—we did think they were carrying more money, though. That was a surprise. But sixty-eight large for less than two minutes' work isn't bad. Tony tries to calculate how much we saved in taxes on each score, can you believe that? Like I give a flying fuck about how much we saved on taxes. The boy is stugatz [crazy]," said Cresta, laughing.

In Phil Cresta's opinion, "Sometimes the more witnesses you have the better off you are. We had a white car . . . we had a red car . . . we had a blue car. We had a panel truck . . . we had a sports car. We had a car following us . . . we didn't have a car following us. Give me a break! The more witnesses, the more pictures they paint, especially when they hear gunshots. Now, how many people do you know who are going to stand there, head straight, taking notes, when a guy in a ski mask is spraying lead all over the area? That was the reason Angelo let go with that round from the semi. Those bullets didn't have anyone's name on them. They were just meant to scare people. And it worked, by the look of all the different accounts of what happened in the papers.

"We called one guy 'Red'? That never happened. But the feds go chasing down every cockamamy story those hicks swear by, which is fine with me. The feds spent two weeks chasing down every Red in the country, all the while announcing they had substantial leads and they'd soon arrest the parties responsible for the VA robbery. That day never came.

"Regardless of what the feds told the press, they didn't have dick. They knew we pulled the score, but they had no evidence. They made those statements to the press just to save face."

After the VA Hospital robbery, Phil decided to take another vacation—a long one, this time. "I really didn't want to push our luck," he emphasized. "We had made over three million dollars between the five highway robberies, a couple of big fur robberies, and a couple of armored car robberies in 1966. I knew, as we were riding out of the VA Hospital, that it was time to relax. We certainly didn't need the money and I didn't need the aggravation of everyone from Hoover to Angiulo chasing us down. Two things I always tried to guard against were complacency and greed. Those two qualities have put more people in jail or in their graves than any police force in the country. We'd just made over three million and nobody had any proof we were the perpetrators. That was the way I wanted to keep it," Phil proudly said.

The Cresta crew went to the farm for a few days as the entire Boston police force and the FBI tried to prove who pulled the VA Hospital job. It was there Phil brought up the subject of taking a break, hoping Angelo and Tony would agree.

After counting the money from the hospital job, Phil nonchalantly said, "You know, guys, I was thinking of taking a sabbatical. What do you think?"

The silence was deafening. Finally Tony responded, "You're the boss, Phil. If you want to hit this sabbatical company I'm with you, but I was hoping to take a little rest."

Angelo and Phil both started to laugh, and Tony joined in, though he had no idea what they were all laughing at. After a few minutes, Phil said, "Tony, *sabbatical* is not the name of an armored car company. It means to take a break—take a vacation."

"Why the fuck didn't ya jest say that, for crissake, Phil? I don't know these big words," Tony said, a little annoyed.

They spent the next week at the farm. Phil relaxed by trying to open new safes and locks that had just been introduced to the market. Tony, still under 110 pounds, relaxed by eating. Angelo went downtown to take in a few double features. It would be a whole year before they resumed their profession.

15

Life Is What Happens When You're Busy Making Other Plans

O THOSE WHO LIVED IN BOSTON, 1967 was the year of the Impossible Dream and Yaz. It was especially hard not to be caught up in the dream of the Red Sox winning a World Series if you hung out only a hundred yards or so from Fenway Park. McGrail's, located in the shadow of the baseball stadium, was the place to be that year.

Phil was not a big baseball fan, but he did like the game and the enthusiasm surrounding the Red Sox was contagious. On July 26, 1967, it didn't dawn on Phil that it had been exactly one year since their last job. Tony and Angelo were with him at McGrail's as always, but things were different during the summer of the Impossible Dream. There was no overriding need to plan scores or meet with moles or other informants: they were all driving fancy late-model cars and dressing expensively.

"It was like we were retired at forty years old," Phil recalled. "We had some great connections in Fenway, with some guys who worked there and drank at McGrail's. We were able to get tickets to any game, which was worth a big deal back then. Those tickets, especially in September, were almost impossible to come by for most people," Phil said.

The Sox won the pennant only to lose to the St. Louis Cardinals in the Series, but it was a great run. During the games Phil and Angelo and Tony talked of going back into business. Their preliminary plans, though, were interrupted by Jerry Angiulo, who had been breeding resentment toward the obviously successful Phil Cresta.

A week after the Sox lost the World Series, Phil, still the same tough-looking and quiet man who had pulled so many successful heists, sauntered into Joe Tecce's restaurant with a pretty blonde on his arm. She was a woman he'd been seeing lately, and was hoping to see more of. They sat at the bar until a table opened up. Most wise guys wouldn't settle for waiting in restaurant, but Phil didn't mind waiting. Making a scene was against his habit of staying as unnoticed as possible. And besides, there was another customer in the dining room whose attention he didn't wish to arouse.

When a table became available he was seated—at a table directly across from Jerry Angiulo. Phil hadn't been in the same room as Angiulo in three years. Phil waved to New England's boss as he took his seat. Angiulo did not wave back. Phil shrugged and sat down.

Midway through their antipasto Phil's date asked her boyfriend, "What's that guy's problem over there? He's been staring at you since we sat down."

"That guy," Phil said quietly, "is Jerry Angiulo. And I think it won't be long before I find out what his problem is."

A few minutes later Angiulo got up to leave. He stopped by many nearby tables and received hearty good-byes from the diners there. He did not stop by Phil's table, nor did Phil attempt to greet the man.

"I'm glad he's gone," the blonde said, "he gives me the willies."

Phil changed the subject and finished his meal as though nothing were the matter.

At the door, he was met by one of Angiulo's henchmen. Phil's sharp eyes caught another piece of muscle a few yards away, and three more nearby. Wishing he hadn't assumed eating lasagna was a safe thing to do, Phil quickly estimated the time it would take to get his gun in the trunk of his car . . .

Too long.

"Nice night for a stroll," he said mildly to man who was already grabbing Phil's arm.

"Yeah, Cresta, why don't you just stroll right this way." It was not a question.

"He just wants to talk," Phil said to his date. "Wait here." He was pretty sure this was true, as the area was too public a place for even Angiulo to whack him. If he was wrong, it didn't matter. There was no way that, unarmed, he could take down five seasoned killers.

Phil and his escort crossed North Washington Street and walked into a parking lot often used by Celtics and Bruins fans when the teams were playing at home in the Garden. Tonight the lot was mostly empty, except for Angiulo, who was standing next to his Cadillac. Phil didn't have to wonder long what this was all about.

"You no-good piece of shit! That is the last time you will disrespect me in public . . . " Angiulo yelled at the approaching thief, and then continued in that vein for five minutes or so, barely stopping to take a breath between invectives.

The thought crossed Phil's mind that Angiulo had gone mad, but then he corrected himself. There must be something Angiulo had heard about, maybe about Phil's heists of the previous year or two, despite his efforts at keeping things quiet.

When he got a chance Phil asked, "Is this about money?"

Angiulo, who had been winding down, went crazy again and launched into a new tirade. A car pulled in nearby and parked, and a couple got out, looked at men in the lot, and hurried across the street to the safety of Joe Tecce's. By this time Phil was pretty sure he wasn't going to die—at least not that night in that parking lot.

So at his next opportunity Phil said, disgusted, "So let me get this straight. You're pissed because I waved at you instead of going over to your table in person?"

"You have no respect, Cresta, and that is gonna cost you. Your brother has respect." Angiulo climbed into his car, done with his lecture.

But Phil couldn't help it. He was not going to take this treatment without a fight. He shouted to the closed car, "Fuck you, you small-minded prick—"

Angiulo jumped back out of the car.

"—You leave my brother out of this, Angiulo! He's got nothing to do with anything!"

"He does now," Angiulo said quietly. Then he smiled, got back in his car, and took off.

"I knew I should've kept my mouth shut, but that little puke pushed me too far," Phil said later. "I knew when I watched him drive away that I'd really fucked up."

When he got back to the restaurant to where his girlfriend was waiting, Phil gave her hug. She was upset from what she'd seen and asked Phil not to leave her alone that night. Phil was thrilled at the invitation.

Since he was pretty sure Angiulo would send someone after him—the only questions were who and when—he stopped by his room at the Fenway Motor Inn to load up. After packing a small arsenal in his suitcase, he took the blonde to her apartment on Commonwealth Avenue. No one came for him that night, but it was the beginning of a continuing relationship for him and this woman who, nine months later, became the mother of his seventh child.

Unlike Phil, his brother Billy "Bad" had accepted the invitation to become a made man. He had shed his blood on the picture of a saint and sworn allegiance to La Cosa Nostra, to Angiulo and his boss, Patriarca. But Billy "Bad" was also Phil's younger brother. Phil had watched him grow up in their awful home, and six years earlier had watched this handsome, gregarious brother fall for a pretty Boston University theater arts student. She was the first—and only—girl Billy had ever fallen head over heels for. But she had refused his offer to "marry me and forget about Hollywood," and Billy had gone off the deep end a little when she left Boston and made it big. He never watched any of her movies and would get furious if Phil reminded him that Billy was probably the only person who had ever told Faye Dunaway she should forget her dreams and settle down with a wise guy from Boston. She was about the only thing the brothers couldn't talk about.

So the next day Phil called Billy to ask what last night had been all about. There was no answer.

Given Angiulo's threat, Phil panicked and went right over to his brother's apartment at the Sherry-Biltmore on Massachusetts Avenue, where the Berklee Performance Center is found today. No one answered his repeated knocks and rings. Now really upset, Cresta gave up and headed back to where he'd parked his car. As he started to pull out, he saw his brother turn the corner. Relieved beyond words, Phil jumped out of his car without even putting it in Park, then had to chase the car halfway down the block. After rescuing his car, he turned to his brother, laughed, and gave him a hug. But he stopped when he saw his brother's stony face.

In an instant Phil understood that Billy had been away because he'd been talking to Angiulo, not because he'd been hiding.

"How bad?" Phil asked.

"As bad as it gets," his little brother replied, avoiding Phil's eyes.

"Who's got the contract?" Phil asked, already knowing the answer.

Billy walked up the steps of the hotel without answering.

But Phil had to hear the words. "Bill," he insisted, "who is he sending after me?"

"You know who," his brother answered. "Me."

Phil's knees buckled. Somehow he'd thought that even Angiulo wouldn't really go so far as to demand that one brother kill another.

Billy gestured for Phil to follow, and when they were in Billy's apartment Billy said, "What the *fuck* did you do to him last night?"

Phil explained what had happened, and Billy shook his head in amazement. "He wants me to kill you because you didn't kiss his ass in a restaurant? Come on, Phil, there's *got* to be more to it than that."

"I swear, Billy, that was *it*."

"What a sick fuck! I should walk right in there and shoot him and all *his* asshole brothers—and see how *he* likes it!"

"If you do," Phil said seriously, "it'll be the last people you *ever* shoot."

"Well, shit, Phil! What other options do I have? I'm not gonna kill *you!*"

Phil laughed, then told his brother to relax. They'd work something out. "Nobody's gonna have to kill nobody," he said. "How long do we have?"

"A few days," his brother said. "I told them I'd have to think it over and I'd get back to them."

"Tell me everything that happened," Phil said.

TWO DAYS LATER Billy called Larry Baione, Angiulo's underboss, who had been with Angiulo when the boss had ordered the hit. "Just me and you, Larry," Billy said. "Come on, Billy. I like you and Phil. This isn't my call. I have no bad blood here," Baione said. They decided to meet in a small North End restaurant.

Billy arrived early and sat with his back to the wall, as Phil had instructed. Ten minutes later Baione walked in, by himself, and motioned Billy into an adjoining room. They had a drink and finally Baione said, "What are you gonna do?"

"One thing I'm *not* gonna do is kill my brother."

There was a long pause before Baione said, "Good. I don't think it's a wise move, and I told Jerry that."

Relieved, Billy asked, "What happens next?"

"Well, we try to talk some sense into Angiulo." Baione smiled. "Tell Phil to relax. We'll get this thing straightened out," Baione said, and he extended his glass in a toast to Billy.

They both drank. Baione led Billy out of the room and into the bar section of the restaurant. The bartender was alone, as the restaurant had officially closed an hour earlier.

"Let's have another one for the road," Baione said. He sat down at the bar, and Billy joined him.

Feeling very good about the meeting, Billy was pouring his beer into a glass when he first felt the wire around his neck. It was not just a warning. Baione dug the sharp wire deep into the skin, trying to finish Billy off. In his struggle, Billy knocked over a few tables but could not get Baione to loosen his death grip. The wire tightened.

Billy knew he had only one last chance. Knowing that since he was younger and stronger, he had strength on his side for a few more moments, he reached around, grabbed Baione's testicles with his left hand, and squeezed until Baione screamed in pain. Then Billy brought his right hand up and over Baione's right hand, coming down hard on his would-be killer's elbow.

Billy heard Baione's wire hit the floor. He turned and hit the man a solid right hand to the jaw. Baione went down like a ton of bricks.

Billy picked him up and hit him again and again. The bartender was nowhere in sight.

Wanting to kill Baione now, Billy continued to beat his opponent. But at the last moment he decided to send him back to Angiulo in that condition, to tell the boss what had happened. So he left him there in a heap and drove back to the Fenway Motor Inn. Finding no one in room nine, he let himself in and called McGrail's.

When Phil saw the blood he started cleaning Billy up, glad that he was comparatively unharmed.

"I'm going to Miami," Billy said a little later. "Won't you come with me?"

"No, I'm staying right here," Phil replied. His anger and disdain were seething. "If he wants me, let him come and get me."

"You know he doesn't have the balls, Phil. He'll just send his little errand boy to do his dirty work."

"Looks like one little errand boy wasn't able to get the job done this time." Phil laughed.

"It's not funny, Phil. You know how it works. They're gonna keep on trying until they get you."

"I can handle myself, Billy. I've been doing it all my life," Phil said. "I'm sorry I put you in this situation. As long as I know you're all right, I can handle Angiulo. And you already handled Baione."

Phil drove Billy to his apartment at the Sherry-Biltmore, where they packed a suitcase. Then Phil drove his brother to the airport, where Billy boarded a flight to Miami.

Within two days, Phil's contacts had calls made to Angiulo by Tony Accardo, from Chicago; and two of Billy's friends also called: Carmine "The Snake" Persico, from the Columbo family in New York, and Johnny Irish, an extremely good-looking guy in Miami who worked for the Columbo family there (until he was later killed by them). Johnny Irish said to Angiulo, "Listen, Billy Cresta is coming back to Boston in two weeks and if anyone even looks at him the wrong way, I'm coming up there. You don't want that."

Angiulo swore to Irish that there was no contract out on any of the Crestas. He said there had been a slight misunderstanding, but now everything was squared. Indeed, Boston's boss did back off the Cresta brothers.

Billy spent the next thirty years living mostly in Miami, visiting Boston annually for a few months. When in the Boston area, he stayed at his Medford home.

Phil never spoke to Jerry Angiulo, his former boss, again.

16
Suspended Sentences for a Fee

T WASN'T LONG before Phil's life was back to normal. A couple of days after Thanksgiving in 1967 Phil, Angelo, and Tony met at Angelo's house in Braintree and talked about working again. "We were all very much on the same page that night at Angelo's house. We hadn't pulled a score since the hospital robbery, which was sixteen months before. The novelty of doing nothing had long since worn off, and we were all itchy to get back in action. We still had a great deal of money stashed away, but this wasn't about the money," Phil recounted.

They put out the word that the Cresta crew was back in action, and within days the tips began to pour into McGrail's.

"We pulled three small scores, just to get back in shape. We wanted to start small. By the time the new year rolled around, we'd made over a hundred and fifty thousand dollars, and we put the word out that we were looking for a big score."

A few days into the new year an old friend named Edward McAleney came calling. Phil knew McAleney from Walpole. He remembered him as a stand-up guy who was trustworthy. McAleney proposed a score in Lynn.

The job seemed easy enough to Phil, but something about McAleney was bothering him. "McAleney was drinking way too much. He wasn't the same guy I remembered. I didn't like dealing with people who were into drugs or alcohol." But Phil listened.

The idea McAleney offered called for Phil, Angelo, Tony, one of McAleney's associates named Michael Reddy, and McAleney himself to enter the Kay Jewelers store in Lynn on an upcoming Sunday, when the store would be closed. Phil asked why McAleney needed so many bodies just to hit one store.

He needed Phil and Angelo to bypass the alarms and open the vault, McAleney explained. He needed Reddy to drive. It would be quicker if McAleney and Tony cleaned out the jewelry displays while Phil and Angelo were opening the walk-in vault, which contained the more valuable jewels.

Phil didn't like the plan. "I knew I should've just walked away from McAleney, but Tony and Angelo were set on a big score, so against my better judgment I went along. I did ask McAleney why we needed Reddy, since I didn't know him and there was no better getaway driver than Tony. What I really meant was, why did we need McAleney? We were used to being given the score, pulling it off ourselves, and giving our informant a split. I would've had no problem with the McAleney I knew in the can, but this was a different guy—a weaker guy. I never liked working with freelancers anyway, unless absolutely necessary, and that job and that guy McAleney weren't necessary by a long shot," Phil recalled.

The Kay Jewelers job was scheduled to coincide with the 1968 Super Bowl Game, which, that year, was held in midafternoon and was between the Green Bay Packers and the Oakland Raiders. McAleney felt, and rightly so, that the majority of Lynn residents would be sitting in front of a television set as Phil and Angelo stood in front of the walk-in vault in the basement of Kay Jewelers. At exactly 4:00 P.M. on Sunday, January 14, 1968, Phil Cresta, dressed in the uniform of an ADT alarm mechanic, headed down an alley that bordered the jewelry store. It took him only a few seconds to disarm the alarm and a few more to pick the back-door lock. Once inside, he and Angelo immediately headed down to the basement and to the vault. The other two persons outfitted as ADT alarm mechanics, Tony and Ed McAleney, headed to the jewelry displays on the first floor. Phil knew they had four to five minutes until the alarm malfunction was discovered by the police and the ADT alarm company. Phil took one look at the old vault and grinned. It would be a piece of cake. "I had opened hundreds of boxes like it. I told Angelo to place our equipment on the floor and check on the other two guys upstairs."

As Angelo started upstairs, he heard a commotion above. "I was too focused on getting into the vault," Phil remembered. "I didn't know anything was going on until Angelo came back and said, 'Phil, we've got problems.' I looked at my watch. We'd been in the building only a minute or so. I knew it was impossible for anyone to respond to an alarm malfunction that soon."

The noise upstairs got louder. Phil and Angelo both knew they had only a few seconds to do something before whoever it was who was up there came down. "I thought some wise guys were muscling in on our score and we'd have to fight our way out. I never for a second thought it was the cops."

Phil and Angelo hid behind some boxes. Less than a minute later, the lights went on and a voice announced that Lynn Police wanted them to come upstairs. "In the dark, I couldn't see Angelo, but I could hear him breathing. I knew he was thinking the same thing I was: if this was really the cops, let them show themselves. We weren't volunteering." When Phil heard Tony's unmistakable voice, he felt better. If Tony was still alive, chances were it wasn't wise guys muscling in.

A few minutes went by and the sound of police sirens and static-filled radio broadcasts proved that the guys upstairs were in fact police. "It was actually a relief in a way," Phil said. "Shit, nobody likes to get busted, but the alternative was much worse. Wise guys shoot to kill."

The cops had the upper floor; Cresta and Angelo were trapped in the basement. They again heard the order to come up. After another minute or so, Phil told Angelo, "Ready to take the pinch? Let's go, I think we'll be all right."

Phil yelled out that they were coming upstairs and that they had no weapons. He led the way up.

What looked like the entire police department of Lynn was waiting. This was a big bust for them and they were all ready to take some credit, especially when the TV cameras arrived. Phil watched as Tony was put into a police car with McAleney, handcuffed and looking pretty depressed. "We got set up," Phil whispered to Angelo. Angelo barked back, "No shit!"

They were transported to the Lynn police station, where they were fingerprinted and booked. The police had arrived so soon and in such numbers that they had even caught Reddy outside in his getaway car. Phil, Angelo, Tony, McAleney, and Reddy were all held overnight in the station lockup.

Phil was livid as he was fingerprinted and booked. The minute he was alone with McAleney and Reddy he exploded. "McAleney, what the fuck *was* that?" Phil yelled. "They knew where we were and what time we were coming in. They knew more about the job than we did. Who the fuck did you talk to?"

McAleney, who desperately needed a drink, just shook his head. "Phil, I don't know how they knew. I didn't tell anyone about the job, I swear," he cried.

"Fuck you, McAleney, you told someone and that someone set us up. Now I want you to sit there and think. Don't say another fucking word until you come up with a name. Do you understand?"

McAleney put his head in his hands and began to cry.

"Real tough guy we got there, Phil. What the fuck were we thinking?" Angelo asked.

"That's just it, we weren't," Phil shot back.

For the next two hours they sat in their cells alone with their thoughts. Tony was the only one who slept that night. "Tony could sleep through an atomic bomb," Phil noted later, laughing.

On Monday morning, January 15, 1968, the *Boston Globe* ran half a dozen stories on the Super Bowl and how Vince

Lombardi's Green Bay Packers slaughtered the Oakland Raiders 33 to 14. There was also a much smaller story detailing how five alleged burglars had been caught inside Kay Jewelers in Lynn.

That same morning they were transported to Lynn District Court, where they were arraigned. They were charged with breaking and entering in the daytime, robbery, and possession of burglarious tools. Then they were released on bail.

As soon as they hit the street, Phil turned to McAleney and said, "I want to see you tonight at McGrail's at seven. You got that?" McAleney just nodded and jumped into a cab. Phil was intent on finding out who had set them up.

That night at McGrail's, Cresta grilled McAleney. "Who knew about the job?" he asked. "Nobody," McAleney replied. "That's bullshit," Phil said emphatically. "I've been in this business long enough to know when I've been set up." Phil continued the grilling for another hour but he was getting nowhere. Then Phil noticed that the more McAleney drank, the more talkative he became. So Phil tried a different approach.

"Where do you drink?" he asked McAleney. By the time McAleney got through naming all the bars he frequented, Phil said mockingly to Angelo, "I should've asked him to name the bars he *doesn't* drink in." Phil was watching Angelo out of the corner of his eye as McAleney rattled off the names of his watering holes. When he finished, Angelo asked Phil, "Can I talk to you for a minute?" Phil was more than happy to get away from McAleney.

Outside, Phil asked, "Whadda ya got?" Angelo showed him a napkin from the Brown Jug and said, "Phil, he told us about every bar in Boston except this one." "So?" "I frisked his coat while he was talking, and found this in it." "And?" "Phil, Tony and I have been there lots of times . . . with Ben Tilley. The Brown Jug's Tilley's hangout." Phil snarled, "You gotta be shittin' me!" and stormed back into McGrail's.

McAleney was chasing his beer with a shot of Old Thompson. "Ed, do you know a guy named Ben Tilley?" Phil asked in an over-innocent tone. "Sure, everyone knows Tilley." McAleney's words were slurred now. "When was the last time you talked to him?" Phil asked, pushing for what he needed to know. McAleney thought for a minute and then said, "Two weeks ago at the Brown Jug." "This is very important now," Phil stressed. "Did you mention anything to Tilley about the Kay Jewelers job?" "Absolutely not," McAleney answered indignantly. "Are you positive?" Phil asked again. "Absolutely," McAleney was defiant now. "Okay, screw," Phil commanded. "But stay by your phone in case I need to talk to you." "Sure, Phil," McAleney said, and he hurriedly left the Kilmarnock Street bar.

Phil waited until McAleney was out of sight and then quickly turned to Angelo and said, "Get Tony over here." Angelo could tell by the tone of Phil's voice that he had better not question why Tony was wanted. Angelo used the pay phone at the end of the bar and dialed Tony's home number.

Phil and Angelo were sitting in their favorite booth, against the back wall facing the door, when Tony came charging in. "Relax, Tony, we're not in a gang fight," Phil said, laughing for the first time that night. "Whadda ya gut, whadda ya gut?" Tony asked. "We gutta take a little ride," Phil said, imitating Tony's diction. Tony was clearly puzzled. In wise-guy terminology, "being sent for" is a serious thing. It usually means there's been trouble and someone's going to get whacked.

Phil saw how anxious Tony was and he quickly moved to dispel his fears. "Don't worry, Tone, nobody's gonna get whacked. We just have a little business to attend to in Mattapan, and I wanted you with us," Phil said.

Tony breathed a sigh of relief and said, "Okay, Phil. . . . There's a great spuckie shop on Blue Hill Ave. Can we stop there for a minute?"

"Unbelievable," Angelo whispered to himself.

The three of them rode down Blue Hill Avenue until they saw the Brown Jug, located in Mattapan Square. "Who are we looking for?" Tony asked. "Information. Do either of you know any of the bartenders here?" Phil asked. Angelo pointed to Tony. "He knows everybody." They parked and entered the crowded bar.

The three men sat at the end of the bar and ordered a round of drinks. Phil asked Tony what he knew about the bartender on duty. Tony told him. The guy was from Lower Mills and his kid was a great football player at Boston College High School and—

"I don't need a family tree, all I want you to do is introduce me," Phil said, shaking his head. "Unbelievable," whispered Angelo again.

Tony introduced Phil and Angelo to the bartender, and Phil began throwing huge tips at the guy, who, they found out, worked as a school custodian during the day. The later it got, the friendlier the bartender got. "Sorry about your pinch, Tony," he eventually said. Before Tony could reply, Phil asked, "How did you know about that?" "I read about it in the paper this morning," the bartender replied. "Of course," Phil said, backing off.

Then the bartender said something that almost knocked Phil off his stool. "I was surprised when I read it. I thought it was just gonna be a break-and-take job," the bartender said.

"What, you knew about the job before you read the paper this morning?" Phil asked incredulously.

"Yeah, we all knew it was going down while the Packers game was going on. Some guys in the bar even made jokes about it as we watched the game here on Sunday," the bartender reported.

Phil couldn't believe what he was hearing. "What kind of jokes?" he asked.

"You know . . . like 'I hope McAleney will be able to pay his bar bill now that he's robbing a jewelry store.' Stuff like that. And 'Lynn, Lynn, the city of sin; you never go out the way you came in,' stuff like that."

Phil's head was spinning. "You mean to tell me that people in this bar watching the game knew that McAleney was robbing that jewelry store at the same time?"

"Sure, we all knew," the bartender said nonchalantly.

Phil held his breath and asked, "Was there a guy named Ben Tilley in here last Sunday?"

"How'd you know that? In fact, Tilley was the one making most of the jokes."

"WHERE DOES that piece of shit live?" Phil asked Angelo as the three left the Brown Jug, speaking of McAleney. Angelo replied, "Somerville."

Twenty minutes later, Phil's car was parked in front of an old house badly in need of repair. "Are you sure this is the place?" Phil asked Angelo. "This is where I dropped him off," Angelo replied. "Did you see him go in?" Phil asked. "I didn't have that much time. It took him two minutes just to stagger out of my car," Angelo remembered. "How the fuck did we get hooked up with the likes of this guy?" Phil asked, ignoring the fact that it had been his own idea.

Phil picked the front-door lock and the three men entered the filthy home of Edward McAleney. "Find the scumbag," Phil barked and both Angelo and Tony went scurrying. "He's in here," Angelo yelled. Tony and Phil both converged on the room Angelo was calling from. "Are ya gonna whack him, Phil?" Tony asked. "He's not worth it, Tony," Phil replied.

They entered the bedroom, where they found McAleney, passed out. The strong smell of cheap whiskey permeated the room. "Wake him up," Phil ordered Angelo, who grabbed the prone body, slapped McAleney's face, and called his name until he opened his eyes.

"Wh-what? Wh-what are you doing?" McAleney screamed.

"Shut the fuck up before we *really* hurt you," Phil said.

Angelo released his grip and McAleney hit the bed hard.

Tony turned on the lights and McAleney began to get his bearings. "Phil, Angelo! What's wrong?" he asked.

"*You,* you fucking lowlife!" Phil yelled.

McAleney looked befuddled.

"I thought you said nobody knew about the score last Sunday," Phil yelled into his face.

"Why? Who knew?" McAleney asked.

"Who the fuck *didn't* know, you asshole!" Phil shouted. He

pulled out his .38-caliber gun and held it to McAleney's head and asked menacingly, "Did you discuss the job with Ben Tilley?"

McAleney tried to jerk away.

"You lie to me and I'll be the last person you ever lie to," Phil threatened. "Now, how did Tilley know about the job?"

McAleney looked around, but there was no sympathy in that room. "I might have told him," McAleney whispered.

"You might have told him," Phil repeated, mocking him. Then Phil cocked the gun.

McAleney cowered.

Before Phil could pull the trigger, Tony grabbed his wrist. "Come on, Phil, we got what we came here for. You said he's not worth it, remember?"

At Tony's words Phil got off the bed and said to McAleney, "Stay away from me, you fucking lush, or next time you won't be so lucky."

They left Somerville and headed to Phil's room at the Fenway Motor Inn to discuss their next move.

PHIL KNEW that the feds, the Boston Police, the MDC police, and just about every other police force in the Commonwealth were going to use the Kay Jewelers pinch to put them away for a long time. Secretly, Phil met with one of his many paid informants, who just happened to be a high-ranking Boston police official.

As they strolled along a circular walkway known as the Sugarbowl on Castle Island, the officer told Phil that the feds were going to ask the judge in the Lynn case to throw the book at them. "You really pissed the feds off, Phil," the cop said. "You made a mockery of them and now's their chance to get even."

Phil wanted to know what kind of sentence they were talking about. "They're asking twenty to twenty-five years for you and Tony. Angelo might skate, since he has no priors," the cop said. "What?" Phil exploded. "Twenty years for a B and E? That's fucking nuts." "Hey, don't kill the messenger," the cop said. "But that's absurd! Nobody gets twenty to twenty-five for B and E. Nobody," Phil groused. "Nobody ever got away with what you got away with, either," the cop said.

"We'll see about that," Phil said. Then he asked the $64,000 question. "Who tipped the police?" he asked straight out.

"I don't know the answer to that," the cop said.

"How did the Lynn cops know we were in there?"

"Nobody's talking on this one; the feds are all over it," he whispered, even though nobody was within a hundred yards of them.

Phil reached into his pocket and withdrew an envelope containing more money than the cop would make in a month. He quickly passed the envelope. They walked off in different directions.

Phil went back to McGrail's and made some phone calls. After the fifth call, he left and walked up Yawkey Way to Brookline Avenue, where he stopped at a pay phone and made another call. Standing near Fenway Park, he talked in low tones to the person on the other end of the line. By the time he returned to McGrail's, Angelo was sitting in their booth, waiting for him. "How we doing?" Angelo asked.

"The feds want to give me and Tony twenty years," Phil said.

"For a lousy fucking B and E?" Angelo gawked. "What's going on, Phil?"

"The feds know what we've done and they're pissed because they couldn't catch us. Now they have us, and they want to make sure we're off the street for twenty years or so," Phil said slowly, as if not believing what he was saying. "You're off the hook, Ange. They're only looking for probation for you, since you have no priors," Phil finished.

"Fuck that, Phil. If you and Tony do a double saw, we're all on the hook." He was silent and then asked, "What about the DA? Is he going along with the feds?" His tone was glum.

"It doesn't matter what that asshole wants, we're all gonna be okay." Phil smiled for the first time.

Angelo's face lit up. "You fixed it?"

"Yeah, the fix is in, but it's not gonna come cheap," Phil remarked.

"How much?" Angelo whispered.

Phil looked around and said, "Seventy-five large."

Angelo just whistled.

"They got us by the short hairs, Ange; we either come up with the scratch or me and Tony go to Walpole. It's only twenty-five large apiece, and we've got it," Phil said as if trying to convince himself along with Angelo.

They each took a long drink of Schlitz and Angelo asked, "Phil, you said twenty-five apiece. What about Reddy and McAleney? Are they in or out?"

Phil smiled. "They'll get taken care of, but I want McAleney to squirm a little first."

The Essex County grand jury had returned one count of breaking and entering in the daytime (a lesser sentence than nighttime) with intent to commit larceny, and one count of possession of burglarious tools against all five defendants. The case was heard on May 21, 1968, in Essex County Superior Court in Newburyport. The presiding judge was Victor Bowman (not his real name). The transcript of the trial reads like this:

CLERK: Philip J. Cresta Jr.: indictment 61532 charges you with breaking and entering in the daytime with intent to commit larceny. Do you waive the reading of that indictment?

PHIL CRESTA: Yes, sir.

CLERK: How do you plead on indictment 61532?

CRESTA: Guilty.

CLERK: Philip J. Cresta Jr.: indictment 61533 charges you with possession of burglarious tools. Do you waive the reading of that indictment?

CRESTA: Yes, sir.

CLERK: How do you plead on indictment 61533?

CRESTA: Guilty.

JUDGE VICTOR BOWMAN: How old are you, Mr. Cresta?

CRESTA: Forty.

BOWMAN: How far through school did you get?

CRESTA: First year of high.

BOWMAN: Do you know that, by your plea, you admit to the facts alleged in these indictments?

CRESTA: Yes, sir.

BOWMAN: Do you do so voluntarily?

CRESTA: Yes, sir.

BOWMAN: Have you discussed this matter with your lawyer and are you satisfied with his advice?

CRESTA: Yes, sir.

BOWMAN: Has anyone made any promises or threats to induce your plea?

CRESTA: No, sir.

BOWMAN: Do you know, then, that your sentence is entirely up to me?

CRESTA: Yes, sir.

BOWMAN: All right, you may be seated.

Judge Bowman then heard the same pleas from Angelo, Tony, and Michael Reddy. Then it was McAleney's turn.

DISTRICT ATTORNEY PETER F. BRADY (Assistant District Attorney for Essex County): Your Honor, a fifth defendant, Edward McAleney, has entered a plea of not guilty on these same charges. His case has been continued until June fourth.

BOWMAN: Proceed, Mr. Brady.

DA: Your Honor, for the record, the testimony you are about to hear will not be given by the officers or officer on the scene. It has been agreed by counsel for the defendants that the story may be read into the record.

BOWMAN: Proceed.

Lynn Police Lieutenant Edward Higgins was then sworn in and took the witness stand.

DA: Do you have the story there, sir?

LT. EDWARD HIGGINS: Yes.

DA: Would you read it for the court?

HIGGINS: This is the report of Officer Holland Bourque: "On
Sunday, January 14, 1968, at approximately four-sixteen P.M.,
Officers William Bochicchio, Thomas McDonald, and myself responded to a call that some men had entered an alley
between the Warner Theatre and Woolworth's department
store. Officer Bochicchio and myself entered the alley from
the Blake Street side. Officer Thomas McDonald entered
the alley from the Union Street side. I found that a side
door to the Kay Jewelers store had been forced. I entered
the building and found five men inside. Two were upstairs
and two were down in the basement, attempting to open a
large walk-in safe. We apprehended all five subjects at gun-
point. I informed each of the men that they were under arrest and I informed them of their rights. Officer J. Peterson
asked each one if they understood what I had told them.
They all said they did. They were then taken to Lynn Police
headquarters, where they were again notified of their
rights.

DA: And what, if anything, did you find inside the Kay Jewelers
store?

HIGGINS: In the cellar we found a suitcase containing a variety
of metal-cutting tools. On the floor we found two iron bars
wrapped in a green window shade. While we were at the
scene, an employee of Kay Jewelers came to the store and
showed us where the alarm had been disconnected. Nothing
was taken from either the first floor or the cellar, but dam-
age had been done to the dial of the walk-in safe. A black
cashmere coat that belonged to one of the defendants was
found on a box adjacent to the safe in question in the cellar.
One hacksaw with blade and ten extra blades, four two-inch
nipples connected to four two-inch couplings to be used,
one heavy-duty crowbar, one jimmy bar, two bull-point ham-
mers, one heavy-duty electric drill, an extension cord, eleven
assorted drill bits of various sizes, one drill bit for cutting
cement and steel, one regular flashlight, one pocket-sized
flashlight, one screwdriver, one crescent wrench, two chis-

els, and one pamphlet on safes were all found in the basement of Kay Jewelers at 285 Union Street, in Lynn, Massachusetts.

ATTORNEY JOSEPH P. McPARTLAND (Counsel for the Defense):
No questions, Your Honor.

BOWMAN: All right, I will hear you.

McPARTLAND: Your Honor, you have four defendants before
you this morning. The first is Mr. Cresta. Mr. Cresta presently supports a wife and six children. Because of some personal domestic problems with his wife, Mr. Cresta does not
reside with his family on Light Street in Lynn, but he has
been providing ongoing support for his children. In addition
to this, Mr. Cresta has taken an active role in their upbringing. My feeling, Your Honor, is that in view of those circum-
stances and his family relationship and the fact that he is
still employed as a car salesman in the summer and he is
self-employed in the carnival business: to incarcerate him, if
I could make a plea to the court, would not serve either him
or his family or society. In spite of what I am aware of in
terms of his record, it would be my feeling that certainly the
court has to consider this in making a sentence. But also, I
would like the court to consider that, to my knowledge, Mr.
Cresta has not been in any difficulty with the law in several
years and that—

BOWMAN: Since 1961?

McPARTLAND: Yes, that is right, Your Honor. And if the court
could consider some kind of suspended sentence, that might
be a sufficient lever over his head to keep him working, to
keep him supporting his family, and to keep him out of trouble with the law.

BOWMAN: There were no arms involved here, were there?

McPARTLAND: No, there were not, Your Honor, and with regard
to the defendant Reddy . . .

For the next twenty minutes, Attorney Joe McPartland issued
the same plea for Reddy and then Tony. In each case he outlined
their support of their families and their employment records,

stating that Tony was self-employed and in the transportation of vehicles, which was coincidentally the truth. Reddy was said to be an employed bartender and was presently residing with and looking after his aged mother. McPartland asked Judge Bowman to give all three men suspended sentences and probation for three years. In regard to Angelo, McPartland asked Judge Bowman to sentence him to two years' probation, since this was his first offense.

The courtroom was packed with supporters of the defendants, per their attorney's instructions. There were friends and relatives of Phil, Angelo, and Tony, all making themselves seen. Michael Reddy's aged mother was there, showing her support. Also in the courtroom were five FBI agents, three Boston police detectives, a few state police organized-crime officers, and a certain sergeant from the Arlington Police Department. Bowman, after hearing McPartland's twenty-minute speech, looked at Assistant District Attorney Brady and nodded.

BOWMAN: Mr. Brady, what is the Commonwealth's recommendation?

DA: You're Honor, in regard to Mr. Cresta, the Commonwealth will be seeking two and a half in the state prison at Walpole.

Brady went on to recommend that Angelo be given a suspended sentence, but no actual jail time. Then, for the Commonwealth, he recommended that Tony be given two years in the Franklin House of Correction, and that Michael Reddy serve one year there.

BOWMAN: Were those recommendations to be served? Have you considered a suspension of them?

BRADY: No, Your Honor. I strongly recommend that all but one sentence be served.

BOWMAN: Mr. Brady, from the police report, it would seem that these men were apprehended before they actually broke into this—

DA: I think that is true, Your Honor. Well, they were actually in the process of breaking in—

Bowman handed his decision to the clerk before Brady had a chance to finish the sentence.

CLERK (reading the judge's ruling): Philip J. Cresta Jr., on indictment 61532, charging you with breaking and entering in the daytime, with intent to commit larceny, and on indictment 61533, charging you with possession of burglarious tools, the court orders that you be punished by imprisonment for a term of not less than two and a half and not more than three years, to be served concurrently. Execution of this term is suspended and the court places you on probation for a period of three years.

The courtroom erupted. The feds, who were hoping for a twenty-year sentence, stood there looking at each other, unable to believe what had just happened. The Boston detectives stormed out of the courtroom, slamming the door as they left. A Lynn police sergeant took out his badge and flung it in the direction of the defendants. Judge Bowman banged his gavel and demanded that everyone be quiet. Phil was happy to comply.

The clerk then read the other three verdicts. Each one was sentenced to time, with sentence suspended, except for Angelo, who was given two years' probation. When the last verdict was read, Judge Bowman stood up and said, "All right, I think we're finished here."

The Kay Jewelers robbers walked out of the courtroom together.

Phil later said, "I'd never seen cops so mad in my life, and believe me I have seen some pissed-off cops before." The feds and the Boston detectives and the state police and the Lynn cops all congregated on the front steps of the courthouse as the four defendants left. "Hey, Phil, how much did that cost you?" one of the feds yelled. "That's justice, guys," he replied smoothly.

"Sometimes you win and sometimes you lose." Then he smiled at the reporters and said, "Sorry, there's no story here for you guys." One of the cops said to Phil, "Oh, there's a story here, all right. It just might not be about *you*."

As Phil was getting into his car he spotted his old friend from Arlington, who looked as if he was ready to explode. "Hey, Sergeant Doherty," Phil yelled. "Nice day, huh? But I hear rain is in the forecast. You'd better watch out."

"Fuck you and fuck your judge, Cresta," Sergeant Doherty yelled.

Phil drove off.

THAT AFTERNOON Phil, Angelo, and Tony went back to McGrail's to celebrate their court victory. Tony was stunned. He had packed a small bag in anticipation of being sent to jail that day. He had explained to his wife that he probably wouldn't be coming home for a while, and had asked friends to look after his family until he returned. "It was the first time since I'd met him that I saw Tony speechless," Phil remembered. "He didn't have a clue."

They were in McGrail's for about an hour when Phil turned to Tony and said, "I'm going to need twenty-five large by tonight. Can you bring it to me at the Fenway?" Now Tony was *really* speechless. "Twenty-five large, Phil, for what?" "You don't think you walked out of that courtroom today because the judge liked your face, do you?" It took a few seconds for what Phil had said to sink in.

"Honest to God, Phil?" Tony's face went white. "You fixed it? No, come on, Phil, there's no way." "Oh, there's a way." Phil laughed. "It's called m-o-n-e-y." "Phil, even *you* can't buy a judge," Tony whispered, looking around to see if anyone might be listening. "Tony, everyone can be bought. It's just that some have a higher price than others," Phil responded. "But a judge!" Tony exclaimed. "Hey, a judge is only human. Judges need scratch too, don't they?"

Tony turned to Angelo and asked, "Did you know about this?"

"No," Angelo lied. Then Tony said, "But, Ange, you were gonna walk anyway, you have no sheet." "Tony, we're all in this together. We split everything three ways, right?" "Yeah, well, I guess. . . ." Then Tony whispered, "Hey, what about Reddy and McAleney, are they in on this?" "Absolutely not, and they'll never find out about it, right?" Phil said emphatically, and then, "When can you get twenty-five for me, Tony?" "I'll go to the bank right now," Tony said, and he got up to leave. "No withdrawals, Tony. It's too easy to trace. All we need is some eager young reporter finding out that we each withdrew twenty-five large on the day we beat the feds. You do have a box, don't you?" "Sure, Phil, I have two boxes," Tony replied. "Well, get going, then. And please . . . make sure you're not followed." Tony left McGrail's, and Phil walked up Yawkey Way to the same pay phone he had used previously.

He dialed and let the phone ring five or six times before the other person answered. "It's Phil—" Cresta started, but he was cut off before he could say anything else.

"I know who the fuck it is! What happened?"

Phil, who wasn't used to being talked to that way, kept his cool. "Whadda ya mean, what happened?" he asked. "Everything went fine."

The angry voice on the other end said, "I just talked to the judge, and there were only four defendants, what happened to the fifth one?"

"He's an asshole," Phil said.

The other man answered, "I don't give two shits about him or his asshole. I do care, however, how this looks. And right now, it doesn't look good. Now, what happened?"

"That scumbag McAleney wouldn't plead guilty, and there was no way I was going to tell him the fix was in. Not with his mouth. Half the city of Boston would've known after he had two drinks, so I left him out there to hang on his own," Phil said.

"Well, that was not the deal you came to me with. That was not the deal the judge bought into, right?"

"Where does that leave us?" Phil asked.

"It certainly leaves *you* off the hook, doesn't it?" The angry man said sarcastically.

"Well, where *does* that leave us?" Phil asked again.

"It leaves *us*"—and he emphasized the word *us*—"with about twenty-five thousand dollars more in expenses," the voice on the phone said.

"A hundred grand? For crissake! Who are the crooks here?" Phil said.

"Don't fuck with us, Cresta. We are not the ones who fucked up here. You said all five of you would plead guilty and that didn't happen, did it?"

"No, it didn't," Phil said, now the sarcastic one.

"Well, here's what you do. Someone will come by tonight and you will give him one hundred thousand dollars in cash, and then you will get McAleney to change his plea from not guilty to guilty and you will have him in court in two days. Is that understood? This case was supposed to be over by now. We don't need it dragging on until some wiseass reporter decides to investigate, now do we? Do you think you can handle the arrangements?"

Phil hesitated and finally said, "Yeah, I can handle them."

The voice on the other end said, "Are there any other problems?"

"Not that I can think of," Phil replied.

"Fine, good-bye." The man hung up.

Phil slammed down the phone and headed over to the Fenway Motor Inn.

By the time Tony returned with his $25,000, Phil had already briefed Angelo on his conversation with "the bagman," as he called him. He was just finishing when he heard Tony's unmistakable knock on the door to room nine. "Don't tell Tony nothing," Phil admonished Angelo. "But, Phil, we should *all* split the extra twenty-five. Why should *you* pick it up?" Angelo said. "Because I made the deal and I fucked up, that's why," Phil replied as he let Tony in. Tony gave Phil the cash and said he had to get home, which made things easier for Phil.

As soon as Tony pulled out of the driveway, Angelo and Phil got in Phil's car and headed to Mattapan Square. Neither of them said a word until they got to Franklin Park. "This is really bothering you, isn't it, Phil?" Angelo asked.

"No, fuck the money. That's not what's bothering me. It's Doherty," Phil said.

"What does *Doherty* have to do with any of this?"

"He made Bowman this morning," Phil said quietly. "And Doherty may be an asshole, but he's not stupid."

"You're talking about that cop from Arlington, right?" Angelo was now totally confused.

"Did you hear what he said as I was getting in the car?" Phil asked, not looking at Angelo as they passed Franklin Field.

"He said 'Fuck you,' didn't he?"

"That was half of it."

"And . . . " Angelo waited.

"And then he said 'and fuck your judge.' " Phil turned to face Angelo.

"I don't get it."

"Before I even knew you or Tony, I had a guy on my payroll who was in Governor Furcolo's office. That guy got me out of a few situations. One of them—remember the DeMarco shooting?—had to do with Doherty, who's hated me forever. After the DeMarco thing, he went to my parole officer and got me busted."

Phil parked his car in Mattapan Square. Neither of them made any move to get out. Phil shut off the ignition, faced Angelo, lit a cigarette, and continued. "Doherty thought I was going to have to serve the remaining two years on my original bit [sentence], and he was happy as a pig in shit that he'd finally busted me."

"How much time did you do?"

"Three weeks." Phil laughed.

"Shit, Phil!" Angelo gasped. "How did you pull that off?"

"I had to pay big-time," Phil said, looking Angelo right in the eye.

Phil could see that Angelo wasn't getting it. "Ange, the guy I paid off, the guy in the governor's office, was Bowman."

"Holy shit, Phil!"

"Bowman was one of Furcolo's top guys back then, before the governor made him a judge. His bagman was a guy named Baker, Nathan Baker."

"That's the guy you called today?" Angelo asked, catching on.

"Yeah, Baker is still the bagman. Only the price has changed." Phil laughed.

"What does any of this have to do with Doherty?" Angelo asked.

"Good question. When I got out of jail, it was pouring out, so I drove over to Arlington and opened Doherty's windows and his car was filled with a foot of water when he got off duty. He went absolutely berserk and ran right to my parole officer, who told him that it was out of his hands. He'd have to go to the governor's office to find out how I got out."

"And Doherty met Bowman when he went to the governor's office, right?"

"He was there every day for a month, and Bowman would call me every day and tell me what he said. Bowman thought the guy was a little crazy."

"And today in court, Doherty saw the judge who let you off is the same guy who let you off before, right?"

"I'm not sure Doherty ever actually found out that Bowman *was* the guy who was responsible for my walking before. But I think he knows now. And that worries me. Doherty is one tenacious bastard, and we don't need him snooping around this case."

"What can we do about it?" Angelo asked.

"We can whack him or we can wait and see what he does. Maybe I'm giving him too much credit, but I doubt it. Especially after what he yelled at me today. He knows *something* about this case smells. Let's just hope for everyone's sake he doesn't become a Jimmy Olsen on us." Phil laughed.

"Well, Superman," Angelo said, trying to extend the metaphor, "you'll just have to put him on a kryptonite diet if he does."

"Kryptonite kills Superman, knucklehead, not Jimmy Olsen."

They both were laughing as they walked into the Brown Jug, which, as always, was crowded.

Phil froze, though, when he saw who was sitting at the bar with McAleney. It was none other than Ben Tilley. Angelo could sense trouble, so he said to Phil, "You get McAleney, I'll take care of Tilley." Angelo headed over to Tilley and started talking to him as if he were a long-lost friend.

Phil motioned to McAleney, who went outside with him.

"He was shaking when I motioned him over to my car," Phil recalled. "I had no use for that piece of shit, and I just wanted him out of my life. But first, I told him, he'd better call his lawyer and change his plea from not guilty to guilty."

"Phil, I've never pleaded guilty in my life," McAleney said.

"Yeah, and a lot of good it's done you, you've spent half your life behind bars," Phil said. "For once, McAleney, do the smart thing," Phil insisted. "Look at it this way: you have two options. Number one, you call your attorney when I leave and tell him you want to change your plea. Or number two, you never make it to court for your trial. Now which is it gonna be?"

"I can't do any more time, Phil," he pleaded.

"You won't do any time if you follow my instructions. That is all I can say, but you know my word on the street is good, right?"

"Absolutely, Phil, everyone knows that." He smiled.

"I don't need you to ball-suck me. I just need you to do what I tell you. Understood?" Phil smiled as well.

"Sure, Phil, whatever you say."

On May 23, 1968, Edward McAleney was standing before Judge Victor Bowman, the presiding justice of the Essex County Superior Court. By the time McAleney's docket number was called, the only people in the courtroom were the judge, a probation officer, the clerk, one police officer—and a small guy sitting in the last row taking notes. He was the man Phil Cresta referred to as "the bagman." There were no feds, no staties, no Boston policemen, and no sergeants from Arlington as there had been before. They didn't care about an alcoholic, down-and-out ex-con who was in the twilight of a mediocre career. Their big fish, Phil Cresta, had again gotten away, forty-eight hours earlier.

McAleney was represented by Attorney Julius Sobil. After agreeing to waive the readings of the two indictments, McAleney was given a suspended sentence by Judge Bowman and he walked out of the court a free man. Ten hours later he walked into McGrail's. "Look who's here," Angelo said as he spotted McAleney. McAleney went to where Phil and Angelo were sitting and extended his hand to Phil. "What's this?" Phil asked. "I just want to say thanks and to apologize for everything. I guess I screwed up," McAleney said slowly. Phil looked at Angelo, who just shrugged, and then extended his hand to McAleney. "No hard feelings," Phil said. "Let's just put the whole thing behind us, all right?" "Thanks, Phil. You're a square guy, like I always heard. Can I buy you a drink?" he asked. Phil nodded, and McAleney went off to get Phil and Angelo a couple of beers.

"Whadda ya doing? I thought you couldn't stand the guy," Angelo said to Phil.

"I just want to plant a seed." Phil smiled.

When McAleney returned, the conversation got back to Tilley. "What kind of car does Tilley drive?" Phil asked. McAleney asked Phil why he wanted to know. "I just thought I saw him riding by Fenway, but I wasn't sure it was him." Phil smiled again. "A green Cadillac," McAleney told him. "Naw, I guess it wasn't him," Phil said, and laughed.

Phil asked McAleney how everything went in court, as if he didn't know. "Unbelievable," McAleney said. "My lawyer was great, he got me off with a suspended sentence. I was sure Brogna was going to send me away, but my lawyer worked miracles." Phil just shook his head. "How much did he charge you?" Angelo asked. "Ten grand, but it was worth it to get off with a suspended." McAleney smiled.

When McAleney went to the bathroom, Phil said to Angelo, "That poor prick is really stupid. He could've had Harpo Marx for his lawyer and he would've gotten the same sentence, but he'll never know it. What a fool." Phil and Angelo left before McAleney returned.

"I never saw him again after that night at McGrail's. It's a shame what booze can do to people. He was a squared-away guy in the joint, but the booze soaked his brain, and he let people like Tilley and that lawyer take advantage of him. It's too bad."

Doing business with McAleney, who shot off his mouth to Tilley, was a costly mistake for Phil as well. He'd had to pay "the bagman" $50,000 of his own money and he lost $25,000 worth of valuable equipment in the basement. And even more of a loss, partly due to Bowman's letting off the Kay Jewelers robbers, came five years later. In 1971 there was a major investigation of superior court judges and bail bondsmen. Bowman and Baker were both investigated and consequently these men who had helped Phil over the years became useless to him. Phil, still in hiding at the time, said of his payees, "I read all about Baker and Bowman and I actually felt bad for them. They were in business for a long time. Shit, they were a better team than the Red Sox. I always wondered what Sergeant Doherty felt like when he watched the hearings."

Phil never found out. He neither saw nor heard from Doherty again, which was fine with him.

17

Brink's Déjà-vu

MONTH AFTER THE LAST of the Kay Jewelers thieves was given his suspended sentence, Phil Cresta began thinking about a bigger heist. When, in June 1968, the Cresta team got news of this potential new job, they decided they needed help from one of the best setup and escape men in the business. Tony and Angelo suggested Red Kelley.

Six years earlier, in mid-August 1962, Jack "Red" Kelley had pulled off the largest mail robbery in Massachusetts history. Known as the Great Plymouth Mail Robbery, it made headlines from coast to coast. The banks on Cape Cod were, at the time, transporting their excess cash to the Federal Reserve Bank in Boston—by way of an ordinary mail truck. When they started, they used state police to escort the money, but by July someone decided they weren't needed. Instead, two postal employees would ride the truck: one a driver, the other a guard. Both would carry .38s. Thanks to that poor decision, the Plymouth mail robbers netted $1,551,277 in a daylight holdup. They were never prosecuted, and none of the money was recovered. Kelley's indictment didn't come up until 1967, the year before Cresta paid off "the bagman" for the Kay Jewelers job. And,

along with that of other Plymouth mail robbery suspects, including Patricia Diaferio's, Kelley's indictment was filed away
without ever going to trial, owing to "insufficient evidence."
These events were still fresh in Cresta's mind in June 1968.

"Just be careful what you tell him," Phil told Angelo before
that first meeting with Kelley, which was set up by an intermediary. "Anyone who's dealt with Kelley in the past has wound up
either in the can or dead—and not from old age."

Phil was not stretching the truth. Within two and a half years
of the Plymouth caper, five men with direct knowledge of the
Plymouth robbery were found murdered around Boston.

Robert Rasmussen, of Dedham, a well-known wise guy, was
found in Wilmington on January 21, 1965, with a single .38 bullet
in the back of his head. Rasmussen's body was dressed only in
underwear, black socks, and a necktie. Several days earlier, another local wise guy fresh out of Walpole, a Jackie Murray, of
the South End, was found dead on Tinnean Beach. On May 4,
1964, Francis "Frankie" Benjamin, of Dorchester, was found
fully clothed, but without a head, by Boston Police. His head
was never found. Leo Lowry, of South Boston, also an ex-con recently released from Walpole, was shot to death and his throat
slit in Pembroke on September 3, 1964. And on December 28,
1964, George E. Ash, of Brookline, was shot and stabbed to
death in the South End of Boston. None of these murders were
prosecuted.

Phil had known the five victims from his own Walpole days,
and he was leery of working with a thief who didn't stop at paying people off to stay out of prison. On the other hand, risk was
part of Phil's business. And except for McAleney, Phil had always come out on top when using accomplices for crimes.

So, though uneasy, Phil agreed to Tony's and Angelo's meeting with Red Kelley on a June afternoon at McGrail's. Kelley,
Angelo was told, couldn't wait to brag to the Cresta guys about
his big score in Plymouth. Though none of the Cresta team
wanted to hear the story again, they were willing to let Kelley

talk in order to get his help on this new potential job of theirs. Kelley was still considered one of the best at what he did—when he wasn't talking.

True to form, Kelley came in and had a few drinks with Tony and Angelo. He wouldn't listen to what Angelo and Tony were proposing until he'd told his tale about Plymouth.

"We clocked the job for at least six months. We even knew what time those guys took a shit," Kelley bragged. "We had the whole job timed for under four minutes if everything went all right—and it went better than all right."

Angelo and Tony listened politely.

After a long swig of beer Kelley told Tony and Angelo, "We were parked across the street from Clark Road in Plymouth. We saw the mail truck approach and everything went into motion. As soon as the truck turned onto Clark Road, one of our guys, who was dressed as a Plymouth police officer, ran over and put a detour sign on the road right behind the truck. We wanted that vehicle to be the last on Clark Road until the real cops arrived.

"The driver had no clue. He drove for two and a quarter miles from where the detour sign was. There we'd staged a two-car accident, making it impossible to get by. In case the mail-truck guys got suspicious and tried to bolt when they saw the accident, we had a woman standing in the middle of the road, acting as if she'd been hurt." Kelley grinned and drank some more beer. "Now who's going to suspect an injured woman, who's pretty cute as well, to pose any kind of threat? Ha! They almost fell over each other trying to get out of the truck to help.

"The minute they got out of that truck, they knew they'd made a mistake—a one-and-a-half-million-dollar mistake." Kelley was grinning from ear to ear by this time. He was also oblivious to who was around to hear him, which made both Angelo and Tony nervous.

"He kept getting louder and louder, and he wasn't telling us about his kid's First Holy Communion either," Tony said later. "We should've walked away right there, and never looked back."

But they didn't, and Kelley went on. "Once those two guards' shoes hit the pavement they were surrounded with heavy fire-power. They were smart, though, and did what we told them. We handcuffed them to one of the two stolen cars we'd used to stage the accident. Two of our guys, who were already dressed as armored car drivers, got in and drove the truck to a spot in Randolph, which we had designated as the drop-off spot. It took us about ten minutes to unload the bags." Kelley laughed so hard he almost choked. Then he excused himself to go to the bathroom.

Angelo said to Tony, "I think Phil's right. This guy's a loose cannon. Let's clam up and tell him we just wanted to hear the Plymouth story firsthand. He's so caught up in himself he won't care. And then we'll be outta this."

But to Tony and Angelo's consternation, Kelley wasn't through. He brought three more beers back with him, and con-tinued. "Those postal assholes and the feds spent more money than we robbed trying to pinch us," he said, laughing. "They charged us with armed robbery of mail, putting the lives of post-al employees in jeopardy, and possession of firearms. I said to my lawyer, F. Lee Bailey, 'No shit. When ya rob someone, you better put their lives in jeopardy or your own'll be over.' . . . You guys should call Bailey, just in case you need him someday."

Angelo looked at Tony and shook his head, meaning, "We both know how much Phil hates Bailey, but don't tell Kelley."

After what seemed like forever, Kelley said, "But here I am: safe, sound, and rich. The indictments have been dropped. The feds never recovered a cent of that money and they never will."

"Speaking of money," Angelo said, deciding to say what they'd come to say and seizing an opening, "we have a proposition for you."

Kelley leaned back confidently. "It better be six figures or I'm walking outta here."

"It's six figures, don't worry, Mr. Big-time," Tony said disgust-edly.

Angelo got to the point. "We have reason to believe that a guard who works for Brink's is looking to make a deal."

The word *Brink's* made Kelley sit up. Like Phil, he thought of hitting Brink's as the ultimate crime, if they could pull it off. Brink's rolled with heavy money, and having an inside guy meant everything. And besides, the Brink's robbery of 1950 was still being talked about. He was all ears.

They outlined the job and asked if he was interested. "I have to eyeball your inside man first and have a sit-down with him," Kelley responded.

"Fair enough," both Tony and Angelo replied.

They shook hands and parted.

That night Tony and Angelo met Phil in the South End and told him that Kelley was in. Then Tony said, "But, geez, what a flake. When he was giving the details of the hit, it looked like he was gonna have an orgasm."

"We have to be very careful of him," Phil said. "He scares the shit out of me. No face-to-face meetings with that Brink's guard, okay? That's why we're bringing Kelley in. If this goes down bad, that guard only knows Kelley. And if Kelley goes down, fuck him; he won't be missed."

Angelo set up the first meeting between Kelley and the guard through a third party. Kelley met the guard, Andrew DeLeary, one evening in the Mede's Log Cabin Bar in Revere. DeLeary was told to wear a Red Sox hat and a blue jacket because all the transactions had so far been carried out by phone and nobody knew what he looked like.

Angelo picked up Kelley at his house in Watertown and drove him to Revere. He waited in his car as Kelley went in and sat in a booth facing the door. About five minutes later Angelo saw a station wagon enter the Log Cabin parking lot. Out of it climbed a man wearing a Red Sox hat and a blue jacket. Andrew DeLeary looked around a couple of times before he climbed the stairs that led into the bar.

Angelo sat there for about forty minutes, praying that Kelley didn't screw this thing up. It seemed like the longest forty minutes of his life. At one point Angelo was tempted to go in and watch what was going on, but he knew Phil would be angry if he let himself be seen.

DeLeary finally came out, went to his car without looking around, and drove off. A couple of minutes later Kelley walked out and got into Angelo's car. Angelo asked him what he thought.

Kelley wasn't sure the man could be trusted. "He seems . . . scared," Kelley told Angelo.

"The guy is a legit guy! Of course he's fucking scared," Angelo angrily replied. "He's gonna rob the joint he works for. Wouldn't you be nervous?"

"I guess," Kelley said, unconvinced. Then he added, "Oh yeah, he wants to meet again next week."

On the next two Wednesday nights, Kelley and DeLeary met at the Log Cabin. At the third meeting they finalized a deal. By then Kelley felt comfortable enough with DeLeary to give the go-ahead to Angelo.

The next piece of the puzzle would be to determine what Brink's truck to hit, and when. Phil cased a bank in Burlington that was on DeLeary's Brink's route. But it was too close to a police station. DeLeary then gave Kelley information about a stop in the Natick Shopping Mall. He told Kelley that the truck would have in excess of $150,000 when it got to the mall. Kelley cased the place for a couple of weeks, but didn't like the setup of the location.

Phil, Tony, and Angelo were getting frustrated. They had a meeting with Kelley in which they voiced their displeasure. A couple of days later Kelley called, excited. "I think I got it," he said. On his own, Kelley had clocked an armored truck run that included pickups at major restaurants and hospitals, then finished by picking up at all three major department stores in downtown Boston.

Phil also became enthusiastic when he heard about this particular truck. It was mid-October by this time, and he looked at Tony and uttered but one word, "Christmas." From that point on, only that job occupied their minds. They decided that Saturday, the heaviest shopping day of the week, as dusk was falling, was the time to hit.

Kelly asked DeLeary about the run. "Yeah, that's a lucrative route. The best of the Saturday trucks," the guard replied. "We call it the Saturday-three run because it picks up from all three big department stores. I don't know who drives it, though."

Kelley said he'd seen one of the three guards carrying a white pearl-handled revolver.

"Oh yeah?" DeLeary said. "I know him. That's Smokey— Richard Haines. I'll find out who the other guards are."

Kelley then asked DeLeary how much money this particular truck would be carrying after its downtown department store pickups.

DeLeary estimated anywhere from half a mil to a million dollars, given the season, but of course the figure would go down after Christmas. Kelley made notes and promised to call DeLeary in a few days.

The team clocked Brink's truck 6280 every Saturday for a month. It started in the morning at Joseph's, a posh restaurant. Then it went to Children's Hospital, the Harvard Coop, and out to Brigham Circle, where there were several hospitals and a supermarket. One of but a handful of trucks that picked up on Saturday, on this particular route it had three guards, as Kelley had observed. Phil studied their mannerisms, their reactions, when and where they ate, how long they took, and how long they spent at each stop on their route. The three guards on 6280 seemed a little more lax than many, making Phil more and more sure this was the truck to hit. They almost always took a break at the same tavern in South Station, then at a diner on State Street, and their last stop of the day was always the same: Downey & Judge's, a bar on Canal Street, near the Union Oyster House. The team thought that might be the best place to hit the truck.

On two consecutive Saturdays Kelley and the team watched two of the guards leave the truck and go into Downey & Judge's, near the Boston Garden. The third guard, alone, stayed in the back of the truck, which was locked, but the team saw no sign that he ever bolted either of the front doors. Kelley, as careful as his reputation, clocked the scene from every conceivable angle, including from the elevated North Station MBTA platform. He wanted to see what kind of view any waiting riders might have of the robbery they planned.

Despite the temptation of the big score and Kelley's apparent care, Phil continued to have mixed feelings about Kelley. He just didn't trust the guy, especially with such a big haul. So Phil told Tony and Angelo that one of them had to sit in on all further meetings between Kelley and DeLeary. "I know it puts one of us in jeopardy, but we have to know Kelley's being square with us. If we have to, we'll kill Kelley and DeLeary after this is over."

Tony and Angelo were silent. Then Angelo said, "I'll go. I think Kelley trusts me."

Phil replied, "Nothing personal, Ange, but Red Kelley doesn't trust his own mother."

At the next meeting at the Log Cabin, Red Kelley introduced Angelo to DeLeary. "Who's he?" DeLeary asked. "He's the guy who's been staking you out." Kelley smiled. DeLeary was shocked. "You guys have been *watching* me?" "Fucking right we have, whadda ya think this is, Ted Mack's *Amateur Hour?*" Kelley laughed. DeLeary turned pale and looked around to see if there were any more eyes watching him. Very nervous now, he asked, "Is anyone going to get hurt?" "That all depends on how it goes down," Kelley said nonchalantly. "Hey, I *know* one of those guys," DeLeary said, producing a sheet of paper with the names of the three guards who rode Brink's truck number 6280 on the Saturday-three run. "Be careful, okay?"

The names were Richard Haines—the one who carried the personalized revolver—John Gillespie, and Joseph Kelly.

Angelo and Red Kelley looked at the paper and Kelley began to laugh. "Joe Kelly, huh? I like that. He doesn't spell it like I do, but I like it a lot. Luck of the Irish, eh?" And then he ceremoniously burned the paper and put its smoldering remains in the ashtray on their table.

ON A BITTER COLD November morning Kelley got word to meet DeLeary on Boston Common.

"You aren't going to believe this." DeLeary was smiling ear to ear. "I just got assigned to 6280's Monday run."

Kelley grinned. Things were starting to look up.

The next Saturday the entire team—seven men—met at McGrail's and then went to the North End. They lunched together at Joe Tecce's, then walked in three groups from the restaurant to the stakeout on Canal Street. Red Kelley and Santo "Sonny" Diaferio, whose wife had been the pretty "accident victim" in the Plymouth robbery some six years earlier, walked in front. Phil, Tony, and Angelo were a block behind Kelley and Diaferio. Stephen Roukous and Carmello Merlino, recently added to the team after Phil had done a count of how many guys would be needed, brought up the rear, a block behind Phil, Tony, and Angelo. It was now the last week of November and the wind whipped down Canal as they waited for truck 6280.

Each group watched from a different vantage point. The truck came to a stop on Canal, in front of the Union Oyster House. Two guards got out and, as was their custom, walked into Downey & Judge's and stayed there for eighteen minutes. The armored truck was locked, with a lone guard in the back who did not bolt the front doors. They all liked what they saw.

At their conference afterward, Kelley suggested they could hit the two guards as soon as they opened the door.

Phil shook his head and said, "Two doors, Red, two doors."

"Oh yeah," Kelley said, and took a drink of his beer.

"Let's just go in heavy, hit all three, and grab the loot," Diaferio suggested.

Phil listened to this cowboy scenario and others until he'd heard enough. Then he said, "Why don't we just get a key and let ourselves in?" Everyone stared at him. Kelley asked, "Are you crazy? Those guards have to sign for all the keys they get, and sign again when they return them. It's impossible unless you're Houdini." Diaferio agreed, saying, "Nobody has *Brink's* keys. Not even the great Phil Cresta."

Phil shook his head again. "You guys with this shoot-'em-up mentality make me laugh. We want to get in and out without anyone knowing we've even been there." Nobody spoke. Phil continued, "Listen, we have a guard on our payroll, right?" "We do?" Diaferio asked. This was news to him, and to the newest team members, Merlino and Roukous. "Shut up and listen," barked Angelo. "Yeah, listen to Mr. Houdini," Kelley said sarcastically. Phil, ignoring Kelley's taunts, said, "Kelley, check with DeLeary and see how tough it would be to borrow a key to truck 6280. A couple of minutes is all I need."

That night Angelo and Kelley grilled DeLeary on every aspect of 6280's Monday schedule. DeLeary told them that he and his two partners took two breaks, one in the morning, at the Bulkie Restaurant near Copley Square, and one in the afternoon, on Commonwealth Avenue. DeLeary stayed in the truck in the afternoon, but not in the morning. The pattern of the breaks was not expected to change.

"So there's a guy in the truck while you take your morning break?" Angelo asked.

"Yes," DeLeary stated. "We always leave someone in the truck."

"Where's the truck parked?" Kelly probed.

"Right there, on Boylston Street."

"So the guard who's still in the truck has you in sight at all times?" Angelo asked.

"Absolutely," DeLeary replied firmly.

Angelo groaned and repeated, "So you're never alone and you're always in sight of each other."

"Yeah," DeLeary said. "Keeping each other constantly in sight is a rule none of us breaks."

"Okay," Angelo said glumly. "We'll get back to you."

On the way back from the meeting, Kelley said to Angelo,

"Doesn't sound too good." "Phil will come up with something," Angelo said confidently. "Yeah, I forgot we're working with Mr. Houdini." "Fuck you, Kelley," Angelo said, a little too loudly. He was really getting annoyed at the way Kelley liked to put Cresta down.

Monday morning Phil and Angelo were in Copley Square. At ten-fifteen exactly the big gray Brink's truck double-parked, and Phil saw Andrew DeLeary for the first time. Laughing and joking with his partner, DeLeary went into the Bulkie Restaurant on Boylston Street. The two men were inside for six minutes and thirty seconds, and came out holding paper bags.

Phil made notations on everything he saw, including traffic conditions and the number of a Boston police car that drove by while the two guards were in the store. On the way to their car Phil said to Angelo, "Go into that phone booth and call Tony. Tell him to meet us at my room in an hour."

Later that night Phil called Kelley and they all met at McGrail's.

Just as Angelo had predicted, Phil came up with a plan. He went over it with Kelley and Angelo, and stressed that nobody else needed to know anything. Kelley instructed DeLeary on what to do the next Monday.

The following Monday, December 9, Angelo was in the phone booth, approximately seven yards from the restaurant's entrance, when the Brink's truck pulled up to the Bulkie Restaurant. As DeLeary and his partner left the truck on Boylston Street and passed the phone booth where Angelo was pretending to be talking to someone, DeLeary quickly slipped two keys into Angelo's hand. The pass-off was perfect, completed in the blink of an eye.

Walking behind DeLeary was Tony, who took the keys from Angelo and quickly went around the corner to a parking lot on Exeter Street. Phil Cresta was seated in the front seat of his Bonneville. Cresta took the keys and began work, using the smoker he kept in his glove box. Within two minutes he had a copy of each key—one to truck 6280's front door, the other to the back.

Angelo was still inside the phone booth when he spotted Tony walking toward him with a big smile on his face. He passed the original keys to Angelo.

A couple of minutes later DeLeary and his partner came out of the restaurant and headed back to the truck. The telephone booth was now empty, and Angelo was hovering by the door as though waiting for somebody. DeLeary, as instructed, told his partner he had to make a quick phone call. The other guard waited by the booth too, as DeLeary put in a dime and dialed a number. As though ready to talk privately, he turned his body to block the other guard's view and casually reached into the coin return slot, where the original Brink's keys lay. He then hung up the phone, told his partner he couldn't get through to his party, and together the Brink's guards headed back to their truck.

Only one more obstacle lay ahead. Phil had Kelley return both new keys to DeLeary temporarily, to make sure they fit the truck's front and back doors. He also asked DeLeary to scratch an *F* on the key to the truck's front door, to avoid any fumbling for the right key during the robbery. When he returned the keys to Phil, Kelley reported smugly, "They passed with flying colors!"

The stage was now set for a crime that would be described by a Suffolk County district attorney in open court as "one of the most interesting, carefully planned, and well-executed armed robberies in the history of Massachusetts." Phil and team, keys in hand, planned the hit for Saturday afternoon, December 14.

PHIL CRESTA awoke on the morning of December 14, 1968, with a sense of foreboding. This was the day that he and his six accomplices planned to make history. They had gone over the plans all week. If something went wrong it would not be for lack of planning. Every man had an assignment and each knew where he and every other team member were supposed to be. Phil had made it clear that the best scores are quick and deci- sive. They were going to take down the Brink's truck in the mid- dle of downtown Boston as thousands of unsuspecting Christ- mas shoppers went about their holiday business. Phil had reminded Red Kelley the night before, "There's no need to go in heavy. Make sure your guys know that." "Sure, Houdini, you're the boss," Kelley shot back.

It was a typical Boston December day, cold but clear. Phil didn't mind the cold, but he didn't like the clear weather. He would much rather have seen snow or rain. The members of the team arrived separately at the Fenway Motor Inn and parked their cars in the vicinity but not in the parking lot. Two cars in the parking lot that morning didn't belong to anyone staying there; they had been stolen the night before from Brighton. These two cars would transport seven men to two locations: one in South Boston and the other in the South End. Those going to the South End location would collect another recently stolen car for Red Kelley and Carmello Merlino to use. All three cars would cross the Broadway Bridge into South Boston, where they would retrieve a fourth stolen car, for Angelo and Sonny Diaferio. Then all four cars would leave for the robbery site.

Phil turned onto B Street in Southie; there was no car. He looked at Tony, who just shrugged and said, "Phil, I dropped the car off right here at ten last night." "Well, the fucking thing isn't here now," Phil, already on edge with that pre-crime tension, said menacingly.

They got out to meet the guys in the other two cars. "Someone must have stolen our stolen car," Tony said to the others. "Unbelievable!" Phil cried to no one in particular while throwing up his hands to the sky. "Can you believe the nerve of these people—stealing our car like that?" Tony asked Angelo. "First of all, numb nuts," Phil barked, "it wasn't *our* car and second of all, what the fuck are we, Boy Scouts?" Angelo couldn't help himself. He started to laugh, and before they knew it they all were standing in the middle of B Street in Southie, laughing hysterically. Everyone, that is, except Red Kelley.

"What's the matter, Red, ya gut no sense of humor?" Angelo asked between guffaws. "You guys are all crazy. All we need is for some flatfoot to drive by and do an FIO [field interrogation observation] on all of us. How would you like that?" "Lighten up,

Red," Phil said, feeling better now. "We live to rob another day."
"It's all right, Phil, I gutta do some Christmas shopping anyway,"
Tony said. Angelo began to laugh again, so hard this time that
he had to hold his side. *"He's gotta do some Christmas shopping!"*
he yelled. "Tony, you're priceless," Phil said as they piled back in
the cars and headed back to the motor inn.

There would be no Brink's robbery on December 14, 1968.

They met in Phil's extra room at the motor inn, the one he
kept for planning heists, on Tuesday, just to stay sharp. Phil was
even more worried about Red Kelley than he'd been before: the
man was starting to show signs of strain. "You gonna be all right
with this, Red?" Angelo asked. "I've been knocking off trucks
since you were in diapers, ya fucking wop," Red yelled at
Angelo. All eyes immediately turned to Phil, who jumped off the
bed. "Kelley, I've just about had it with you, ya fucking prima
donna. I'll take my chances with Angelo any day. As far as I'm
concerned, you're all talk." Phil glared at Red Kelley. "Yeah,
about a million and a half sentences, Mr. Houdini," Kelley said,
alluding again to his Plymouth success. "You'd better stop living
in the past, Kelley, or you're gonna get us all hurt," Phil said,
and he started to walk out of the room. "Are we through, Phil?"
Tony asked. "Yeah, see everybody back here on Thursday night."

They got through the Thursday night session with no more
flare-ups. They were to go into action on Saturday, December
21. This time rounding up the cars went like clockwork. They
were all in place, and even the weather seemed to be cooperat-
ing: there was a slight dusting of snow, which made Phil feel a
little better.

Kelley and Merlino were down the block, ready to pull up behind the Brink's truck when it turned onto Canal Street. Sonny
Diaferio and Angelo were already parked across from the Union
Oyster House on one side of the street, and Steve Roukous was
parked opposite them on the other side. Phil and Tony were
standing at the top of Canal, waiting to spot the Brink's truck as
it turned the corner. About three minutes before it was due,
Phil heard someone from behind say, "What the fuck are you

greaseballs doing down here? Someone let you out of your cage for the day or something?"

Tony and Phil spun around and stood face-to-face with detectives Gary Bowman and Robert Chenetti, who worked out of Boston Police's organized crime unit. Phil started sweating but hoped they wouldn't notice how shook up he was. "Hey, Chenetti," he said loudly, making sure it sounded like "Chinshitty," which he knew pissed the cop off. He was hoping the other guys could see what was going on; with two cops standing there, they didn't need anyone jumping out with their semis. Then Phil said, still loudly, "Come on, Tony. Let's get some Joe and Nemo hot dogs." Turning to the detectives, he added, "Sorry ya can't come, guys, but Joe and Nemo's don't sell doughnuts."

"Fuck you, greaseball," Bowman shouted as the thieves moved down Canal Street.

Phil held his breath, afraid the two detectives would spot other team members. They'd surely figure something was going down if they spotted Kelley, Merlino, or Diaferio. But everyone caught the play and hid as the two dicks strolled by. Though the Brink's truck then pulled around the corner, Bowman and Chenetti never even looked at it. The team made no move on the truck, since the detectives were still in the vicinity.

Nobody had to be told what to do. They met at the motor inn. Phil could tell from the moment Kelley walked in that he was through. "This fucking job is jinxed," Kelley said in disgust. "You want out, Red? Tell us now so we can get someone in quick," Angelo said. "I'm not saying I'm out, but I think we'd better reevaluate the situation," Kelley said, looking around for a friendly face. "Reevaluate this!" Angelo said, holding his crotch. "You're just a fucking coward, Mr. Big-Shot-Million-and-a-Half." Kelley turned and said to Phil. "I don't have to take this from some amateur B-and-E man." He picked up his hat and left.

They were all depressed—especially Phil. He knew that those two cops had probably cost them between a quarter and a half million dollars. A Brink's truck rolling four days before Christmas had to be loaded. Because they'd clocked 6280's Saturday routine only, the one time they could take the truck now would be after the Christmas holiday shopping frenzy, and the odds were that the loot would then be considerably less.

A few nights later Phil asked the remaining five men if they wanted to go ahead or not. Kelley, who was not officially out, had not been seen during the three days following their second aborted attempt. When Phil had called him at home, Kelley had used the excuse of a cold to avoid attending the next strategy session. "He's got a cold, all right: cold *feet*," Angelo said disgustedly. They went over two sets of plans that night, one with Kelley and one without. It was the latter that they used on the following Saturday, three days after Christmas.

PHIL COULD HEAR the rain as he began to stir from his fitful sleep. He was in fine spirits as Tony, who always arrived first, knocked on the door. There was a calmness about everyone that day. Everyone knew that the hit would go today, December 28, 1968, or never at all! They were ready.

The car pickups went perfectly. They arrived at the Canal Street site ahead of schedule and took their places. There were now three cars instead of four. Phil was in the first, which would park in front of the Brink's truck. Tony also was in that first car, but only Phil was visible. With a perfect view of the front of 6280, Tony was in the car's trunk, looking through a hole that had been drilled that morning. Angelo and Sonny were parked directly across from where the armored truck's driver usually stopped for his eighteen-minute break. Roukous and Merlino brought up the rear. Kelley had told Phil that he was staying at home in bed.

Heavy rain pelted down that evening as Phil, looking in his car's rearview mirror, spotted the Brink's truck turning onto Canal. It was just after six o'clock. Phil hit his horn once, the prearranged signal. He got out of the car and stood behind it, near its trunk. The Brink's truck, on its last stop of the day, double-parked in front of 122 Canal Street, the Union Oyster House.

Guards Joseph Kelly and John Gillespie headed into Downey & Judge's (For the benefit of the news media, Kelly and Gillespie would claim to have taken their break at a nearby Hayes Bickford cafeteria.) Through his peephole, Tony kept close watch on the third guard, Richard Haines, who, as usual, made no move to bolt the front doors. Tony was to bang on the door of the trunk if he saw Haines move toward the front, to bolt the door, which would render the key they planned to use completely useless.

Phil was waiting as Tony watched. After thirty seconds Phil took off his hat, a signal to Angelo and Sonny to move in on the truck. They were both wearing fake beards and stocking caps that they would pull down into ski masks when they got within a few feet of the truck. Sonny was carrying a semiautomatic in his long trench coat. Angelo had a .38 in his right coat pocket.

As they began to walk the twelve feet from their car to the Brink's truck, a couple came out of the Oyster House and got into their car, which was being blocked by the double-parked truck. When Phil saw them, he thought to himself that maybe Red was right about this job being jinxed. It was too late for Angelo and Sonny to retreat, so they moved into a doorway next to the Oyster House and waited for the car to leave. The guard got into the driver's seat, pulled ahead to let the car out, then stayed in the cab.

Once again, it was Tony's call, and he watched to see if this time the driver threw the bolt. Phil walked over and put his foot on his stolen car's back bumper as though tying his shoe and waited. No sound from Tony. He turned around and again took off his hat. Angelo and Sonny quickly moved to the truck's passenger-side door.

Phil held his breath, hoping that the key would fit as promised. There was no turning back now. As though in slow motion, he watched Angelo take the key out—and then was startled by a noise behind him. Quickly turning, he saw a drunk stumble out of Downey & Judge's. The drunk, fortunately, went the other way. By the time Phil turned back to see if the key had worked, his men already were in the truck.

Once in the truck, Angelo took control. "Do as we say and you'll live to see your grandkids. You fuck up once and I'll blow your fucking head off," Angelo told the guard. "Please, I have asthma, don't push me down," Haines begged. "Just sit the fuck down, then, and keep your mouth shut," Angelo told him, keeping his gun trained on the guard. Sonny, by that time, already had the truck in drive and was ready to pull out.

Phil retreated to his car and headed down Canal, followed by the armored truck, then by the third vehicle with Merlino at the wheel. The stolen car Sonny had driven to the crime scene was left there.

Boston streets have changed since 1968, but newspaper reports are clear that all three vehicles took a left onto Causeway, which until that night had been known only as the street on which the Boston Garden sat, and a right onto Nashua Street. From there they pulled into a parking lot directly behind the Massachusetts Registry of Motor Vehicles. At the time, this was a dark and deserted area, especially on a Saturday evening.

As they turned into the parking lot Phil spotted the other car that had been stolen earlier that day. This was for Angelo and Sonny, who were still in the armored truck. They were out of sight of any traffic on Causeway and Nashua streets, and totally removed from any foot traffic. A perfect spot for what the Brink's robbers had in mind.

It was dark and rainy, just the way Phil liked it, and his adrenaline was pumping, his heart racing, as he jumped out of the car to release Tony from the trunk. "How'd we do?" Tony wanted to know. "We're doin', Tony, we're doin'," Phil said. So far, everything seemed to be going exactly as they'd planned, and the weather was a bonus.

Phil figured that by this time Angelo would have the guard handcuffed and blindfolded in the back of the armored truck. The vehicle with Roukous and Merlino in it pulled into the parking lot a few seconds later, and everyone ran to prearranged positions. The station wagon driven by Merlino backed up so that its rear bumper almost touched the back bumper of the Brink's truck. With the guard safely blindfolded and handcuffed, the Brink's robbers quietly went to work transferring the money.

One metal container, four feet by three and three feet deep, was labeled JORDAN MARSH and was so heavy that it required two guys to carry it. The side of another heavy foot locker had FILENE'S written on it. It too was too heavy for one man to carry. RAYMOND'S was clearly marked on a suitcase-sized box. Boston Police later stated that, besides these three big department stores' containers, the truck contained forty-eight other bags with money from smaller downtown businesses. They estimated the take to be a million dollars.

The transfer of the money was completed in less than two minutes. In the truck that only moments before had contained so much money, the robbers left only a cardboard box, a living guard, and a guard's hat. Since they'd worked through 6280's back door, no one noticed that the key they'd used to get into the truck, back on Canal Street, was still in the truck's front door. And nobody cared either. As Boston Police Commissioner Edmund McNamara would later say, the robbery was clever, quick, and well planned.

When the last bag had been put into the station wagon, Phil began to relax. "I knew it couldn't have come off any better. Everything went right. Everything," he said. Once Steve Roukous got the nod from Phil, he and Merlino slowly drove out of the parking lot. Right behind them were the other two stolen cars. Haines was left in the back of the Brink's truck, handcuffed to the side door. The three cars, in sight of one another, drove four miles to Somerville.

There they put the next part of the plan into effect in a deserted parking lot behind the old Ford plant. There was one car already in that lot. It belonged to Steve Roukous and had no parking tickets or other kinds of violations outstanding. Phil had made certain of that a few weeks before. The last thing he needed was to steal a million dollars and have his driver get pulled over on an unpaid parking ticket warrant.

Nobody spoke, but nobody had to. Each knew that getting the money out of Boston before the cops knew what had happened was essential. It took less than two minutes to transfer the money from the station wagon to Steve's car. Once the switch had been made, Roukous and Merlino took off in one direction, the other two cars drove a different route.

Phil and Tony went over the bridge into Charlestown and headed to the projects, followed by Angelo and Sonny. Phil's stolen car was abandoned there. Tony and Phil got in the car with Angelo and Sonny and headed to Brockton, where Phil had rented a room for the next two days in a Holiday Inn. The room was in the back of the motel, so nobody could see it from the street. When Tony, Phil, Angelo, and Sonny arrived, Roukous and Merlino were already inside.

They took all the bags from Steve's car into the room, and separated the checks from the cash. While Phil, Merlino, Roukous, and Sonny Diaferio counted the money, Angelo and Tony got rid of the third stolen car and returned to the Holiday Inn. Now they had two clean cars—Steve's and one Phil had left at the inn the night before, when he'd rented the room. They also had almost a half million dollars in cash, and another half million in checks. Moving quickly under the cover of darkness, the robbers placed the empty moneybags and the three boxes in Phil's trunk. Roukous and Merlino, with a half million dollars in their trunk, headed to a safe house that belonged to Steve's cousin. They hid the money there. Phil and Tony drove to the Blue Hills Reservation, where they dropped the boxes, bags, and canceled checks over the side of an embankment.

BY THE TIME Phil was dumping his stolen car in the Charlestown housing development, guard Richard Haines, a former Tewksbury police officer, had fashioned a makeshift key out of the tin foil from a candy bar wrapper he had in his pocket. After a number of unsuccessful attempts, he managed to open the cuffs that had secured him to the door. Then Haines walked five hundred yards to the MDC Lower Basin police station, near the Museum of Science.

At 6:56 that evening Officer Eugene Innocenti looked up from his desk. A cold, wet Brink's guard looked directly at

Innocenti and said, "I've been hit for half a million." Innocenti immediately called his superior, George McGarrity, who unlocked the other handcuff on the guard's wrist. As McGarrity was freeing Haines, Innocenti was calling the Boston Police. One of the MDC cops noted, "While we were waiting for Boston to get down to our station I had a few minutes to talk to Haines and I could tell you the guy was pretty shook up." He said that after the robbers had transferred the money and left, he managed to hit the truck's alarm with his nose, but it was such a desolate area nobody heard it. He then told them how he'd managed to fashion a key to free himself. "It was the most amazing bit of ingenuity under stress I've ever seen," the detective declared.

Boston Police Commissioner McNamara, upon getting the report of the Brink's million-dollar robbery, immediately called in the FBI. At a one A.M. press conference, the commissioner, wearing a sports shirt and looking bleary-eyed, admitted that authorities had only the barest description of the holdup men. McNamara told a horde of press that when the two guards looked out of the window and didn't see their Brink's truck, they figured that Haines had gotten tired of waiting for them and driven the truck to the nearby countinghouse by himself. When he didn't return in twenty minutes in his own car, though, they began to panic but still didn't notify authorities. Finally, after half an hour, Gillespie called the Brink's office. He was told to stay where he was. Boston Police picked up both Gillespie and Kelly minutes later.

McNamara assigned fifty Boston detectives to the case, and the Brink's company offered a $25,000 reward for information leading to the arrest and conviction of any party involved in the robbery. Brink's spokesman Thomas F. Horrigan admitted that if the robbery had occurred a week earlier there would have been several million dollars in that truck.

PHIL KNEW that those two Organized Crime dicks had cost him, but he didn't know how much until he read Horrigan's statement in the evening paper the next night. They were on their way back to the Holiday Inn in Brockton. "Those two fucking assholes cost us at least a million dollars," Phil remarked sullenly.

Angelo tried to calm him down. "Come on, Phil, we got away with half a mil, nobody got hurt, they have no clues, no leads—they're fucked."

"Yeah, now we just have to worry about that fucking loudmouth Kelley. I don't intend to be his next victim."

Angelo nodded in agreement. Tony snoozed in the backseat.

"Do you believe this fucking guy?" Phil said, looking back at the snoring Tony and smiling.

"I just hope his Christmas shopping went okay," Angelo said, chuckling.

"Ours did," Phil said, and laughed too.

When they got to the Holiday Inn, Phil called Steve and told him to bring the money back to Brockton. They divided the take and put it in stacks of $50,000. When they had finished, there were ten stacks with a few hundred left over.

Phil gave Kelley, who had undergone a miraculous recovery, his stack of $65,000 and another stack of $51,000 for Andrew DeLeary.

"You'll be able to pay your doctor now, Red, for that miraculous cure he gave you," Angelo sniped.

Kelley stared at Angelo and walked out of the Holiday Inn.

"I hope it's the last time I see that piece of shit," Angelo said.

"We'll see him again," Phil said. "You can count on it."

IT WOULD BE more than five years before Phil would be in the same room with Kelley again but he heard from him much sooner than that. Three months after the robbery, Phil got an alarmed call from Kelley. He started with, "We got trouble."

"What's this *we* shit? What are you, French?" Phil said.

"I'm serious, Phil. I've been calling DeLeary for the past six days and he's not around," Kelley whispered.

"Well, where the fuck *is* he, Red? You were supposed to watch him."

"I did. And I told him to lay low, just like you told me. Told him not to spend any money or draw any attention to himself. Told him that *and* kept an eye on him. Honest," Kelley whined.

"When *was* the last time you spoke to him?" Phil asked coldly.

"About ten days ago."

"*Shit!*" Phil said into the phone. After a moment of furious silence he went on. "Listen, Red, if the feds got to him, we all go down, you understand? Find him before I do," Phil threatened and hung up.

Three days after that telephone conversation Phil was sitting in McGrail's when he spotted Angelo coming in. He could tell just by the look on his face that there was trouble. Angelo gestured with his head for Phil to meet him outside.

"What's the good news?" Phil asked, knowing only too well that there would be no good news coming from Angelo that day.

"It's fucking DeLeary," Angelo spat out. "You know why that fuck-face Kelley couldn't find DeLeary?"

"No, but I have a feeling you're going to tell me."

"Because DeLeary was in the Bahamas, that's why. He was in the fucking Bahamas with his whole fucking family and all his fucking in-laws, *that's* why."

Now Phil knew they were *really* in trouble. He groaned and said weakly, "Kelley told me DeLeary was laying low."

"Ten days in the fucking Bahamas with all the fixings—is that what that fucking mick calls laying low?" Angelo cried in frustration. "What are we gonna do, Phil?"

"Let's wait and see what develops," Phil answered. But he knew they had lost control of the situation. The feds had to have found their leak.

He also knew that DeLeary could finger not only Kelley, whom he didn't care about, but Angelo. Phil cared a lot about Angelo and was angry at himself for letting Angelo go to those meetings with DeLeary. Phil had said he'd take care of both Kelley and DeLeary if it ever came to this, and now he looked for a way to do just that.

AFTER DELEARY'S BAHAMAS EXCURSION, the feds indeed knew who the inside man was and they turned the screws on him. Upon his return from vacation, they moved in quickly, making it obvious they were watching his every move around the clock. This made Phil's decision to whack DeLeary difficult to accomplish, and whatever hope he might have had that the cowardly Kelley would whack the guard to protect himself also disappeared. Phil received a frantic late-night call from Red Kelley near the end of April 1969. "Phil, it's Red. We got more trouble."

"What the fuck are you doing *calling* me, asshole? Your phone is probably bugged and now you're dragging me into this mess," Phil shouted.

"Dragging you in? You were the one who dragged *me* in," Kelley said.

"What now?" Phil asked.

"DeLeary called me and he's about to crack," Kelley whispered.

"*He called you?* That stupid fuck has everyone but Efrem Zimbalist Jr. tailing him and he *called you?* He's fucking dumber than I thought," Cresta yelled into the phone.

"If he turns, Phil, we all go down."

"What do you mean, Red? DeLeary doesn't know dick about *us*. The only way we go down is if *you* roll."

"Oh, don't worry about me, Phil. I'll just deny everything, but he did meet with Angelo, you know," Kelley said quickly.

There it is, Phil thought, that's the reason for the call. Kelley was dangling Angelo out there to see if Phil would take the bait. There was a long pause. "You want me to take out DeLeary, Red? Is that what you're saying?"

"Either that or your wop buddy with the big mouth takes a tough fall."

PHIL WANTED to leave Tony out of this development since DeLeary didn't know about him. Hoping to keep it that way, Phil called only Angelo, and they met that night at McGrail's. "I just got a phone call—" Phil started to say, but Angelo interrupted.

"Kelley?"

Phil nodded.

"What's the deal?" Angelo asked.

"He wants me to whack DeLeary."

"I knew I should've killed that Irish cocksucker that night in the planning room," Angelo spit out, his eyes and face showing contempt for Red Kelley. "Has DeLeary rolled?"

"No, but he's about to," Phil said. "That's why Kelley wants me to whack him before he implicates you and him. I'm sorry, Ange. I never should've let you meet DeLeary."

"Why doesn't Mr. Tough-guy whack DeLeary himself?" Angelo asked.

"The feds are watching both of them. DeLeary, for fucksake, called Kelley at home!"

"So Kelly wants you to do his dirty work? Fuck it. Let's do what we have to do. I don't feel like spending my life in Walpole."

They headed out onto Kilmarnock Street, just as the Red Sox crowd was letting out.

THE FEDS, certain that DeLeary was their man, closed in. First they began to interview his friends and neighbors, and they left no doubt as to their intentions. Everywhere DeLeary went he was tailed. The feds acted like incompetent, low-rent private eyes as they made sure DeLeary saw every tail and heard the clicks on his home phone, but they knew what they were doing. They wanted DeLeary to know they were on to him. They hoped that their scrutiny would crack him, and it did.

Phil got word through a source in the Boston Police Department that they were bringing DeLeary to the new Area A station the next day. As soon as Phil got off the phone with the cop, he called Angelo and made plans to meet again. Angelo had been brought into that same station, on New Sudbury Street in Boston, a week earlier but had said nothing. The cops had been rounding up anyone and everyone they considered a suspect. Angelo knew they were just fishing, but he was pretty shaken nonetheless. He'd recounted that experience for Phil as the two of them walked around Castle Island in South Boston the day after he was released. "DeLeary has more tails than a dozen donkeys," Phil had told Angelo that day. "I've been looking for a place to whack him, but the feds are everywhere. It would be suicide to try it."

This time they met at McGrail's and when Phil told him DeLeary would be in custody the next day, Angelo said, "We're screwed now." He frowned.

"Maybe not," Phil said. "I have a plan."

The two of them left the bar and headed downtown. They parked the car on Congress Street and walked to New Sudbury Street, only a block away from the where they had robbed the Brink's truck four months before. The Area A station was new, replacing the one Phil had hit in April 1966. It had opened just that past summer, on July 31. Phil had never been inside. He hoped Angelo had been paying attention to his surroundings when he was questioned there.

"Do you remember where they took you for interrogation?" Phil asked Angelo.

"Second floor."

"Back or front?" Angelo looked a little puzzled and didn't answer. Phil tried again. "Were there any windows in the interrogation room?"

Angelo nodded.

"Did you look out any of those windows?"

Angelo thought for a moment and then smiled. "Yeah, they left me alone for a couple of minutes and I went over and looked out the window."

"What did you see?"

Angelo pointed to a parking garage that was under construction.

"You sure?" Phil asked.

"Positive."

The first four floors of the garage had been completed. It looked as if there were going to be nine or ten stories to the structure. Phil was concerned only with the garage's second floor. He and Angelo walked up the stairs to it and Phil asked

Angelo to show him the window. Angelo did. Phil walked back and forth and studied the layout for fifteen minutes and then turned to Angelo. "All right, let's go."

It was while they were heading home that Angelo said, "Phil, you're not thinking of hitting DeLeary while he's *in* the police station, are you?" "It's our last chance," Phil responded. "You'll never get away with it, Phil. We're talking about hitting a guy who's in a room with four cops: two local and two feds. That's insane."

"I think it's a lot more insane to be looking at twenty-five years at Walpole. You ain't been there yet, Ange. Trust me."

There was dead silence in the car for the rest of the ride. Phil parked in front of Angelo's house and Angelo turned and said, "Phil, why don't we wait? What if DeLeary doesn't roll?" Phil laughed and said, "That guard is going to roll faster than a fat man down the G Street hill, and you know it." Angelo wasn't convinced yet. "Phil, I don't give a flying fuck about DeLeary. I'd whack him myself if I could, but hitting him while he's in a police station is another thing entirely." Phil didn't respond. "Will you at least think about it before tomorrow?" Angelo implored. Phil said, "Yeah, I'll call you in the morning."

The next morning Phil called Angelo at home and said, "Let's just hope he doesn't roll."

Angelo knew this was Phil's way of telling him that he would not try to hit DeLeary.

"Have you heard from Kelley?" Phil then asked his friend.

"Not a peep."

"Let's batten down the hatches," Phil said. "This could get bumpy."

It did. The following day the ship began to take on water. A Suffolk County grand jury was meeting with DeLeary. Assistant District Attorney Lawrence Cameron was slated to present the state's case. Also giving grand jury testimony would be Boston detectives Ed Walsh, Thomas Connolly, Alan Crisp, John Carter, Gregory Mazares, and Patrick Spillane.

At around ten that morning, May 14, 1969, before Larry

Cameron said word one to the grand jury, Phil received a call from one of his allies on the inside. Something big was happening, Cresta was told, and it probably had to do with the Brink's job. When Phil learned how many officers were scheduled to address the grand jury, he knew the case was strong. Those guys were the cream of the crop. Still, since DeLeary had never met him, Phil didn't think he'd be indicted yet.

But a little after twelve-thirty that same day Phil got another call from his contact in the police department. "Red Kelley gave you up," the person on the other end of the line whispered. "They just handed down secret indictments for you, DeLeary, Kelley, and Angelo. The arrests are being made immediately." Then the caller hung up.

"That fucking rat bastard," Phil said out loud, referring to Kelley. He immediately called Angelo and said, "Ange, Kelley gave us up. They're on their way." There was silence as Phil waited for Angelo to tell him what he'd do.

"I'm gonna have to take the pinch, Phil," Angelo finally said. "I can't leave my family and hide for ten years. I'm just gonna have to take the pinch."

Phil had been pretty sure Angelo would decide that way. "I'm outta here, Angelo. You know I love you."

"Yeah, and I love you. Now take care and don't worry about me." And then Angelo said, "What about Tony?"

"He wasn't named, thank God. Gotta go, my friend. Take care of yourself."

According to the front-page story in the *Boston Evening Globe* that day, May 14 had been a busy day. The Boston Police picked up Cresta first, it said. The story told of how they arrested him at his home on Headland Way in Medford and how he was booked at Boston Police headquarters. Boston Police, it went on to say, had received a call from attorney F. Lee Bailey, indicating that his client, John "Red" Kelley, would turn himself into authorities at nine A.M. the next day. Angelo and DeLeary were also under arrest

Attorney Chester Paris, representing Angelo, received permission from Judge Rueben L. Lurie to present his arguments on bail in the judge's chambers. There, Paris complained that the arrest of his client had already been the subject of numerous radio and television reports and that photographers had been pursuing his client. Judge Lurie, no Bowman, then listened to the arguments from Assistant District Attorney Lawrence Cameron, and thereafter set bail at $250,000. He gave Paris thirty days to file motions.

On May 15, 1969, Kelley, accompanied by an attorney from Bailey's office, was arraigned. He too was held on $250,000 bail.

In between Angelo's and Kelley's arraignments, the police brought Cresta to the Suffolk County Courthouse. He also was held on $250,000 bail, and sent back to the Charles Street Jail, where Kelley and Angelo were incarcerated.

The next day the *Record American* ran a huge front-page picture of Cresta being taken out of the back of a patrol wagon on his way to his arraignment. The caption read, "William Cresta, in custody of a detective as he was taken into Boston Police Headquarters. He was one of four men named when a Suffolk County grand jury returned secret indictments in the $800,000 hijacking of a Brink's truck in the North End last December."

18
On the Run

HIL SAW THAT PICTURE as he was having his shoes shined in a Pennsylvania barbershop on his way to Chicago. "When you're on the lam, the last thing you want to do is to draw attention to yourself. But as soon as I saw my brother Billy on the front page of that paper, I just started to laugh." The FBI and the Boston Police wouldn't think it was all that funny.

All the detectives who worked Organized Crime had been at Superior Court testifying when the indictments had been issued. They had sent regular cops to round up the suspects. The only known address listed at police headquarters for Cresta was Billy Cresta's house. When the cops had gone to his house they'd asked, "Is your name Cresta?" Billy, who just happened to be away from Miami on one of his stays in the Boston area, had answered, "Yes, it is." And he was placed under arrest. It wasn't until that picture appeared in the paper that the Organized Crime guys realized they had the wrong Cresta. By the time they got to Phil's last-known address—in Lynn—he was long gone. That extra twenty-four hours had given Phil ample time to tie up some loose ends before he headed to Chicago.

Boston and federal authorities had converged on Phil's house, armed with subpoenas and search warrants, but they were a day late and in the wrong place. Phil was, of course, separated from his wife, and had been living at the Fenway Motor Inn for over five years.

At the same time that police were converging on the Lynn house, another team of police, also armed with subpoenas and search warrants, was charging into a number of Boston area banks, trying to confiscate the contents of Phil Cresta's accounts and a number of safe-deposit boxes. The first bank was located in Coolidge Corner, two doors down from where Phil had unlocked a Skelly armored truck and driven away with $58,000 in 1966. The agent in charge explained to a teller why they were there. After some confusion, two safe-deposit boxes were placed on a table by the bank president and unlocked. There was one single piece of paper in the box that read, *"Ha, ha! Kilroy was here!"* The same thing happened to other policemen when they opened Phil Cresta's other safe-deposit boxes in South Boston, East Boston, Charlestown, and Revere.

Phil left Boston with more than half a million dollars in cash. He paid a friend five thousand dollars to drive him to Pennsylvania. When he arrived there, a driver and a room were waiting for him, courtesy of his Chicago friends. The driver would later say, "He was as cool as a cucumber. I was shittin' my pants. We keep hearing on the radio how he's a fugitive from justice and considered armed and extremely dangerous. He's laughing at the news reports, but I'm still scared that we'll be stopped. As we're heading into Pennsylvania, there's a multiple-car crash on the road ahead of us! I'm going to speed up and go around the accident but Phil tells me to stop. I can't believe it! He gets out of the car and starts helping people who are still trapped in their cars. I keep looking for the cops, but he's totally unconcerned. Here he is, one of the most wanted fugitives in America, and he's in the middle of a huge accident with television cameras and police on their way! Finally I grab him by the arm and pull him back into our car and get out of there. When I dropped him off at the designated spot in Pennsylvania, he gave me the five thousand dollars we agreed on, and twenty-five hundred more *for my conversation*. He was unbelievable."

Phil wasn't worried about himself, but he felt bad about Angelo. And he believed it was only a matter of time before Tony was pulled in. All the crime cops knew that Tony and Angelo were part of his team, and that if Phil and Angelo were involved in something, it was a pretty sure bet that Tony was there, too.

What Phil didn't know was that Red Kelley was already singing like a canary, and he had given up Tony, Merlino, Roukous, and Santo Diaferio. Kelley thought his high-priced lawyer could get him off on any pinch, as long as he rolled on his accomplices.

"Ben Tilley must've been laughing his ass off, since all three of us took the hit," Phil said. "I knew I screwed up by not killing Kelley when I had the chance. Angelo was right, we should've taken that asshole out the day he walked out on us. By not killing Kelley and DeLeary we set ourselves up for a big fall. I shouldn't've let them off the hook."

THE BRINK'S ROBBERY TRIAL for the available defendants took place in June 1969. The state's two leading witnesses, Red Kelley and Andrew DeLeary, buried the two defendants who stood trial at that time: Tony and Angelo. There was never any question as to their guilt, only to what sentences they would get.

Kelley and DeLeary pleaded guilty to conspiracy and were given three to five years.

Angelo and Tony received sentences of twenty-five to forty years each, to be served at Walpole State Prison.

Carmello Merlino, who evaded capture for more than a year, was later found guilty and sentenced to twenty-five to forty years.

Santo "Sonny" Diaferio suffered a heart attack as the opening arguments of the trial were just getting under way. His case was continued until June 23, 1971. Diaferio's doctor told Judge James C. Roy that his client had only five to six years to live because of his heart condition. Roy was apparently unswayed; he gave Diaferio ten to fifteen years in Walpole State Prison. Diaferio died April 15, 1981, after his release.

Sonny Diaferio's attractive wife, Patricia, was also indicted, but she was never tried. She said that she was on welfare and had been forced to sell the family home to pay medical expenses.

Bench warrants were issued on June 12, 1969, for the arrests of Stephen Roukous and Phil Cresta. Like Cresta, Roukous was placed on the FBI's Most Wanted list. When apprehended in 1972, he was tried and sentenced to twenty-five to forty years in Walpole.

PHIL CRESTA was a lot smarter than your average wise guy. He had planned for the day when he'd have to flee as meticulously as he planned every score he was involved in. He'd kept his safe-deposit boxes in places easy to get to when going on the run. He'd nurtured his contacts, devised ways to stay in touch with family and friends back home, created aliases, studied disguise. Throughout the years that Cresta and his team had done their jobs, Phil never lost touch with the fact that there was always someone out there trying to take him down.

When he hit the bricks on May 14, 1969, Phil tapped into contacts he'd made while living a shadow life in Chicago (unbeknownst to everyone in Boston except Angelo and Tony) for almost ten years. His sister Mari, through her husband, Augie Circella, and his Follies Burlesque Theater, was tied in pretty well with Anthony "Big Tuna" Accardo, Joseph "Joey O'Brien" Aiuppa, Jackie Cerone, and Joseph "Joe Negall" Ferriola—men who ran the Chicago mob as well as the Las Vegas, Milwaukee, Miami, Kansas City, and St. Louis operations. Mari became especially close with Joe Ferriola, who watched out for her and who later took over Chicago.

Years later, Mari reminisced about an evening after she and Augie had split, when she was getting ready to go out on a date with a local wise guy. Before her date came to pick her up she got a call from Ferriola. "Mari, are you going out with so-and-so?" he asked. "Yeah, how did you know?" Mari asked. "Never mind that, just don't go out with him tonight," Ferriola, the boss of Chicago at the time, told Mari. She'd been around long enough not to ask any more questions. When the wise guy came to pick her up, she told him she wasn't feeling well and apologized. He said he understood and left. The next day his body was found in the trunk of his car. Ferriola had saved Mari's life. Mari knew that everything around Chicago was probably bugged, and that mentioning Ferriola's phone call to anyone could implicate him in the murder and that she'd end up in someone's trunk just as her almost-date did.

In 1969, while Mari and her connections were helping Phil hide in Chicago, his whereabouts and ultimate capture became an obsession of a very powerful man in Washington: J. Edgar Hoover. Hoover and his Special Agent in Charge (SAC) in Boston would begin a massive paper trail concerning the whereabouts of Philip Joseph Cresta. In an internal FBI memo dated June 12, 1969, the FBI gave this description of Cresta (which made him somewhat smaller-than-life):

SEX: Male

RACE: White

HEIGHT: Approximately 5'9"

WEIGHT: 165 pounds, January, 1968

BUILD: Medium

HAIR: Chestnut-brown

COMPLEXION: Dark

EYES: Brown

DATES OF BIRTH: March 2, 1938; March 2, 1928

PLACES OF BIRTH: Boston, Massachusetts; Everett, Massachusetts

SCARS AND MARKS: Scar right middle finger; scar left thumb; scar left ring finger; scar near point of left elbow; scar over right eye

OCCUPATIONS: Counterman in restaurant; plumber; car salesman; salesman; mechanic's helper

ADDRESSES: 16 Light Street, Lynn, Massachusetts, January,

1968, October, 1961, February, 1960; 1 Nelson Street, Lynn,
Massachusetts, November, 1959; 56 Fountain Street,
Medford, Massachusetts, November, 1959, November, 1955,
March, 1945, June, 1942

SOCIAL SECURITY #: 030-20-4003

RELATIVES: Philip, father; Ruth, mother

MARITAL STATUS: Married, November, 1959

FBI IDENTIFICATION #: 4349239

NCIC FINGERPRINT CLASSIFICATION: 1612010611180906TT12

OFFENSE CHARGED: Fugitive from justice

U.S. CODE TITLE AND SECTION: Title 18, US Code Section
1073

WARRANT ISSUED BY: U.S. Commissioner R. Robert Popeo

DATE ISSUED: 6/12/69

Another memo, dated November 1, 1969, from the SAC in
Boston to the FBI director, said that Cresta was believed to have
driven from Boston to parts unknown in a 1967 yellow Bonneville sedan, license plate number G2140. The feds thought they
had a break in the Cresta case and they plastered his picture
and one of the gold Bonneville all over the country.

The FBI offices in Boston were located directly across the
street from Boston's Area A police station, where Phil had
thought about hitting DeLeary as he was undergoing questioning by the Boston Police. For a year and a half, the memo from
the FBI was posted in every police station in Boston. While the
feds were looking all over the country for the gold Bonneville
with license plate number G2140, a Boston police officer, working in Area A, was driving that very car every day and parking it
twenty yards from the FBI offices.

The cop driving the gold Bonneville was a loudmouth whom
Phil never liked. Two days before Phil went on the lam, the cop
was drinking in McGrail's and Phil approached him. "Hey,
Cresta, you're not in jail yet?" the cop said loudly enough
for everyone in McGrail's to hear. Phil laughed, but deep inside
he was fuming. "Now what would I be in jail for?" he asked. "I

can think of a hundred things," the cop said, laughing. "You got me all wrong," Phil answered. "As matter of fact, I'm thinking of opening a new restaurant." Intent on needling Phil, the policeman said that he hoped this time Phil was going to buy his meat instead of stealing it. "Your last restaurant didn't last too long," the cop said, laughing. By now he was really irritating Phil. "Well, I know how much you like my car, and I was going to see if you wanted to buy it from me. But if you're not interested, I'll sell it to someone else," Phil said, drawing the cop in. "Whoa, whoa, whoa," the cop said. "Are you serious?" "Yeah, I got to come up with fifty large to open the restaurant," Phil lied. "How much you asking for the car?" "A grand," Phil said. "Just one?" The cop smiled. "Yeah, I need the money tonight," Phil said sadly. "You got the papers?" the cop, now beaming, asked. "Of course. This isn't hot, you know that. You've already checked it out." "How'd ya know that?" The cop blushed. "I have my sources," Phil returned. "I'll be back in an hour. You gonna be here?" the cop asked. "I'll be here," Phil said as the cop hurried out.

Forty minutes later the cop was back with a thousand dollars in hand. Phil had all the papers ready and the exchange was made quickly. The cop, who loved the gold Bonneville loaded with extras, was thrilled with his new possession. "So long, sucker," he yelled to Phil as he left McGrail's. "We'll see who the sucker is," Phil said under his breath, knowing that DeLeary was close to breaking and he himself was close to fleeing.

The cop Phil sold his car to didn't bother to reregister the license plates. Thinking himself above the law, he simply put the bill of sale in his glove compartment. Two days later all hell broke loose and Phil beat the cops out of town. The cop reported nothing. Just because Cresta was gone was no reason to give up his new prized possession.

On April 8, 1970, a year after Phil fled, another internal memo sent from the FBI field office in Boston to Director J. Edgar Hoover stated, "Subject: Cresta (FBI # 4347) was last known to be driving a 1967 Pontiac Bonneville, hard-top sedan, yellow, bearing current Massachusetts License G2140 issued to himself." This FBI memo was put in the police stations throughout Boston, and was posted in the Boston FBI office, on top of the similar one posted the previous November. On May 12, 1970, a young FBI agent parked his car on New Sudbury Street and was walking to the back door of the FBI offices when he noticed a 1969 gold Bonneville parked in one of the spaces reserved for cops assigned to Area A. The agent ran upstairs.

Within minutes he had found what he was looking for. He raced back down to New Sudbury Street, approached the gold Bonneville, and was pleased to see that the license plate said G2140. He couldn't believe his luck. He told his boss about the Bonneville, and showed it to him from the window. Three FBI agents then walked across the street, where the police captain in command of Area A told them that the officer who owned the vehicle was working a detail at the Boston Garden.

The officer was summoned to the station, where the FBI and some high-ranking Boston police officers anxiously awaited his arrival. After hearing his explanation, the department held a disciplinary hearing. The officer who had called Phil Cresta a sucker immediately "retired" from the Boston Police Department. Phil Cresta, in Chicago, laughed like hell when he was told the story.

WHILE BOSTON'S FINEST were hushing up the story about Phil's car being driven by one of their own, the feds were putting the heat on Phil's family and friends. The FBI had moved Phil to their Ten Most Wanted list and his picture regularly appeared on the popular show *The FBI*, hosted by Efrem Zimbalist Jr. Hoover was creating a mountain of paperwork with the same theme: find Phil Cresta.

Phil's younger brother Bobby knew he was under surveillance. He responded one day by pulling into the parking garage next to the Area A police station. "I was directly across the street from the FBI offices. I parked the car on the fourth floor and could look into their offices from there. I knew the feds wouldn't follow me into the garage. There was only one way out, so they'd wait across the street until I came out, which I did about fifteen minutes later. I could tell they were surprised as I drove out onto New Sudbury Street. They'd figured I'd be walking, I guess, but they quickly followed me. I traveled down Congress Street and over to Stuart. I parked on Berkeley Street, directly across from Boston Police headquarters. I walked down St. James Avenue and into the Greyhound Bus terminal. I quickly ran to a bus that was headed for Florida, and removed from my pocket the bug that I'd taken from my car in that parking garage. I placed the bug under the cushion of one of the seats and ran off the bus before it left the terminal. I ran into the men's room and stayed there for an hour. When I returned to my car on Berkeley Street, the tail was gone. It was the last bug I ever found on or in my car," Bobby said.

Bobby Cresta knew, too, that his phone was being tapped. But he and his brother Phil stayed in contact by telephone, by using an intricate system that Phil had devised long before he fled. Phil had given Bobby a list of twelve pay phones, each in a different part of Boston. Next to each phone's number and address was the phone's location. Part of it looked like this:

1. 269-0080—460 West Broadway, South Boston; next to South Boston Savings Bank
2. 265-66378—1120 Dorchester Avenue, Dorchester; in front of Fields Corner MBTA station
3. 242-7897—312 Main Street, Charlestown; next to Warren Tavern

The plan worked as follows. On January 1 at one P.M., Bobby Cresta would be standing in front of a pay phone located at 460 West Broadway. At exactly one o'clock the phone would ring and Bobby would talk to his older brother Phil on the other end. Their conversation would be brief and straight to the point. Phil would probably say, "Anything I should know?" Bobby might answer, "No, everything is cool." Phil would hang up and Bobby would be on his way.

The next month the second listing would be the one to use: On February 2 at two P.M. Bobby Cresta would be in front of 1120 Dorchester Avenue and at exactly two o'clock the pay phone at that location would ring. Bobby would pick it up. And so it went.

The conversations varied from seconds to minutes, but the feds never had the time or the expertise to track where the call originated, and even if they had, it would have done them no good. Phil always used a different pay phone to call from, just as Bobby used a different pay phone to answer. If Bobby missed a call, Phil would wait until the next month to call again. If Phil had to reach Bobby for an emergency, everything was to go through Augie, but that happened only once.

WHILE THE FEDS were looking for Cresta, three indictments were handed down by a Suffolk County grand jury in October 1969 for the VA Hospital job, naming Phil Cresta and, of all people, Ben Tilley—and Jerry Angiulo as an accessory after the fact. The indictments went nowhere and nobody ever went to trial. Phil, of course, was already long gone from Boston.

Angiulo, though, was extremely annoyed that his name was in the indictment. He was trying to lie low at the time, and was dealing with more important things: a gang war going on in Southie, Charlestown, and Somerville that threatened to compromise Angiulo's power. Nobody ever won in those kind of battles, as Angiulo, who had been involved in a few, knew only too well.

Still, people were disappearing left and right, both in Southie and Somerville, and the two names that kept cropping up were Whitey Bulger and Howie Winter.

Bulger was known to be a fitness freak who had served time in Alcatraz and Leavenworth for bank robbery, and now was back home in South Boston, teamed up with people like Steve "The Rifleman" Flemmi. He had met Phil Cresta through mutual acquaintances, and while they weren't close friends there was a mutual respect. Many people saw Bulger as trouble and there were a few attempts on his life, which he somehow managed to escape. The attempts were thought to have been made by Angiulo's men, but that was never proven.

Howie Winter, who was the leader of the Winter Hill Gang in Somerville, was also seen as an up-and-coming player who had a lot more in common with Bulger than with Angiulo. Angiulo was clearly having problems, and his boss in Providence, Raymond Patriarca, the head of New England's La Cosa Nostra, was having serious problems too. The last thing Jerry Angiulo needed was the kind of publicity that the VA Hospital indictment brought.

Phil had no sympathy for the man he had once worked for, the man who had tried to get him killed—by his own brother. "I understood that Jerry Angiulo wasn't too pleased with me when he got pulled into the hospital rap," Phil said, smiling. "Tough shit."

J. EDGAR HOOVER died in 1972 but the FBI continued the search for Phil Cresta. Cresta, however, had been quietly swallowed up by his friends in the Chicago syndicate. He now answered to the name Joey Paul Zito, and he was the owner of a toy store in Chicago.

While Phil was lying low in Chicago, Tony and Angelo were serving their sentences in Walpole. "It really bothered me that they were in the can, but they understood why I was in no hurry to join them," Phil said. Every Christmas both Angelo and Tony would receive huge goody packages from different states. An accompanying card was signed, "*a friend.*"

Phil had been in Chicago for a year before the intense heat started to subside a little. He made a lot of friends while there: some legitimate, some not. One person whom Phil (aka Joey Zito) became very friendly with was none other than the mayor, Richard Daley. There had been rumors circulating around Chicago that Mayor Daley was "in bed" with the mob ever since some well-known wise guys gave Daley some serious campaign money in 1955. It was rumored that Daley had more direct ties to the Chicago mob, and it was a well-known fact that the Chicago Police Department was owned lock, stock, and barrel by gangsters.

Phil had been introduced to Mayor Daley through friends of Augie. "The mayor and I hit it off," Phil said. "He never for a minute knew who I was or that I was wanted by the FBI. He knew me as Joey Zito, the guy who owned Toy World downtown. He knew I had some connections, but that was a plus and not a minus in Chicago. Mayor Daley personally gave me what was called a legislative aide's badge, which, he told me, would come in handy at times. And it did," Phil said, laughing. "I was stopped for speeding on three different occasions. Each time, when I produced my license and registration, I also produced my badge, which got me a warning instead of a ticket. Police or anyone else in Chicago didn't fool around with Mayor Daley."

Phil became even closer to his sister Mari while he was on the run. Mari and Augie knew almost everyone on the hustle in Chicago. It was not uncommon for Joey Zito to have dinner with Mayor Daley on a Wednesday and then dine with Tony Accardo or Joey Aiuppa on Thursday.

In 1972, after Phil had been on the run for three years, the feds began to focus on Chicago and to tail Mari. She had a beautiful apartment in one of Chicago's most fashionable high-rise buildings and Phil often stopped by unannounced, after work or on the weekends, to visit his sister. On one of those occasions, he was just about to walk into the lobby when he spotted a man conspicuously trying to be inconspicuous. Phil headed out the door to his car.

He waited and watched for thirty minutes. The guy who was sitting in the lobby left Mari's building along with three other guys; they got into two cars and left. Phil waited another ten minutes and then went to see Mari, who was shaken up. "They know you're in Chicago," she cried. "They might *think* I'm in Chicago, but they don't *know* anything," Phil replied, wondering how the feds had figured out where he was. He headed home to his new wife, Molly.

Phil called some of his new friends in Chicago and asked them to do a little snooping to see if there were any new memos about his fugitive status. "After a week or so, I got a call from a well-known Chicago wise guy who asked me to meet him at Augie's theater. As I stepped from my car, I could see feds everywhere. It was too late to do anything, so I just got out of my car and walked right past the place. I figured they had compromised the wise guy and knew I was coming there to meet him.

"I was wrong. They never looked at me because they were there to bust a guy named Jackie Cerone, who I saw being led out of the Follies in handcuffs a few minutes later. It could've been a pretty good twofer if they'd done their homework. Here I was on the Top Ten list and not one of those feds—and there had to be at least twenty of them—even looked my way. I walked around the block and came back just in time to see them leading Jackie away. That was too close. I went into the Follies and met my guy."

The Chicago wise guy was sitting alone at the end of the bar, pretty shook up. His eyes went wide when he saw Phil approach. "Phil, I'm glad you're okay." "I thought you'd set me up," Phil told him in a menacing tone. "Believe me, Phil, I had nothing to do with this. But I knew if they grabbed you on your way in here, I was a dead man." "You thought right," Phil said seriously. Then he sat down, paused, and extended his hand to the gangster, who was instantly relieved.

The wise guy told Phil that his sources in the Chicago Police Department knew absolutely nothing. It was almost as if they had been purposely left in the dark. Then he'd talked to some of the guys on the mob's payroll who worked with the feds. The FBI had gotten a tip from a police informer about Phil's whereabouts.

"I knew it," Phil said. "Where did the tip come from?"

"Boston," the wise guy answered.

Almost to himself, Phil murmured, "Tilley."

"What?" the Chicago gangster asked.

"Nothing, it's just a score I have to settle," Phil said.

FOR THE NEXT SIX MONTHS the feds were everywhere, and Phil, using his Joey Zito passport and some of the money he still had left from the half million he'd had when he ran, took off until things quieted down. He asked Augie to make an emergency phone call to Bobby Cresta and tell him Phil would be incommunicado for several months. Then Joey Zito took his new wife on a cruise around the world, where the only thing he had to worry about was whether to eat five or six times a day.

He returned to Chicago in March of 1973 and went back to his toy store as if nothing had happened. The people who'd missed Phil the most while he was away, beside Mari, were members of the Chicago Police Department. They were used to getting special half-price deals on Christmas toys at Toy World. He continued his life in Chicago through Christmas 1973 as the most popular businessman in the eyes of the Chicago Police.

The feds continued to harass Mari. "One day in December Phil contacted her and asked her to meet him in a downtown lounge. She checked for tails and was sure nobody was tailing her when she went into the place. She sat down in a booth and waited for Phil. As soon as she ordered a drink she saw two men enter the lounge. Both were wearing suits that might as well have said FEDS on the sleeves. She panicked, knowing Phil was due momentarily.

Not knowing what else to do, she continued drinking her drink and smoking her cigarette. A minute later a hippie with long hair and a scraggly beard, who looked like he hadn't bathed in a week, came over and asked Mari, "Hey, lady, got a light?" She looked him straight in the eyes, tapped her cigarette on the ashtray, and in a hard voice told him that she didn't smoke. The hippie got the message and left. Phil never showed up.

After a while Mari went back home. The phone was ringing when she let herself into her luxury apartment. Mari, frightened for her brother, said, "Phil?" He just laughed in reply. "What's so funny?" she said. "So you don't smoke, huh?" It took Mari a few seconds and then she screamed, "You have *got* to be shittin' me. Tell me you weren't that hippie." "I confess. . . . And by the way, you weren't too friendly."

"I don't believe you, I just don't believe you!" Mari was laughing now. After a while she asked, "Why did you do that?" "I just wanted to see for myself if they were still tailing you," Phil said.

"Couldn't you have watched from across the street?" Mari asked. "What fun is that?" Phil asked, still laughing. But Mari could sense that Phil was getting restless, even careless. It was almost as if he were challenging the feds to catch him. Maybe being an ordinary citizen no longer satisfied him. "I think part of him wanted to get caught," Mari recalled later.

"A few weeks after the hippie incident, in January 1974, Phil called and asked me to accompany him to get some snow chains for his tires. There was a huge snowstorm predicted for the Chicago area. So we drove to Sears Roebuck, where we both went our separate ways, promising to meet in half an hour at a designated spot. Later I saw Phil at the spot but was surprised to see he didn't have anything in his hands. I asked him where the chains were and he said he didn't like what they had in the store. When we got into the parking lot, I heard some kind of noise and I asked him what it was. Phil opened his coat; he had the snow chains under his coat. I went crazy," Mari recalled. "He had a couple of thousand on him and he stole snow chains worth only twenty bucks!" Mari was upset that he'd taken such a risk. But Phil just laughed his head off. Mari couldn't help herself. He was having such a good time, she had to laugh with him. But not without fear that Phil wasn't adjusting well to such a tame lifestyle.

19
Surrounded

N 1972 OR SO, Phil had married a woman named Molly, though he still had no formal divorce from Dorothy, back in Lynn, Massachusetts. The new couple bought a house in a Chicago suburb. A house with a white picket fence. Phil commuted to the toy store every day. To their neighbors, the Zitos seemed like the perfect suburban couple: successful, in love, and with a great future. They had no children. Molly didn't know anything about Joey Paul Zito's past. At least not until March 1, 1974.

On that day two dozen federal agents surrounded Toy World. Joey Zito was inside the store, totally oblivious to what was going on outside. A Chicago television station had gotten wind of something transpiring downtown and had sent a TV crew to cover the event.

If Phil was oblivious to what was happening, so too were the members of the Chicago Police Department—who were purposely kept in the dark. The FBI had rightly figured that the Chicago Police were much too fond of the owner of Toy World. As the feds got into position to take Phil down, though, the Chicago cops arrived on the scene too, and a near shootout ensued between members of the two law enforcement agencies.

Phil's wife Molly had turned on the television set expecting to see the nightly news. What she saw drove her to a nervous breakdown. All three Chicago television stations were on the scene reporting the apprehension of one of the FBI's Ten Most Wanted fugitives, a man from Boston named Phil Cresta—her husband.

Phil figured out that the game was up before the first federal officer stepped through the door and handcuffed him without a struggle. "I saw the television cameras before I saw the feds, but I knew they had to mean the feds were out there somewhere. I called Augie from the store and told him I was going down. I asked him to make sure a good attorney was at the police station when I arrived.

Augie didn't disappoint him. With TV camera lights blazing, Phil was led into Chicago's U.S. District Court to be arraigned. Waiting for his new client was the famous mob attorney Julius Echeles.

BAIL WAS SET at $625,000. Phil waived extradition and the paperwork began. On the evening of March 1, 1974, the Boston FBI SAC received the following memo from his Chicago office.

NR 002 CG PLAIN

445PM NITEL MARCH 2[1], 1974

TO: DIRECTOR

         BOSTON

FROM: CHICAGO

PHILIP JOSEPH CRESTA JR. AKA JOE ZITO   IO NUMBER 4347

SUBJECT APPEARED THIS DATE BEFORE UNITED STATES MAGIS-TRATE JAMES T. BALOG AND WAS REPRESENTED BY ATTORNEY JULIUS ECHELES.

MAGISTRATE BALOG SET BOND IN THE AMOUNT OF $625,000 COR-PORATE SURETY AND REMANDED CRESTA TO CUSTODY USM, CHICAGO. CRESTA TO REAPPEAR BEFORE MAGISTRATE BALOG, 1:45 P.M., MARCH 7, 1974.

ARMED AND DANGEROUS

Later that day another memo was dispatched across the country from then-FBI Director Clarence Kelley:

PLAINTEXT   TELETYPE   NITEL

TO   ALL SACS

FROM   DIRECTOR, FBI

  CHANGED [SIC]: PHILIP JOSEPH CRESTA, JR., AKA JOE ZITO—
IO NO. 4347,

  SUBJECT ARRESTED MARCH I, 1974, BY BUREAU AGENTS, CHICAGO,
WITHOUT INCIDENT USING ALIAS JOE ZITO.
  <u>ARMED & DANGEROUS</u>.

BEFORE THE TRIAL could start, Phil had to be returned to Boston from Chicago. To say that the wheels of justice move slowly is a major understatement, at least in regard to this case. Cresta was held in a federal lockup in Chicago from March 1 until March 30, when the papers involving Case No. 74 M 177 were sent to the office of the United States Marshal. These directed the marshal to transport Cresta to Boston, where he was to stand trial on armed robbery charges. There was only one problem. The Suffolk County Superior Court could not find the bench warrant that had been issued on June 12, 1969, for Cresta's arrest.

Attorney Julius Echeles went before Judge Balog and asked for the immediate release of Phil Cresta. Echeles presented a petition that stated, "The United States Marshals Service has been unable to produce any kind of warrant which would detain or hold Mr. Cresta. Therefore I request the immediate release of Mr.Cresta pending the $625,000 cash/surety, which will be presented to the Clerk at 9:00 A.M. tomorrow." Suddenly the wheels of justice went into overdrive. By the time Attorney Echeles returned to federal court at nine the next morning, the warrant had been found and Cresta was already on his way to Boston. They were not taking any chances.

ON APRIL 11, 1974, forty-six-year-old Phil Cresta stood before Judge James C. Roy and asked for bail reduction. Suffolk

County Assistant District Attorney James Sullivan told Judge Roy that if Cresta was allowed to get out on bail, he would never be seen again. Sullivan stated, "Your Honor, this man has just been returned from Chicago where, under the alias Joseph Paul Zito, he knowingly and willingly fled prosecution for the crime he now appears before you on. He is the worst kind of bail risk. Your Honor, this man who appears before you today is no ordinary run-of-the-mill defendant. Just the fact that he disappeared for over five years while the FBI and every other major law enforcement agency in the country was looking for him should tell you something about the man and about the resources he has at his disposal. We fear that if Mr. Cresta is allowed to meet bail, he will again use his resources to flee. We strongly urge you not to decrease his bail but to hold Mr. Cresta without bail."

Phil Cresta's attorney, Alfred Paul Farese, railed against the DA's plea for no bail. Farese said, "Your Honor, Phil Cresta is an innocent man who fled this state to avoid being persecuted, not prosecuted, by the likes of a career criminal named Red Kelley, who will be the only witness to testify against my client. Mr. Kelley has a personal vendetta against my client, who is totally innocent of the indictment, as set forth. He has no intentions of fleeing. In fact, Mr. Cresta is glad to be back home with his family and friends and is anxious to clear the record and his name. To hold an innocent man without bail is unconscionable and we know that you are a fair and decent man, Your Honor."

Attorney Farese may have laid it on a little too thick but it worked, at least they thought it worked. Judge Roy reduced Phil's bail from $625,000 cash/surety to $100,000 cash/surety. He set the trial date for June 19, 1974, in Suffolk County Superior Court.

Getting the $100,000 was no problem for Phil. He had what was left of his money in a few safe-deposit boxes in Chicago. He called Augie from the Charles Street Jail, where he was held pending trial. Augie promised to get the cash and bring it to Boston personally.

Phil just wanted to get out of that hellhole. But Suffolk County District Attorney Garrett Byrne had other ideas. Byrne put the word out that Cresta was not to be bailed under any circumstance. He made it clear to any bail bondsman who might think of putting money up for Cresta to think again. Byrne let it be known that any bondsman who helped Cresta would find a call on bond; that is, bonds that any of their clients had forfeited in the past would become immediately due for payment.

Augie carried the money from Chicago as he had told Phil he would. Phil couldn't understand why he was still in jail until he got a visit from his brother Bobby. Bobby explained how no bail bondsman in the state would touch the money. "Have you asked Cosmo Gilberti?" "Phil," Bobby explained, "I'm telling you: I've tried just about every bondsman in this city, and the word is out. Nobody's going to jeopardize their livelihood for you or anybody else."

Phil listened to what Bobby had to say and then told him to go call Cosmo Gilberti. An hour later bail bondsman Gilberti appeared in Suffolk Superior with $50,000 in cash and the deed for Phil's younger sister's house. Byrne went ballistic, but he had no choice but to order Phil to be released immediately from jail.

"Gilberti had some balls," Phil said later. "He and I had done a lot of business and I knew he'd stand up to Byrne if I asked him to." So, knowing that the feds and the IRS would be snooping around, trying to find where he came up with a hundred large, Phil told Bobby to instruct Gilberti to put up fifty large in cash and the other fifty in surety. Phil's sister Rose was more than willing to put up her house as surety after being guaranteed that her brother would stand for trial.

Phil hit the bricks on the twelfth of April and immediately went to McGrail's. Nothing had changed except that Tony and Angelo were no longer sitting in the last booth, and that was hard for Phil. It was great, however, seeing all the other old faces and reliving some of the old times. They treated Phil like some kind of star that day, even the guys who'd sat in that bar for ten years and never spoken to him. One guy, after a few beers, came over to Phil and said, "Shit, I always thought you were a car salesman or something. I never knew you were a big-time thief." Phil didn't know whether to say thanks or what.

The next day Phil boarded a flight to Chicago—after he cleared it with the authorities. He didn't need Byrne to hear he was gone and revoke his bail. So he walked into Byrne's office and told them that he had some business to clear up in Chicago and that he'd be gone for two days. Byrne's assistants didn't like it, but they had no choice: he wasn't leaving the country or anything. Phil gave them Mari's address, got a cab to Logan, and flew out. The toughest part for Phil was his current wife's situation: she had thought she'd married a single man, a toy store owner, not a man who was still married to his first wife and on the FBI's Ten Most Wanted list. She was not doing well.

Phil later said of her, "Molly was a good woman and she didn't deserve that." She was still hospitalized at the time of Phil's visit to Chicago, because of the nervous breakdown she'd had after seeing her husband arrested on television. He knew enough not to visit her. Phil's first wife divorced him that same year, 1974. Molly followed through with divorce, without ever seeing Phil again, in 1976.

Back in Chicago, Phil made the rounds, thanking friends and taking care of many of his legal and illegal ventures. "It was toughest saying good-bye to Augie and Mari," Phil recounted. "We'd become very very close and that was very difficult."

On the plane returning to Boston, Phil Cresta started planning how to wrap up the last piece of his still-unfinished business. It was too late to off Kelley or DeLeary, but there was one other guy who had ratted on Cresta who was still at large. Maybe some kind of atonement could be demanded of him.

20
Settling Scores

HIL GOT OFF THE PLANE at Logan around five o'clock on the afternoon of April 15, 1974. He grabbed a cab and directed the driver to Fenway Park, one place every cab driver knew how to get to, regardless of where he was originally from. Cresta walked down Yawkey Way but did not go into McGrail's. Instead he headed into the Fenway Motor Inn parking lot, got in Bobby's car, which he'd borrowed, and drove to Mattapan.

As he drove, he thought of nothing but how many times Ben Tilley had screwed him or attempted to screw him, especially since Phil had "stolen" his gang and become successful while Tilley had remained small-time. The more Phil thought about it, the more convinced he became that all the bad things that had happened to him had started with Tilley: his betrayal of the Kay Jewelers job . . . Tony and Angelo in the can . . . and Phil's likelihood of joining them.

Phil was getting worked up more and more. Now he was thinking of how his own failure to get rid of DeLeary and Kelley wouldn't have mattered if Tilley hadn't talked. Phil's almost-perfect method of hiding from the feds had been ended by this last betrayal. Phil would most likely go back to the last place on earth he wanted to be—and Tilley would remain free. Was that justice? Tilley didn't deserve freedom.

As Phil drove down Blue Hill Avenue, just as he and Angelo had done years before, it did not enter Phil's mind that he had no proof for or against Tilley's guilt. Like his father, when Phil Cresta Jr. was angry he acted.

He parked his car and headed into the Brown Jug. Phil forced a big smile when he saw the man he had come to see. Ben Tilley was standing at the bar.

Tilley saw Phil about the same time Phil saw him. There was fear in Tilley's eyes as Phil walked over to him.

But when Phil got close to his nemesis, he extended his hand and said, "Ben Tilley, how the hell are ya?"

Tilley was caught off guard by this gesture of friendship and he instinctively extended his own hand, which Phil grabbed and shook.

Phil asked if he could buy Tilley a drink.

"Sure, a Seven and Seven," Tilley said, now beginning to lighten up.

Phil continued to buy Tilley drinks and Tilley continued to throw them down. As the man got drunker, Phil, who was drinking only beer, became more sober, more focused on the job at hand.

Braggart that he was, Tilley spun story after story of his recent coups, which Phil knew to be false or embellished. Phil continued to laugh and ply Tilley with whiskey. The drunker Tilley got the more obnoxious he got, and the more Phil wanted to strangle him right there in the Brown Jug. Finally Cresta managed to steer the conversation around to cars.

He talked in glowing terms about his gold Bonneville, and he waited for Tilley to take the bait. Slurring his words, Tilley loudly said, "There's only one kind of car for me and that's a Cadillac. That's all I ever drive, yes sir. I'll take a Cadoo any day." "I'm partial to gold cars," Phil said, "how about you?" "Green, that's always my color. Yes sir, get a new one every year, but I never change the color or make."

Ha! Phil thought to himself. He really never *does* change! Still bragging, still drinking, still driving a green Cadillac, like he was when he spoiled our Kay Jewelers job. And still ratting people out!

At about one in the morning Phil told Tilley he had to go to the bathroom and he'd be right back. By that time Tilley thought Phil Cresta was one of his closest friends.

Phil headed in the direction of the bathroom, which was by the front door, but when he got there, he went outside instead. No one saw him leave. He headed to the parking lot and immediately spotted a new-model green Cadillac. He reached into his coat pocket and brought out an object that shone in the moonlight.

Phil dropped his cigarette and rolled under the Cadoo, shined a small flashlight on it, and within thirty seconds he was out from under the car and back on his feet. He brushed himself off, looked around, and headed back into the bar.

When Tilley saw Phil walking toward him, he shouted, "Hey, Phil, did everything come out all right?" and began laughing.

"Yeah, Ben, everything came out just fine."

Phil bought Tilley yet another Seagram's 7 and 7Up, and watched as he downed it. Phil couldn't believe anyone could drink that much and still be standing.

Ten minutes before the tavern's two A.M. closing time, Phil told Tilley that he had to be getting home. Tilley slurred, "Phil, let me buy you one drink before you go?" Phil declined, saying it was *his* night to buy. He ordered one more drink for Tilley and a beer for himself, which he never touched. Tilley, who still had three drinks on the bar, turned to Phil and said, "Where'd ya get so much money? What'd you rob, another armored car? Or was it a bank this time?"

The bartender came over and asked Tilley if he was all right. "Sure, I'm fine. Right, Phil?"

"Right, Ben," Phil said. He turned to the bartender and asked if Tilley really would be all right driving home like that. The bartender, who didn't recognize Phil from the last time he'd been there, some six years before, said, "Oh sure, God takes care of drunks and Irishmen, and Tilley happens to be both."

"I was just worried about him," Phil reiterated.

"Don't worry, pal. He leaves here almost every night like that and he always makes it home."

Phil tipped the bartender and left.

In his car, Phil waited another half hour until just about everyone had left the bar. Finally, at 2:25 A.M., Ben Tilley staggered out and just made it to his Cadillac. Phil watched as he fumbled about, trying to get his keys in the ignition. Once he had the car started, Tilley left rubber getting out of the parking lot. He headed right into traffic on Blue Hill Avenue and barely escaped a head-on collision. Phil followed him, hoping that Tilley wouldn't get arrested.

Continuing up Blue Hill Avenue past American Legion Highway, Tilley took a left at Franklin Park. He was traveling at a high rate of speed as he passed the golf course. Phil followed the man's car as it went past Shattuck Hospital and headed onto the bridge that would take its driver into Jamaica Plain. As Tilley was accelerating down the bridge, Phil could tell from the way the car handled that the brake line he'd cut in the parking lot had now let go completely. Tilley continued to pick up speed. At the bottom of the ramp, at the head of the Arborway, he swerved to the right, careened off a parked car, hit a tree, flipped over, and came to rest on the Arborway.

Phil headed back to the Fenway Motor Inn, assuming that Tilley was dead. But the next day he scanned the papers, and there was no report of a car crash on the Arborway.

Phil phoned the Brown Jug and asked the bartender if he had any news on Ben Tilley. "Yeah, but it's not too good," the bartender said. "Is he dead?" Phil asked. "No, but he's close to it." "Do you know what hospital he's at?" Phil asked with just the right note of sadness. "Carney," Phil was told.

Phil had nothing to worry about. The next day Ben Tilley died without ever regaining consciousness. The hospital's death report listed his death as the result of severe trauma to the head. The police report said that Ben Tilley died as a result of a car accident on the Arborway at 2:35 A.M. on April 16, 1974. Both reports were true, in a sense. But in Phil's opinion Ben Tilley also died because he had a big mouth—and he opened it when he shouldn't have.

Phil later said, "I feel no remorse for Tilley. I felt sorry for his family, but he tried to take me down on at least ten different occasions. I did what I had to do." On April 18, 1974, the *Boston Globe* ran a story on page thirty-four in which the reporter wrote, "Benjamin J. Tilley, 64, of Mossdale road, Jamaica Plain, died at the Carney Hospital in Dorchester Tuesday, following an automobile accident in Mattapan. He lived in West Roxbury before moving to Jamaica Plain ten years ago. For several years he was involved in the contracting business in Allston, but retired five years ago." The article went on to list the Tilley family members and the arrangements for the funeral. Ben Tilley's death is still listed on the books of the Boston Police Department as an accident. But Ben Tilley's death was no accident. It was what the wise guys call a payback.

SOMETIME BEFORE HIS TRIAL Phil Cresta met several times with a former acquaintance, the infamous James "Whitey" Bulger, who, knowing his day to run would come, listened carefully to all Phil had to say about how he had managed to hide. Their marathon sessions would pay off many years later—for Bulger.

On April 21, 1974, two prisoners at Walpole State Prison each received a letter. Inside each envelope was Ben Tilley's obituary from the *Boston Globe*. Although there was no return address on either letter, both prisoners knew who had sent the clipping and what its significance was. They knew that their friend and mentor Phil Cresta was back in town and thinking of them, though he had never visited either of them in prison. "I just didn't want to see them behind a glass partition," Phil said. "I hated everything about Walpole, and I wasn't going to go there until they dragged me."

That was exactly what the state intended to do.

PROCEEDINGS AGAINST Philip J. Cresta Jr. were set to begin on June 19, 1974, in Suffolk County Superior Court. Before the trial got started, however, Assistant District Attorney James Sullivan telephoned Phil's attorney, Al Farese, and asked if they could meet in Sullivan's office at Pemberton Square. Farese, who called Phil, was baffled by Sullivan's request for a meeting.

When they met, Sullivan got right to the point and offered to plea-bargain the case. If Phil would plead guilty to the charge of armed robbery, Sullivan told Farese, the state would recommend a term of not more than seven years and not less than five.

Farese was so pleased with the offer, he called Phil from a pay phone nearby, the one in front of the Steaming Kettle on the corner of Cambridge and Court streets.

Phil listened to the offer and said to Farese, "Tell Sullivan to stick it up his ass."

Farese was shocked. He reminded his client that he could be facing up to forty years in prison if convicted.

"Why are they offering this kind of deal?" Phil asked.

Farese told him that the only thing he could figure was that it had to do with Red Kelley. By that time Kelley had become the poster child for the state. He had testified in a number of high-profile cases in which he'd rolled on former associates. And he was seen by some lawyers as having about as much credibility as a boatload of used-car salesmen. Farese speculated that the state was leery of trotting him out once again in what was sure to be another high-profile case.

"That rat bastard," Phil said angrily. "I want him to look me in the eye when he's on that stand. I want to see what he has to say."

Farese advised Phil to think it over. "Listen, Kelley had no problem taking the stand and turning on Patriarca," he said.

"He's certainly not going to have any problem sending you away for forty years either. Please think about this and call me back."

"No deal. Tell Sullivan we go to trial as planned."

"Are you positive, Phil?" Farese asked.

"Absofuckinglutely," Phil replied.

His family and friends pleaded with him to take the seven years and not look back. But Cresta had accepted his mistake of thinking he could control Kelley, and the result of that mistake: his partners being sent to prison and his own eventual capture. He was adamant about going to trial.

"Nobody around me could understand why I didn't take the plea," Cresta recounted. "But I just couldn't. Angelo and Tony were doing twenty-five to forty, and they wanted me to do a seven-year bit? If I went to trial and beat it, that was one thing, but I couldn't take a plea and do seven while they were doing twenty-five–to–forty bits . . . I never told Farese or anyone else why, but I just couldn't do that. Being a man of honor, which was something Red Kelley had no idea about, was a lot more important to me than anything else. So I told Sullivan to get it on and let the chips fall where they may."

Phil knew there was a chance he'd win. None of those now in prison—Angelo, Tony, Diaferio, Merlino, and Roukous—would testify against Phil. DeLeary didn't know him from Adam. Kelley, and Kelley alone, was the state's only chance to put Cresta anywhere near the Brink's job that had led to sentences for all the other participants.

Phil had read the transcript of Angelo and Tony's Brink's robbery trial and knew every word Kelley had said against them. Cresta prepared his lawyer for what to expect. He'd take his chances.

The high-profile trial of Phil Cresta, the last Brink's robber to be tried, got under way in Suffolk County Superior Court on June 19. Attorney Al Farese and Assistant District Attorney James Sullivan settled on a jury made up of three women and thirteen men, all of whom would be sequestered for the length of the trial and for deliberation and disposition. James C. Roy was the presiding judge.

In his opening arguments Sullivan outlined for the jury the same case that the state had presented five years earlier against Angelo and Tony, again denoting Kelley and DeLeary as the prosecution's star witnesses.

Farese, in his opening, told the jury that Andrew DeLeary would testify that he'd never met or seen Phil Cresta. Farese argued that Red Kelley was a professional witness who would say whatever he was instructed to say by his handlers. "Red Kelley is a coward and a liar. He will be the only witness who'll tell you that Phil Cresta was involved with the December 28, 1968, Brink's robbery. Neither the Boston Police nor the FBI can stand here, in this court, and tell you that Phil Cresta was involved in the Brink's robbery. Not one prosecution witness other than Red Kelley will stand before you and tell you that Phil Cresta was in any way involved in the Brink's robbery. You will hear a mountain of information about a robbery that was committed on December 28, 1968. None of that information has anything to do with Phil Cresta."

Testimony began the next day, June 20. District Attorney Sullivan's witnesses, just as Al Farese had said they would, told the jury about the Brink's robbery, but none of them placed Phil Cresta at the scene. The jury heard from Richard Haines, the guard who had been tied up inside the truck. Part of his testimony provided an inkling of Phil's expertise and prowess as a keymaker. This is a partial transcript of Haines's testimony:

DA JAMES SULLIVAN (Assistant District Attorney for Suffolk County): Mr. Haines, is this key, to the best of your knowledge, the same key that the thieves used to enter armored car number 6280?

RICHARD HAINES: Yes, sir, it is.

DA: How do you know that this is the key used in the robbery? Are there any identifying marks on it?

HAINES: "Yes, sir, there's an *F* scratched on the bow of the key.

DA: Do you know what that *F* stands for, Mr. Haines?

HAINES: I would assume it stands for the front door?

DEFENSE ATTORNEY AL FARESE: Objection, Your Honor.

JUDGE JAMES ROY: On what grounds?

FARESE: That answer calls for personal knowledge, Your Honor.

JUDGE: Sustained.

DA: Do you know from your personal knowledge if that key with the *F* scratched in its bow opens the front door of armored car number 6280?

HAINES: Yes, sir, it does.

DA: Did you personally try this key in the front door of number 6280 at any time after the robbery?

HAINES: Yes, sir, I did.

DA: And this key [he held up the key] is without a doubt the key that let two armed, masked robbers into number 6280 on the night of December 28, 1968. Is that right, Mr. Haines?

HAINES: Yes, sir, and I might add that it opened the front door a lot easier than the key the Brink's office gave me every day.

The courtroom erupted in laughter. Judge Roy banged his gavel repeatedly, demanding quiet. Phil Cresta did not admit in court that he'd made that key, but he later said that it was one of the best picks he'd ever made.

After Haines left the stand, the DA paraded witness after witness, from Boston police detectives to FBI agents to MDC policemen, each of whom told his story about the Brink's robbery. Then the jury heard from Andrew DeLeary.

DeLeary told about meeting Red Kelley and Angelo and about his $51,000 cut from the robbery.

After each prosecution witness finished his testimony Judge Roy would turn and say to Al Farese, "Mr. Farese, do you have any questions from this witness?"

Each and every time, Farese stood up and asked the same question—"Do you know this man?"—as he pointed to Phil

Cresta. Each time the prosecution witness answered, "No." Farese would then ask, "Have you ever seen this man before today?" And again each witness would answer, "No." Farese would then say, "That's all I have, Your Honor. Thank you very much."

On June 24, all that changed. At nine A.M. a Suffolk County Superior Court officer led a man with glasses and white hair to the witness stand. The man looked as though he could be everyone's grandfather. He was, in fact, a cold-blooded killer with a police record dating back to the 1940s. It had been sixty-six months since Phil had last seen Red Kelley, when they split the Brink's money in a Brockton Holiday Inn room.

District Attorney Sullivan asked the man on the stand his name. "John Kelley," he answered slowly. "Are you known by any other name, Mr. Kelley?" Again very slowly, the elderly man said, "Yeah. Red."

"Do you know that man?" Sullivan asked, pointing to Phil Cresta. "Yes," Kelley answered. "Do you know his name?" Again Kelley nodded.

"Cresta. Phil Cresta." "How do you know Phil Cresta?" Sullivan continued. Kelley identified Cresta as one of the bandits who robbed the Brink's truck and further testified that it was Cresta who used a key-making machine to copy the truck's key that Andrew DeLeary turned over to Angelo in a phone booth on Boylston Street.

Kelley told of clocking the truck's route for three or four Saturdays, and of making two aborted attempts before the robbery was accomplished. "Was Mr. Cresta involved in the planning of the robbery?" Sullivan asked. "Yes." "What role did Mr. Cresta have?" "I assigned him to be a driver," Kelley lied. "I watched from a station wagon as Angelo and Diaferio used the key Cresta made to enter the Brink's truck." "What happened next?" Sullivan asked. "We followed the route I had designed, from Canal Street to the parking lot behind the Registry of Motor Vehicles," Kelley said. "Where was Mr. Cresta at that time?" Sullivan asked. "He was following me in one of the cars," Kelley said, looking directly at Phil for the first time since he'd started manufacturing his testimony.

Phil said later that he was thinking, "That son of a bitch didn't even have the balls to be there when we took the truck down, and there he was on the stand lying about how he'd masterminded the job and how he was in the lead car, when he was at home faking an illness! What could I do, stand up in front of the jury and say, 'You're a fucking liar. You weren't even there'?

"I don't know what made me madder, his taking me down or his lying to make himself a big shot, when he was nothing but a turncoat coward. I knew that Kelley had set up Bobby Rasmussen, Jackie Murray, Leo Lowry, Frankie Benjamin, and Georgie Ash. They were all killed because they'd trusted that rat-bastard Kelley. And there he was trying to kill me by taking away my freedom for a long, long time. I should've whacked him when I had the chance. I never should've gotten involved with him in the first place. It turned out that we only needed him to meet with DeLeary—anyone could've done that."

Phil sat through two days of Kelley's bravado-filled testimony. "It was the most difficult two days of my life," Phil recalled, "having to sit there and listen to that rat bastard making himself the mastermind when he wasn't even there." Not only did Phil have to listen to Kelley's fabrications of Cresta's Brink's robbery, he had to look at them in print. On June 25 the *Record American* headline read, $1M BRINKS HEIST MASTERMIND TELLS OF PLANNING, BANDITS' ROLES.

Farese went after Kelley's credibility. He basically let the jury see what kind of man Red Kelley was and how he had spent his life. Farese was able to introduce some of the things he wanted the jury to hear but was not allowed to discuss others. He knew it was a crapshoot anyway, and Phil's fate would rest on whether the jury believed Red Kelley's story or not. Farese rested his case on June 26.

On June 28, 1974, a memo was sent to the director of the FBI:

TO:　DIRECTOR, FBI

FROM:　SAC, BOSTON

SUBJECT:　PHILIP JOSEPH CRESTA JR. AKA JOSEPH PAUL ZITO

On 6/28/74 Suffolk County, Boston, Mass. Jury returned guilty verdict re PHILIP J. CRESTA, former Bureau 10 fugitive, and CRESTA then received a State Prison term of 25–40 years.

Phil was taken from the Suffolk County Courthouse immediately after the verdict was read and transported to Walpole State Prison, where he was reunited with Angelo and Tony. They were in the fifth year of their own twenty-five-to-forty-year sentences.

ON THE INSIDE, Phil Cresta's brain, which had helped him outwit authorities during hundreds of jobs, went to work helping other convicts. Phil became what is known as a jailhouse lawyer, and he filed brief after brief with courts throughout Massachusetts on behalf of convicts doing time at Walpole. Regarding his petition to overturn his own verdict, Phil received a letter from a Harvard Law School student, who said that Phil's argument to overturn, based on the seven-year plea that was offered, was absolutely brilliant.

One day, in the prison waiting room, Phil ran into F. Lee Bailey, Kelley's defense lawyer both for the Plymouth mail robbery and for Cresta's Brink's robbery. Phil couldn't help himself. All the old bitterness came out—at Kelley, and at Bailey. Their argument had to be broken up by guards, but not before Cresta spit in Bailey's face.

Other than that confrontation, Phil Cresta became known as a model prisoner during his last stay at Walpole. His only crime in jail was picking the lock of the candy machine once a month, which drove the prison guards wild. It was a crime, like most of the others he committed, that has not been solved until now.

AFTERMATH
The Main Characters

POLICE RECOVERED $35,360 from ANDREW DE-LEARY's share of the 1968 Brink's take, buried outside a little cottage in New Hampshire owned by DeLeary's father-in-law. No other Brink's money was ever recovered.

ANGELO and TONY are alive and free; hence their real names have not been given.

PHIL CRESTA served twelve years at Walpole State Prison. Following his release in 1986, he moved to Chicago, where he stayed in an apartment that his sister Mari continued to rent but seldom lived in. She, by that time, had divorced Augie and moved to Miami, where her brother Billy "Bad" was living. Phil did not get along with some of the Miami wise guys Billy hung out with, so he preferred Chicago. Besides, Phil thought, he'd done enough time, and if he hung out in Miami with Billy and his friends, chances were . . .

Phil had had enough of prison.

While in Chicago Phil was treated at University Hospital for a heart condition. In 1990 he moved back to the Boston area and lived with his mother and his sister Rose, in Malden. Just about all his savings had been spent.

Then, broke, he moved in with Billy Crowley in South Boston, where he lived from March 1991 until July 1994. In August 1994 his heart problems intensified, so he decided to go back to Chicago, to be near the doctors who had previously treated him. There he lived with friends for the last few months of his life.

On January 8, 1995, Phil Cresta, the man who stole more than ten million dollars in his lifetime, died in Chicago's University Hospital. He was penniless.

AFTERMATH
Other Characters

N FEBRUARY 1972, Harvard Law professor Archibald Cox, who would be the special prosecutor in the Watergate scandal from 1973 on, served for three months as counsel to a Massachusetts legislative committee investigating charges of judicial impropriety against two state Superior Court judges, Edward J. DeSaulnier Jr. and VICTOR BOWMAN. The committee had the sole power to remove either judge from the bench. In January of that same year, the Massachusetts Supreme Judicial Court had ordered disbarment as a lawyer for Judge DeSaulnier, but DeSaulnier subsequently resigned from the bench, so Cox declared that case moot. That same Supreme Court had censured Judge Bowman and referred the case to Cox's legislative committee for decision.

On April 11, 1972, on the basis of Cox's investigation, the legislative committee recommended no further action against Judge Bowman. Bowman continued to serve as a judge of the Massachusetts Superior Court until March 1982, when he resigned, citing low salary as a reason. In his letter to then-governor Edward J. King, Bowman stated, "The salary of a Superior Court judge may be enough to live on if one has no dependents; unfortunately, it is not enough to die on." Victor Bowman took up the practice of law as a defense attorney.

On December 2, 1982, according to the *Boston Globe,* minutes after payroll driver "Andrew DeLeary drove away from an East Boston bank with his company's weekly payroll—almost $4,200 in cash—he was held at gunpoint. One of the robbers grabbed the money and ordered DeLeary into the trunk of his car. He was rescued 20 minutes later after a bystander who had witnessed the incident called police." Given that it was DeLeary who originally approached Angelo and Tony about the 1968 Brink's robbery, one might wonder—was this also planned? Or was it some kind of odd retribution?

JERRY ANGIULO is presently in prison on federal racketeering charges.

JOHN "RED" KELLEY was placed in protective custody on June 4, 1969. He became one of the FBI's top witnesses against the mob. He apparently was held under heavy guard at Pease Air Force Base in New Hampshire when needed for testimony. In March 1970, after having testified in several other cases, he helped put Raymond Patriarca, the head of La Cosa Nostra, in prison. He was then placed in the witness protection program. Nobody knows for sure if he is alive or dead today. If he is alive, which is highly unlikely, he would be in his eighties.

AUGIE CIRCELLA, along with his brother Nicky and other Chicago mobsters, was arrested on a charge of extortion in connection with a million-dollar scandal involving the International Alliance of Theatrical Stage Employees and 20th Century Fox. Augie's brother was found guilty and deported to Mexico, where he ran a fleet of shrimp boats until he died. Charges against Augie were dismissed for lack of evidence. He returned to Chicago, where he died.

Phil Cresta's older brother, MIKE, became a Medford police officer, and pretty much separated himself from most of his family.

The date of MARI Cresta Circella's divorce from Augie has not been established, but it is known that they continued to spend time together. She lived in various cities after leaving Chicago, including Miami, where she dated Johnny Irish for a while. She died in Las Vegas, Nevada, on March 25, 1998.

Phil's younger sister, ROSE, took care of her mother until she died in 1999.

His younger brother BILLY "BAD" CRESTA became well-known in Miami and New York, and was considered to be close to Columbo's Carmine Persico and Johnny Irish. He died early in the year 2000.

His youngest brother, BOBBY, like Phil, became an expert pick man. He was arrested in December 1983 and did six years for conspiracy to import twenty-five tons of marijuana. He is presently free and living in New Hampshire, and contributed greatly to this book.

EDWARD MCALENEY is no longer living.

SERGEANT JIM DOHERTY is alive and well, living on Cape Cod. He has vivid memories of "that Cresta kid" as being the "toughest son of a bitch" he ever met. He especially remembers the night Phil fought the entire on-duty staff at the Cambridge police station, when Doherty was trying to arrest him.

LOUIE "DIAMONDS" COHEN, Phil once said, "reminded me of Ben Tilley. He liked to hang around with wise guys and he loved the action. But he didn't want to take any of the risks involved. Like Tilley, he also kissed Angiulo's ass—which made me sick." Phil was not sympathetic when he heard that Louie Diamonds, who always seemed to be a phone call away from being whacked, disappeared. It is not clear whether he was killed, or whether he took off before being killed.

After Phil was released from his last prison term, he received an invitation to meet WHITEY BULGER at a bar in Southie. As usual, Phil arrived early. While drinking a beer in Triple O's, he noticed a lot of punks and druggies hanging out there. Uneasy, Phil left, telling the bartender to tell Bulger he'd been there. He never heard from Whitey again.

In late 1994 Whitey Bulger, anticipating indictments from the feds he had informed for from 1971 through 1990, went on vacation. It was a good idea. On January 4, 1995, a federal warrant was secretly issued for him, for extortion. A federal racketeering indictment followed a week later. Bulger was placed on the

FBI's Ten Most Wanted list. Phil Cresta's advice helped prepare Bulger to run.

"Whitey Bulger was always two steps ahead of everyone else," Phil said before he died. "Before my trial we talked often about how I'd avoided the feds for so many years. He wanted to know everything: how much money I had when I left, what kind of contacts I had, how I got in touch with friends and family back home, what aliases I used, whether I used disguises. . . . He was like a sponge, taking everything in with those ice-cold blue eyes. Bulger, like me, knew there's always someone out there trying to take you down. Sometimes it's the cops, sometimes the robbers, but it's always someone. He knew that when the time came —and it will always come for guys like us—he'd have to be ready to go on a minute's notice. How long you stay gone depends on how much preparation you've done before."

Both Whitey Bulger and Phil Cresta were masters of preparation. As of this writing, Bulger, who has been seen here and there, remains at large.

Index

Acknowledgments

I want to thank especially my wife and best friend, Laurie Wallace, who always believed in me when others didn't. Without Laurie's support and encouragement, this book would never have been written. I also want to thank Brendan and Cullen McGoff for their love, support, and friendship and for keeping me grounded.

Thanks as well to Joe Timilty, who got me started and showed me the way, and to my friends at Northeastern University Press, Bill Frohlich, Jill Bahcall, Ann Twombly, and Sarah Rowley. Many thanks to an expert editor, Diana Donovan, who taught me a great deal about writing, and to Gil Geis, who also helped to shape the book. Thanks to Coley, Helen, Eddie Wallace, and Jack Geary, who never lost their faith in me. Thanks also to Dennis Lehane, Robert Parker, Gerry O'Neil, and Robin Moore, four great writers who wrote such nice things about our book. Thanks to my other family, the Flynns, and to the Greeleys, the Grahams, and the O'Keefes. Thanks to Dan Horgan, who gave me the opportunity to write. Thanks to my good friend Steve Sweeney. Thanks to Sheriff Richard Rouse, Councilor Mickey Roache, and Bill Ferney. And a very special thanks to all my friends in South Boston.

BRIAN P. WALLACE

Special thanks to my mother, Mary Crowley. Thanks to Bobby Cresta, Zack Piscitello, Joe "Pint" Panetta, Mary Mills, Mary Toland, Paul Gagliardi, Bobby, Simone, John Blute, Eddie Correia, the Crowley family, and the O'Connor family.

BILL CROWLEY